MONDAY
THROUGH
FRIDAY

Day Care Alternatives

MONDAY THROUGH FRIDAY
Day Care Alternatives

JANE MERRILL FILSTRUP
with Dorothy W. Gross

Teachers College, Columbia University
New York and London   1982

Published by Teachers College Press, 1234 Amsterdam Avenue, New York, N.Y.
10027

Copyright © 1982 by Teachers College, Columbia University

Library of Congress Cataloging in Publication Data

Filstrup, Jane Merrill.
  Monday through Friday.

  Includes index.
  1. Day care centers. 2.   Baby sitting.
I.   Gross, Dorothy W., 1929-   II.   Title.
HV851.F5   362.8'283   82-3364
ISBN 0-8077-2670-2   AACR2

Manufactured in the United States of America

87   86   85   84   83   82   1   2   3   4   5   6

To one mother who stayed home,
one who stayed home but yearned for something more,
and two daughters who will have it all

CONTENTS

109287

INTRODUCTION

*Before I got married I had six theories about bring-
ing up children; now I have six children, and no
theories.*

Lord Rochester

When I began investigating nursery schools, day care centers, and "tot drops" in our area as day care alternatives, I expected to be able to rate them according to objective standards. The basement nursery school with a rickety staircase, the day care center furnished like a first grade classroom were unacceptable. The *au pairs* of the town and country set were un-affordable. The laboratory school at a nearby college was gloriously appointed and refined, but what would I do during the month-long vaca-tions, provided the children could get in?

The more I looked and considered the more I began to realize that selecting child care hinged on my answering questions that were manifold and subtle. And individualistic. What was I looking for: full-time or part-time care? How many hours a week did I need free in order to pursue my part-time writing career? How did the advantages of having a caregiver come into our house stack up against the advantages of a change of scene outside the home? How important was it for the twins to play with other children? Should I rely on independent caregivers or an institution? What was the right balance between expenditures and earnings? The questions proliferated. In the asking, a profile of concerns and expectations emerged.

I came to realize that I had to analyze and weigh my needs as much as those of my children.

Talking with neighborhood parents, I was struck by how various the child care patterns were. The wife of an investment broker who traveled every other week was trying the nanny route. A nonworking mother hired babysitters only to go out evenings and otherwise looked to a playgroup for outside companionship. One two-career couple used full-time day care. Another, two schoolteachers, relied on a combination of grandmother and nearly full-time babysitter. Each family was expert in its own needs, and collectively they knew a great deal about child care services in the area.

My discussions with these parents were a great help to me in analyzing the needs of our family and finally deciding on a day care arrangement. Having gone through this experience, I began to realize that many other parents might find similar help from a book in which a number of families describe and comment on their own responses to the need for outside assistance in raising children.

The mothers and fathers who tell their stories in this book are trying to balance the welfare of their children with their own desires for career, education, or other involvement outside the home. These parents, especially the mothers, want to raise children but do not want to devote themselves totally to the nursery. They believe that a mother is capable of assuming responsibilities outside as well as inside the home. The want something of both worlds.

This book presents alternatives to nuclear family self-sufficiency. The different ways in which outside assistance is used constitute a critique of the nuclear family as the child-rearing unit of America. The parents interviewed speak from experience about the practice—the nitty-gritty as well as the grander emotions and consequences—of raising children in a complex society. Although each commentary deals with the particulars of a family and its arrangement for care giving, the full chorus of families assert that the nuclear family needs help. It is not dead—there is no chapter on communal households—but it is too frail to do the job alone. The stay-at-home mother who bears almost sole responsibility for raising the children is not only a luxury of a more affluent time; it is a misguided striving for self-sufficiency.

These families argue in different ways that what is best for the parents is also best for the child. Reliance on alternative caregivers not only frees the parent to pursue other interests, it brings the child into an intimate relationship with at least one nonparent. If done with understanding, handing over a child to a surrogate mother for part of the day starts the pattern of separation and return that is basic to growing up. The problems of separation are obvious because they are so public. The family that relies on an alternate form of child care has not created the problems, but it has confronted them at a younger, possibly tenderer, age than those who wait for kindergarten. These parents teach their children that love is not a cloister. It is a railing that leads into the world, and back. Monica Ball (chapter 5) charges to the playground her first day of public school. She has learned that her parents love her and support her even though they go to their respective jobs. Experientially, she understands that separation is part of growing up. At age five, she is ready for the unknowns of public school. She has achieved a major step toward becoming a citizen of the world.

With an alternative form of care giving, not only is the child exposed to different people, new locales, various schedules, and more complex relationships than in just the home, so are the parents. To find good child care in the marketplace, parents have to develop their abilities to judge character, to evaluate institutions, and to balance factors of money, travel, and psychological needs. Then these mothers and fathers must form strong relations with nonfamily in order to share child-rearing responsibilities. The parents have to learn to communicate with outsiders about the mysteries of individualization—vital dialogue about what to *do* with a child. This interaction helps the parents come of age. The cooperative nature of the nursery school in chapter 8 benefits the parents as much as the children. Through their nanny Myra Dalrumple, the Whites (chapter 4) have a larger vision of themselves as family. They have taken Myra under their wing, not out of sympathy, but out of a combination of gratitude and need that transcends monetary considerations.

The book begins with the problem of separation. In chapter 1, Dorothy Gross discusses the psychology of separation and the potential for growth that lies within the initial tension. Starting with chapter 2, successive parents discuss the particular form of day care each selected, and caregivers comment from their perspectives. The arrangement of the book moves from at-home to out-of-home care giving. In terms of sex roles, the househusband (chapter 2) is a radical alternative. In fact, this stay-at-home daddy not only has expanded his domestic perch to include several other children, but he is intent on keeping his children out of school for their education. Still, he is "family." So is Mrs. Mair (chapter 3). She is extended family, living and child caring in her own apartment. Like the househusband of chapter 2, she also takes in other nonfamily children. The nanny (chapter 4) comes into the child's home and becomes "family," not only to the child but to the parents as well.

In chapters 5 –7, multiple caregivers enter the scene. The playgroup (chapter 5), as traditional as apple pie, gives mothers and children companionship and can be extended to operate like a cooperative tot drop. But outsiders step in for mothers and fathers very little, if at all. Babysitters have been traditionally used to allow parents evenings out and other leisure-time activities. Chapter 6 demonstrates that a crew of babysitters can come regularly to support a mother working part-time. The Balls (chapter 7) use a babysitting cooperative to support a full-time working mother. They "pay" for the sitting by sitting themselves, and the children go to the sitter's home rather than vice versa.

The last three chapters deal with more institutional forms of child care. Unlike the babysitting co-op, the cooperative nursery school (chapter 8) is not free. But the use of voluntary labor reduces the fee and involves parents in running the organization and working with the children. The book ends with two chapters on full-day care. These are truly homes away from home. Family day care (chapter 9) is like staying with a nanny in her own home. She is paid to be a substitute, daytime parent. In the last chapter, full-day care moves to neutral, institutional territory. Here the child must deal with many other children and several caregivers. This seems to be the most "modern." The long hours and nondomestic space accommodate the needs of two-income families and single, working parents who combine parenthood with a full-time commitment to career. Here the burden on the caregivers is greatest.

To weigh the alternatives in day care you have to see the whole situation. I believe the personal tone of each chapter gives this book universality. This is not a "how-to" text because the solution to a day care problem pivots on self-understanding. The answers are there but fully clothed in particulars. My approach is that of a lay anthropologist: to take you into people's homes where you can see the many forms that day care takes. Then you must design your own.

MONDAY THROUGH FRIDAY

Day Care Alternatives

HOW CHILDREN DEVELOP: IMPLICATIONS FOR CHILDCARE

by Dorothy W. Gross

In our complex society, parents cannot always provide the continuous loving care needed by their children. . . . I am suggesting that other significant adults, along with parents, can help to provide, in varying amounts and in a variety of settings, the caring relationship that allows a child to have his childhood, fully and freely, as a whole person.

Frances Vandivier, "Developing
Child Caring Skills for a Network
of Child Caring Services"

As mothers of young children are increasingly going to work outside the home, families are more and more finding themselves in need of child care. Many factors come into play in the search for good care—convenience of location, flexible hours, cost. Here we are taking the position that the needs of children are the most important considerations, and that the very young—infants, toddlers, preschoolers—are particularly vulnerable to who cares for them and to the environment in which they live. The implication of this position is that choices of child care should be based primarily on whether a given setting can foster optimal development.

Let us look at the meaning of optimal development by addressing four questions. First, how do young children grow and learn? Second, how do these ways of growing and learning—the processes of development—relate to child care arrangements? Third, what specific features of a child care setting are most pertinent to a child's potential adjustment to that setting? And finally, what can parents do to make the care arrangements optimal for their child?

Growing and Learning

During the early years of life, children make dramatic changes in their appearance, their physical skills, their understandings, and their capacity for maintaining close relationships with others. They evolve in the first five or six years, the early childhood period, from the relative helplessness of infancy—toothless, wordless, unable to walk or to sort out people or ideas—to an impressive level of initiative, thought, and sociability. In these years between birth and entry into kindergarten or first grade, a number of important processes take place as a function both of children's natural endowment and of how they are cared for. These are *separation, building human relationships,* and *thinking.* They interact with each other in one overall pattern of development, but for ease of discussion, let us take them singly.

Separation

Separation is a life-long process (as, indeed, are the other two). It has both an internal and an external aspect. Internally, each human being develops a sense of his or her self as separate from all others, with the self's own special quality, talents, limitations, style—that is, a sense of personal identity. Externally, there is the growing ability to move away from familiar and loved people and environments to new and challenging experiences and relationships. The two aspects feed each other: the more secure one's sense of personal identity, the more one is able to explore new

2

avenues; conversely, new experiences tend to sharpen and define one's sense of unique selfhood.

In the early weeks of infancy, it is thought that a child has no sense of separate self at all, not aware even of his or her own body as the source of many pains and pleasures, living in a world of sensation without boundaries. This is soon followed by a period of "doubleness": now it is as if, for the baby, the mother has entered his or her personal cocoon. A beginning boundary has indeed appeared, between the infant and the world, but he or she does not yet feel separate (alone); the nurturing parent is internally present. It is this sense of dual selfhood (which emerges only out of the ministrations of a loving parent) that is the foundation of later independent identity, as well as of the capacity to maintain intimate relationships.

By the middle of the first year of life, if all has gone well, babies demonstrate an awareness that the source of loving care is, indeed, "out there." Five- and six-month-old babies are often seen staring at their mothers' faces, fingering their noses and mouths, playing with parts of their bodies, their clothing, their eyeglasses, as if to say, "I see that you are somebody else out there, not in here with me. How amazing!" Separateness grows and is furthered by the baby's own drive to creep and crawl, to explore the world around, and eventually and joyfully, to stand up and walk away. Such expeditions can be joyful only if the baby has developed a clear sense of security in his or her separateness, and that of his or her mother. One can see here the integration of the inner and outer aspects of separation. At the same time that secure separateness is growing, however, feelings of emotional attachment are becoming stronger (an area to be discussed later). As a child nears two years old, this conflicting pull, so characteristic of this age, may make it very difficult either to leave or to be left by a loved parent. The two-year-old ambivalence, likely the primary reason why many parents find it such a challenging age to live with, is, in a certain sense, mirrored in all subsequent human encounters with separation from loved ones: going to school, to camp, away to college; leaving for marriage; seeing one's children leave; divorce; death.

Nevertheless, the underlying foundation of the capacity to be a separate individual is, for most of us, achieved by the third year of life, given close nurturing and appropriate opportunities for exploring. Subsequently, what we call the preschool period, ages three, four, five, becomes both a time of consolidation of that sense of separateness and a time to discover new people, places, and experiences. Increasingly, children are able to spend time away from their parents with other adults and children in new settings. Preschoolers increasingly feel comfortable and secure when separated from their parents, because their sense of independent identity is growing.

Building Human Relationships

The development of human relationships, the second of our processes, is clearly intertwined with separation: without a sense of oneself as separate from others, there can be no true building of bonds because there would be no separate entities to be linked. Another way of saying this is that if a baby continues with that sense of doubleness referred to above—a kind of Siamese twinness in relation to parents, siblings, peers, others—then no relationships exist at all, only a kind of self-love. What is suggested here is that the development of human relationships surely involves separation, as discussed above, but it also involves the capacity for closeness. That capacity is probably an inborn part of human nature, but it needs nurturing and it goes through stages.

During the "Siamese twin" stage of early infancy, babies tend to show their pleasure in others in generalized ways, for example, smiling at all friendly faces or accepting being held by many people. In this way, if they have been held and fed and lovingly cared for, they are freed to demonstrate their basic social nature as human beings.

Then, they are able gradually to make the distinction between themselves and familiar others, and to move on to a stage characterized by a growing capacity to differentiate between familiar and unfamiliar people. Have you seen a seven- or eight-month-old baby girl, for example, study a new face, then shift gaze to her mother, then stare again at the stranger? It is as if the infant is musing, "Now is this somebody new? He looks familiar, but . . . let's see. Oh, here's my mother! I know her! But . . . let's check it out again." Whether the sequence ends in tears or giggles is likely a function of how much trust the baby has developed, largely related to how she has been nurtured, but the process of differentiation is similar. The universal peek-a-boo is, in a sense, a separation, "now I see you, now I don't" game. It reflects both the excitement and the anxiety of the separation process—and the pleasure and relief of the return to the loved one. At this stage, increased capacity for a caring relationship is demonstrated by the infant's preference for the parents, not by a continuation of the earlier smiles-for-everyone reaction. The well-known "stranger reaction" of the latter part of the first year, far from being a negative event, is another such demonstration, an indicator of developing attachment.

As the infant becomes a toddler, that attachment serves as a secure base from which to explore the wider world. Other people, both adults and children, become increasingly attractive, as long as the parents are present or available, and new relationships can develop. These provide opportunities for toddlers to develop both a widening range of feelings—gentle affection, intense devotion, jealousy, anger, acquisitiveness—and a growing language capacity, the primary tool for communication. But the relationships also are often occasions for conflict, both internal and external.

It is difficult for many youngsters in the second year of life to integrate internally the exciting new stimuli, relationships, experiences, emotions that are part of developing toddlerhood. The struggle for integration appears to be most poignant in relation to the primary nurturer. "Should I do what she wants? Or what I want?" many two-year-olds appear to be asking, as they veer between autonomy and dependence. "Is she a bad mommy (when she leaves me with the sitter or doesn't buy me a toy)? Or a good mommy (when she reads me a story or plays with me)?" Gradually, the two-year-old, if well nurtured, learns that "good" and "bad" coexist in mothers, fathers, and indeed, themselves. They learn that autonomy and dependence are both part of relationships with parents. Then they can transfer this growing understanding of human complexity to peer relationships, where control and yielding, bossiness and cooperation, anger and affection all interact. Such understandings are helpful in resolving the external conflicts two-year-olds have with each other over toys, cookies, and who goes first on the slide. Certainly, in addition to struggles for primacy, toddlers often play alongside each other in relative peace, taking pleasure in the mutual company. And as toddlers become preschoolers, other children are less and less competitors or parallel players, and more and more true play companions. By age four, many children are able to maintain intense attachments to each other and even to select favored "best friends." Genuine cooperative interaction grows, with each child more and more able to see and defer to others' preferences, while appropriately explaining one's personal views.

Thinking

The ability to perceive and adapt to others' views is also part of thinking, the third development process. In infancy, that ability exists only as a potential: as suggested above, babies cannot yet sort out their own selves from others as existing entities, let alone understand or adjust to different views. That is the meaning of being egocentric, the lack of awareness that there are different ways to view the world, that one's self is, indeed, only one part of a much larger, more complex environment.

Infants think about the world through moving about in it, looking at everything with great attentiveness, tasting and touching as they go, smelling and listening. They formulate ideas out of these sense experiences. For example, they come eventually to understand *to and fro* through millions of times of going back and forth and a notion of *hue* through much looking at the varied colors of objects they encounter. In the human sphere, concepts like *reliability, trust,* and *intimacy* are not likely to be truly learned by a child who has not been dependably nurtured. The point is that in infancy *thinking* and *experiencing* are almost interchangeable. Later on, in the toddler period, children draw on these experiences to create mental images that serve as symbols for what they do and see and feel. They are able to remember earlier events by drawing on these images and expressing them in two major ways: make-believe play and language. As they become preschoolers, three-, four-, and five-year-olds, children become very skilled in both forms of thinking. Play is their way of experimenting with what they have mentally absorbed: they act out parental roles, adult work tasks, baby behavior, even the movements and sounds of inanimate objects. They try out their notions on each other, working out contradictions and distortions through experiments, arguments, discussions, and compromise. In this way, understanding grows, with play acting as a bridge between direct sense experience and more abstract mental operations.

Language is also related to thinking, in a more precise and efficient way. Children's first words, like their first play, express their first experiences. These are experiences with being cared for, with play, with moving about in the world, with autonomy and separation—"ma-ma," "ball," "car," "no," "bye-bye." The very use of these words helps in understanding what they refer to because language makes important distinctions; for example, "ma-ma" refers to a special female person ("da-da" means the special male); "bye-bye" means leave-taking, not greeting; "I wanna cookie" is not a request for orange juice. Further, as children communicate with each other, they exchange meanings and so expand their knowledge: "ma-ma" can stand for many mothers, "Katy Sue" refers only to one particular person; "let's play with the blocks" and "supper's ready" have an assortment of meanings related to different households, preferences, and personal styles.

As children advance into the preschool years, their facility with language expands and deepens, thereby enriching their thought processes. Now they can use words to formulate plans ("Let's go to the zoo"), to frame questions ("How did words get in the world?"), and to express understandings ("Vacations are when you don't work"). Play continues to be an important medium of thought because it gives children the opportunity to act out their confusions and growing knowledge in concrete ways. This is evident in the complex dramas of nursery school and kindergarten in which themes of family life, the marketplace, and the world of work are tackled. But increasingly, as the ability to think abstractly grows, children use language as a primary thinking tool. By the time they reach age seven or

6

eight, children are thinking and talking about moral issues, like fairness and truth, and political ones, like cooperation and leadership.

Relation to Child Care

Having taken a brief look at a few of the principal developmental processes of the early childhood years, we now return to our second question: How do early developmental needs relate to child care arrangements?

Child care is experienced differently according to a child's developmental period. It has one set of meanings for an infant, another for a toddler, and still another for a preschooler. (Naturally, the individual nature of a child is important, too, but here we are emphasizing children's general developmental stages.)

For very young infants, in the first weeks and months of life, the world is food for the senses, and through these, for the mind. Babies learn their parents and their first home settings primarily through their senses—the touch of a caressing arm or a crib mattress, the aroma of a body, the taste of a nipple or a rattle, the look of a face, and the sound of a voice. In these ways, they become sensitive to the familiar and dependent on it for security and stability. Therefore, child care in a new setting by caregivers other than familiar parents is experienced primarily as a shift in basic sense experiences, the foundation of the infant world, and is more or less discomfiting depending on the baby's nature. A baby who is cared for at home has only the caregiver to adapt to, of course, since there is no change in setting. In either case, child care needs to be gradually introduced so that babies can become accustomed to any new sights, sounds, or smells—the very feel of the new environment and/or person. In addition, caregivers need the opportunity to learn the baby's ways and preferences, first from the parents, then from direct observation, so as to adapt any new routines to the baby's needs.

In later infancy, when babies have formed attachments to their parents, can quickly distinguish them from strangers, and may demonstrate discomfort with the latter, issues beyond the sensory alone are involved. Babies often need a period of time in which to observe their parents and their caregivers interacting, as if to see a stamp of approval being issued from one to the other. But this interaction has even deeper implications for the baby. Infants between six and twelve months, while demonstrating clear preference for their parents and open pleasure at their appearance, are not yet able to remember them well in their absence. Out of sight is truly out of mind (although the capacity to remember is growing during this

7

period). A parent who spends time in the child care setting, home or other, becoming, for a while, part of the routine and sharing child care with the caregiver, helps bridge the mental gap by establishing personal points of reference for the child, "memory hooks." In this way, each part of the room and the program becomes infused with the face and identity of the parent. It is a process that takes time, during which the infant and the caregiver have an opportunity to get to know each other and to form an affectionate connection.

For toddlers, fresh issues are involved. Now, assuming the achievements of basic attachment to parents and a growing sense of comfortable selfhood, toddlers are joyfully exploring the wider world. A good child care situation can provide safe and stimulating opportunities for that exploration, supporting children's natural interests. At the same time, there are risks involved: fear of loss of parents ("Will I find them again? Will they come back?); difficulties in managing new challenges ("I need help!"); and need for approval of new achievements ("Who will admire me? Give me support?"). When parents are not available during this new exploratory period, children sometimes appear to be mourning their absence and to have their enthusiasm dampened. Therefore, the caregiver has a special role during this time—to be there and not there, to allow or encourage exploration while providing a welcoming lap, to provide both stimulation and comfort. It is a complex role and a very important one.

As young toddlers grow, so, too, does the sense of security in being separate, making child care more viable. They are growing in the capacity to keep images of parents in mind, so that their physical absence is more bearable. They are beginning to use play to enact and symbolize important relationships and experiences, thereby strengthening mastery and understanding of the child care situation. It is no coincidence that the most common play themes of many two-year-olds relate to aspects of mommy-daddy-baby interaction and separation-return: feeding and being fed, being put to bed and awakening, going "bye-bye" and coming home. Further, since language is increasingly a medium of expression of feelings and ideas, other children are increasingly important, both as sources of pleasure in shared experience and as companions in communication.

On the other hand, older toddlers and two-year-olds tend, in general, to struggle with the challenges of their newly burgeoning autonomy. In some ways, they enjoy and can cope with child care; in others, they need the reassurance that they will be allowed to return to the comforts of infancy. This ambivalence, sometimes expressed in clinging, tantrums, or sleep disturbances, may complicate a two-year-old's adaptation to a child care situation, particularly if it is perceived as a demand for "maturity" on adults' terms, not on his or her own.

By age three or four, however, most children, having resolved the issue of autonomy-dependency, are able to find in child care experiences of satisfying opportunities for play, friendships, learning of new skills, and testing of independence. Caregivers often become important supplementary attachment figures and models of behavior, particularly if they have introduced themselves with care and show sensitivity to children's needs. An important need in this period is to maintain a sense of parents' presence and availability, even while separated from them in a child care setting. Children often want to know where their parents are and what they are doing. Even in their own homes, they may need to speak to them on the telephone or carry a parent's handkerchief or glove. This need demonstrates a capacity for actually being separate while utilizing symbols to make connection in a concrete way. In this way, the child care situation in itself becomes a symbol of both separation and attachment, and can provide rich sources of new experience to support healthy maturing. What is implied here is that in all child care experiences, the potential exists for both pleasurable stimulation and anxiety for children, primarily because of separation stress. The latter must be worked through before the positive aspects can be enjoyed.

Features of Child Care Settings

The theme of the previous section has been that child care arrangements are experienced by children according to their developmental needs and characteristics. Therefore, and this was our third question, what are some of the specific features of child care settings that are most relevant for children's healthy adaptation?

A setting for the care of young children must demonstrate an understanding of developmental needs. The key in such a setting is the *quality of the caregivers*. When the children are young infants, particularly sensitive to consistent nurturing, they need caregivers who take special pleasure in being with babies: the physical caring and touching; responding to small, nonverbal cues; the one-sided conversation that babies love. Older infants and young toddlers need caregivers who take special interest in the children's new explorations and are excited about their discoveries, while being careful not to overwhelm them: they must understand both the importance of the first venturing into the world and the need for providing a secure base. Caregivers of two-year-olds are dealing with children in the throes of struggle: they are reaching for autonomy and intimacy at the same time. Special understanding is called for, along with patience, humor, and flexibility. By the time children are preschoolers, they need caregivers who understand their need for interesting experiences, for opportunities to interact with other children, and for new adults to relate to.

The point is that developmentally oriented caregivers make efforts to separate their own personal styles and preferences from the needs of the children, adapting themselves to those changing needs as the children grow. Training in early childhood education and child development or sound experience in caring for young children is necessary for such a difficult task, and child care settings have a responsibility to parents to select caregivers with that training or experience. Such caregivers tend to continue their studies and/or to work at careful observation of the children in their care in order to strengthen their professional abilities.

The *number of caregivers*, particularly in formal day care centers, is another important feature. There should be enough people to prevent overfatigue and boredom, both of which interfere with sensitive caregiving. Further, children need opportunities to select favorite caregivers and to spend uninterrupted time with them. Only if there are enough people are such opportunities possible. But there should not be so many that the children become confused or insecure, particularly during the toddler and two-year-old period, when relationships with new adults are being established. In addition, the caregivers need to establish relationships with each other, so that there is a common framework of goals and understanding when planning for the children. Too many adults tends to interfere with such a framework and emphasis often shifts to scheduling instead of communication.

Similarly, the *number of children* affects adjustment. Large groups, even with a high adult/child ratio, in home or center, tend in themselves to be confusing for young children. Crowdedness, noise, competition for adult attention, struggle over toys, and lack of privacy are conditions that interfere with the development of secure selfhood. Therefore, groups should be small enough so that children can move freely and investigate their world without interference, play with each other without interruption, and have leisurely opportunities to build warm relationships with their caregivers.

An additional factor is the *extent of individualization* of the setting— that is, how the differing needs of each child are met. Are children encouraged to bring favorite toys and objects? Do meals and snacks reflect personal preferences? How flexible are routines regarding naps, outdoor jaunts, time to complete tasks, and arrival and departure? This is another way of suggesting that developmental needs are best assured of fulfillment in a setting dedicated also to personal style, taste, and pacing.

Finally, there is the *home-child care setting relationship*. It is important for young children's healthy development that the child care environment be reasonably consonant with their experiences at home. This has different meanings at different ages. Infants, for example, should have similar physical routines in both places and should be handled in similar ways (given nonabusive treatment, naturally). Although toddlers and pre-schoolers may enjoy new experiences in their child care settings, they need similar approaches by their parents and their caregivers regarding limit setting, sexual behavior, expression of feelings, and the basic values of child rearing. In order to achieve such consonance, child care settings need to maintain close communication with parents, involving them in plans for initial entry, consulting them on all matters regarding the child, and planning activities for the children that support and deepen connections to home and/or parents.

What Parents Can Do

The last question we raised at the beginning of this chapter was what parents could do to make child care arrangments optimal for their children. Here are three general paths to that goal.

1. *Keep a close relation to the child care setting.* This means a variety of things: sharing concerns about the children's behavior and development so that caregivers can adapt their routines; asking questions about how the children felt and their activities during the day; listening to caregivers' observations, views, concerns; allowing children occasionally to call them on the telephone. (The needed sound of that special voice can maintain the important link and help a child over a difficult moment. Even though there may be tears during the call and a bit of sadness afterwards, making a connection during the day is worth the momentary pain. If a call causes hysterics or inconsolable grief, parents and caregivers should not take it lightly; mutual discussion is called for.)

In addition, it may mean spending time at the center or other facility, both at the beginning to ease the children's separation and entry, and throughout the year. (If parents are not allowed to do this at a center they are considering, they should not enroll.) At the same time, it is important to demonstrate to the children that there is trust between parent and caregiver in order to facilitate the shared child rearing. For the children's sake, this means that parents will have to stay close while they relinquish some of their control, no easy task. The objective is to build three-way connections between child, parent, and caregiver.

2. *Help children leave home (or say goodbye to parents if staying at home) by providing symbols of home and parents.* These may be pictures of parents, a small object belonging to a parent or sibling, favored toys, and

special tokens of home, such as a pillow or a blanket. Some preschoolers may enjoy keeping a "letter" from a parent in a pocket during the day. Others who are cared for at home and see their parents leave for work may enjoy occasional visits to the place of work, taking away a small object, such as a notebook or some colored rubber bands. In this way, children are helped to visualize their parents and the comforting image bridges the separation. The point is to help children keep a sense of their parents' loving care while absent.

3. *Finally, talk to children about the caregivers and the child care setting.* Encourage them to tell their reactions and feelings about their experiences. Play "child care," read stories about children who have caregivers, and tell about other people's experiences away from home. In these ways, both play and language can be used to help children cope with and understand the separation and the new environment.

2

HOUSEHUSBAND

*The best way to make children
is to make them happy.*

Oscar Wilde

A strong humanities education in linguistics, a wonderful ability to do goldsmithing, well-developed carpentry skills, a typically male sense of humor, and atypical, for a man, insouciance about getting ahead—all these Barry Kahn brings to bear in caring for small children. Five-plus days a week, while his wife Jean is at nursing school, Barry has exclusive charge of his daughters, Jocelyn, two, and Heather, four. Additionally, he provides full and part-time day care to five other children, ages fifteen months to seven years. Self-employment has always suited Barry, both temperamentally and philosophically. When his daughters were born he found them so *interesting* that he decided to buck convention, scale down his goldsmithing and old home renovating, and be their caregiver *primarily*. Barry Kahn is a stay-at-home father become professional caregiver. Or as he grins and puts it, "I'm a day care daddy."

The Kahns rent the second and third floors of a mid-Victorian house converted to two apartments, located in a tranquil pocket of nearly downtown Portland, Maine. Across the street lies Westbrook Community College, where Jean, whose desires to "prove herself" and attain a meaningful career are stronger than Barry's, has gone back to school to become a nurse and, eventually, a midwife. The home has a big porch and backyard, and borders a confluence of campus walkways on which the children trike.

At thirty-three, Barry has a slender, wiry frame, is of medium build, and wears a thick, well-kept brown beard. His face is unlined, and his manner merry. He said he welcomed—"just like *any* housewife"—the chance for long conversation with an adult. Talk he did, and dazzlingly, giving the impression of both *joie de vivre* and a sharp cutting edge of personal restlessness.

His commentary that follows includes in places asides to the children in his charge. These remarks, which are enclosed in parentheses, have been included because of the inkling they give of his unconscious style of relating to children, a very "awake" style that saves him utterly from being the bored househusband. Five, nonconsecutive days from his daybook follow the commentary. Barry uses the daybook both to structure his experience as a caregiver and to record "the amazing things kids say." Maybe someday he will develop it into a book.

Barry Kahn's Commentary

I was born in Los Angeles, the second of five children. My older brother is five years older than I—we had a good gap. I helped out with my younger brothers and sisters, but not to any excessive amount. You wouldn't say I identified with my mother's role, or had a special affinity for babies.

For a long time my father was a maverick in the work force, a little like me. He almost had a bachelor's degree in math from the University of Chicago. He joined the army in World War II, a semester away from graduating, and never returned to college. He was a math genius. He could play blindfold chess and was a master's quality chess player. He used to read books and play chess without looking at the board. *Once* my older brother and I beat him because he forgot where a piece was while reading a book. And he was pissed as hell when he lost. He played bridge the same way. He could keep track of all these things; he had that kind of brain.

Until there were five kids in the family, he had all sorts of strange jobs, highly unprofitable. Then he finally fell into a job that brought in much more money, computer programming. After he became a computer programmer, he was truly happy, but I don't think he did a particularly great job as father. We moved around the country every five years because of a deal he made with the company, and then we moved back to California because both my parents hated the snow and rotten weather. My father died young, at 48. Basically he worked himself to death, very happily. He used to get up really early in the morning and drive to work, so he could be there an hour or two before the place opened and play with his computer. He'd come back after rush hour so he could miss the traffic, eat dinner, and then go down into the den where he had his pile of computer printouts, two-feet thick, and fiddle with his program for the rest of the evening.

I don't think he was bad, but he didn't much care. Running the family was my mother's job, and he was there as a presence. He used to yell at us and make lists of things to do, which we never did. We didn't have a big house, but we filled it up!

I had the advantage of being number two, being only eight when my father finally got a decent job. My older brother was very scarred by our poverty before then. From when I was young enough that it didn't matter, I can remember taking peach crates and painting them and that is what we sat on. The place where we lived in Los Angeles that overlooked the freeway was a dump. But if you are young enough it doesn't matter, you don't care. So I missed a lot of the insecure stuff my brother felt. My brother has an ulcer, and I don't.

I've also said jokingly, but I think there's a lot of truth to it, that my parents tried to raise my older brother and screwed him up royally in the process, and then just gave up with the rest of us. We all went our various directions.

(Don't write on your shoe. I thought you were going to ride on your tricycle wicked fast. You did? I didn't see you, you'd better do it again. Are you going to ride your big shoe with Heather? . . . Why don't you and

Jocelyn make a bouquet? Show Jocie how. I don't think she knows what a bouquet is) Another five minutes!

I raised myself, I think we all did to a large extent. Partly as a matter of inheritance, partly because of the way we were raised or allowed to raise ourselves, all five of us are very individualistic. As long as I can remember, I never felt pressure to do what the other kids did. Often I thought what they did was stupid, and I *didn't* do it. We were also, my whole family, pretty bright. It was easy for us to get good grades in school, which really takes the heat off. If you can do what the teacher wants with 5 percent of your brain and spend the rest of the time doing whatever you want, your life is easier. We were all that way.

Relatives on my wife's side of the family all think I'm a bit crazy, but I know they respect my fathering. I *know* my family is crazy, which doesn't bother me either! But every now and then when I hear some cousin talk about how he just started his new job and the bottom rung of the ladder is $15,000 a year, which Jean and I might in the next year or two make between us if we worked hard at it, I get a twinge—to get richer. It would be nice to have more money, but at the same time I see other things that the relatives do. I know where their money goes—to buy color television and the other folderol. I just can't be bothered.

I also see how they shortchange their families. Heather and Jocelyn were both born at home. After Heather's birth, when she was four days old, Jean's parents came to visit. It was a terrible visit because her mother wanted to help and there was nothing for her to do. She couldn't warm up formula or hold a bottle, since Jean was breastfeeding. And Heather basically wanted to be with Mommy. The only good thing about the visit was that a lot of emotional things were aired. At one point I was outside with her father, and he began to ruminate. He said that he loved his kids very much and got along with them very well until they reached kindergarten age. Then he felt that they were, not taken away, but that the responsibility for them was transferred. It was no longer his but the school's. From age five the gap was created and never closed, and he sorely regretted it. As I listened to that, my first child was four days old, and I thought, "I don't ever want to say that for myself."

Some things in your life you can later change or do differently. You can get into a career that "sucks" and change careers, but you can't re-raise your children. That part of your life you can't do over. Jean's father was saying in effect, "This part of my life I blew for twenty years." And the consequences will go on until he dies. That gave me a message.

One of the children brings over a box of 48 crayons. I turned around one moment and there were Kristin and Heather carefully breaking all Kristin's new crayons in half. Jocie PEELS them.

For my part I wish I hadn't had an education. I dislike formal schooling intensely. I resent it. I wish my parents had never sent me to school. And we attended lots of them! I went to public schools all over creation. I went to five schools in the fourth grade. One of them was for one day, until they discovered I was in the wrong division of the school system. That was the day before Valentine's Day. All the kids gave me Valentines, which I wasn't able to return.

From fourth grade to the end of eighth grade, we moved to New York, New Jersey, Wisconsin, and Massachusetts. Then starting in ninth grade I was back in California. I went to high school in the San Fernando Valley and college at UCLA [University of California, Los Angeles]. Then I was in the Peace Corps for three years, in Senegal from 1970 to 1973. I taught English, and on the hot days I "baked." One day it hit 115 degrees on a day when I was teaching. I remember leaning against one of the walls of my brick classroom for about two seconds, and then I lept away, and all the students stared at me. They were sitting there lethargically in puddles of sweat and couldn't figure out why all of a sudden I was so active. I seldom grouse about coastal Maine weather because my thermostat remembers being *hot*.

In 1973 I came back to the United States. I had been married since my second year of college, to a classmate at UCLA, and we got a divorce after we were back. Then I met Jean in Connecticut, and we moved to New Hampshire.

Another thing that happened, that was important: When I was in Senegal I learned jewelry making, which I'm retiring from this year, thank God, although it has been a very good job for many years. But it started as a hobby. I never cared about jewelry. I can remember my ex-wife going out shopping for earrings, and thinking what a waste of money. I never noticed jewelry, I never cared. The second year I was in Senegal some of my students said there was a great jeweler who was back in town; he had been in the Ivory Coast. We used to buy things for presents to bring home, so I met him in his hut where he worked, near one of the places where I taught. I used to go and watch him. We extended for a third year, and before I left for a vacation break in the United States, I asked, "When I come back would you teach me to make jewelry?" He laughed a lot at the idea of any white man, an American particularly, wanting to make jewelry, but he said, "If you are crazy enough to want to, I'll teach you." So I learned to do filigree, which is the predominant style there. I still had no idea that there was money in jewelry. I was totally innocent about the whole thing. It was a hobby. I came back and was still learning how, teaching myself, and people started asking me to make things. Before I knew it I was in business.

So I became a jeweler, and the first year I did it I also was a long-distance operator for the telephone company part time. Only one guy was working there at the time I was hired. The government had said they had to get some men in. That was strange! I quit after ten months and became a jeweler. In the meantime I had met Jean who had been working in the phone company for six years.

At first I made jewelry at home. Then when I decided I was going to do it to earn a living I found a delightful shop in New Haven, walked in, and asked the owner how he would like to have a resident jeweler. I started working in this cellar, a dank cubicle, at Group W Bench, named after the Group W bench in *Alice's Restaurant*. The boutique sells a bit of everything. Since the owner has had kids, it has a lot of toys. The store changes as his life changes. A nice, very successful store. I worked there for quite a while, until Jean quit the phone company, and we moved up to New Hampshire. By that time I had done Rhinebeck, the big crafts show in New York, for two years in a row.

Then we lived in various places in New Hampshire and finally married, after Jean's mother had answered to "Guess what?" on the phone a million times with "You're pregnant?" No, she wasn't pregnant. Then when she finally was, and Jean called up and said, "Guess what?" her mother couldn't guess!

For a long while Jean was so happy to have quit the phone company that she didn't think about a career path. At the phone company she had been a secretary in sales, so she had to put up with the typical syndrome of the guys chasing the girls, American corporate manners at their worst. She helped me with the jewelry, and we lived in all sorts of houses.

One of the first was near Alton, New Hampshire, where we had friends in the crafts business. The house, nearly 200 years old and in a half-restored state, was only a five-minute walk from a lovely lake. But the carpenter ants were so bad we had to run plastic across the ceiling to keep the sawdust from falling down on us. Sometimes flying squirrels or mice ran across the floor. Jean was pregnant by this time. When the pipe that ran from the well under our driveway froze, there was no way we were going to spend the rest of the winter in an open-air house, so we moved into a communal-living situation.

Then, shortly after Heather was born, we moved to East Rochester, New Hampshire, which is just over the border from Maine, because we had friends who were renting space in a factory. That way I could rent space in the factory too, which I did. I started a crafts photography business along with my jewelry business, because to get into shows you have to submit slides. I'd been doing it for my own jewelry for quite a while. I'm out of that field too! I have a lot of exprofessions. I still own an embarrassing amount of camera equipment.

As parents-to-be Barry and Jean had already struck out against conventional practices. The home-birth movement caught their imaginations and earned their firm allegiance.

The reason we moved to Maine was our involvement with home birth. My staying home with Heather and Jocelyn now is no radical shift but a continuum from the initial decision to do birth differently. So I've been involved with my children a lot from the time *before* they were born.

When Jean was first pregnant with Heather, I felt very much left out of the pregnancy. That was when we were still planning a hospital birth. I felt I did my bit, got her pregnant, and there was no more part for me to play. The changes are happening inside the woman's body, and the man can't feel anything. Then when we made the decision for a home birth, all of a sudden we shared the responsibility. We had to find a midwife and take a class. It made a tremendous difference for me. It reinvolved me. This was *my* baby too. The OB pats you on the head and says, "Eat the right food, do what I say, see you next month. Don't worry about anything. Don't read too many of those books. Take your classes at the end." But *everybody* worries about everything, you have to. In choosing to have a home birth it became very clear to us that the responsibility was on our shoulders.

That's when I really started getting involved. We didn't want to merely have our baby and quit. So we went through a training program to become home-birth teachers ourselves, under the aegis of the Association for Childbirth at Home International (ACHI). We taught home-birth classes until Jean entered school last year, and it became too much.

How did Jean get started in her career path?

She had met a nurse-midwife from Maine who was doing home births. The midwife had an apprentice who left so she let Jean accompany her to a couple of births. Then the midwife said, "Would you like to be my apprentice?" We were living too far away for it to be practical, so we moved to Maine and lived up in Raymond, a winter rental, for nine months; then on to Gorham, another of these *deals*, a year's free lodging in exchange for my helping build the apartment where we were going to live. I learned on the job and met a good friend, an English fellow who was the carpenter. I learned a lot; I could build something now if I had to. The work was half rough and half finishing, which I enjoyed. But there were problems with the owner.

Jean worked for the nurse-midwife for a year and a half. She originally had planned to be a lay midwife. Then she decided she needed more

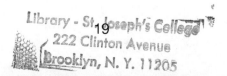

19

training than that to be competent, and that she couldn't get it doing two or three births a month. So she decided to go to nursing school to study to become a nurse-midwife. That gave her a career ambition, which is more than I have, and I said, "Great."

I never have been one to ask, "What am I doing next? What's going to happen next year?" I don't worry about it. I just turned thirty-three, and I've felt as far back as I can remember I could learn to do anything I wanted to if I put my mind to it. I still feel that way. The only difference lately is that I realize more than I did when I was younger the amount of energy it takes, and the sacrifice, particularly having a family. I considered trying to go to medical school at one point and decided there was no way. If I wanted to desperately enough I could, but I would lose my family in the process, which wasn't worth it at all. Working eighty hours a week is not my idea of the good life. I don't care how much money you get someday out of it, if you're a doctor, you keep working the eighty hours.

It was an interesting juncture when Jean decided nursing school was what she wanted. I graduated fourth in my class from a big California school. I didn't try at all. One of the reasons I resented school was that it never challenged me. I think it's inevitable in a school situation that you do with rare exceptions whatever the teacher wants you to do to get whatever grade you think is adequate. And I did. An exception is if you study something that turns you on and you don't care about the class. But it would have been hard to be self-motivated, to know what I wanted to do and get all crazy for things then. The way my ex-wife thought she knew what she wanted to do, to be an English professor. She worked her tail off at UCLA, while I sat around playing my guitar on campus. But she was exceptional. I knew no one else like that. I could have spent those years much more wisely if I had either directed my own studies or had had teachers who said, "You're a lazy bum. If you want a C you're going to have to work."

Jean's school experience was different from mine, and not good either. She attended Catholic elementary and junior highs, and didn't like school or excel. She wasn't ready for the public high school and had terrible grades there all through. Jean came to Westbrook because it has a two-year R.N. program. Her father had thought all women should be secretaries, which is why she was at the phone company. Then at Westbrook they wouldn't accept her into the nursing program until she took certain college courses. In the classes she took she got A's, 100s, both in math and chemistry. It was great for her ego. This is one of the reasons I'm glad she went back to school. Jean is one of the top four or five students in her nursing class—it's super for her. So they let her in, and she did great, although it was very hard. Jocie was about six months old when Jean finished the algebra and chemistry and started nursing school.

That's when Barry and Jean had to make a decision. The question was, should he go out and get a full-time job? Or should he try to think of a way to earn a living and still stay home?

If Jocie had been two, I might have considered going out and working full time, but I didn't and still don't feel that little kids benefit from full-time day care. So I went through the little bit of red tape to become a state-licensed family day care home, and started advertising.

(Can't beat those Granny Smith apples even if they do cost twice as much as the others. Right, kids?)

For quite a while it was slow. Right off I got one girl, Kristin, who is Heather's age, and her older brother, Matthew, who is in first grade. That was in September. Then one more child came for a while until her mother quit her job. Since February things have picked up. I've been busy. Now I get two calls a week and have been turning people away right and left. Presently I have Heather and Jos—that makes two. I have Gabriel, who is three and a half, Kristin, four, Matthew, seven, and Carmen, two, and will have Rachel, who is one year old, starting in July. It's quite a pile of kids! They are all full time except Matthew who comes after school during the year.

There is a strong push in this state to do away with licensing for day care. The providers haven't succeeded; I don't know if they will. A lot of them feel it is silly interference. On the other hand, some of the licensed people are scared of someone putting thirty kids in a room and locking it. The way I feel is that the parents who care will check to make sure that people are taking care of their kids well. And the people who don't care won't go to licensed providers anyway because licensed providers usually charge more. And there is always somebody who will take the kids for $25 or $30 a week, and they have one or two kids of their own. These sitters might be fine, or terrible, but they are not going to come into the system anyway. So I don't care; that is to say, it doesn't bother me to be licensed or not.

Recently the state of Maine raised the limit on the size group you can have. They increased it to six full time including your own, and two after school. This is *more* than I could handle. This spring I hired a fourteen-year-old, who is working out great, to come in the afternoon, and my wife's working evening shifts so she is here until two this summer. So it is working out well.

Before I was licensed, they inspected. The woman who runs the licensing for southern Maine came over with a checklist of questions that I had a hard time answering with a straight face. Social service rulings are always so two sided. On the one hand, they were perfectly legitimate questions to ask somebody who wants to take care of other people's kids. On the other hand, since I know me and the way we raise our daughters, the interview made me laugh. Like, what is your policy on potty-training? When they are ready, they do it, that's my policy. What is your schedule of activities during the day? That one really floored me. I don't say, "Well, from 9:00 to 9:30 we are going to paint, and from 9:30 to 10:00 read." That's school! That's bad school—when the message is, "I said you are going to paint. If you don't feel like painting, you are going to paint anyway." So to that question I replied, "When it's nice, we will go outside, and we'll do indoor things when it's ten below zero; what do you think?" She checked for lead paints around the house and asked what kinds of supplies we had. Lots, and we have acquired additional immense amounts since we started.

Behind the informality of the day's curriculum lies Barry's very definite ideas about child rearing.

Before Heather was born, I did a lot of reading about childbirth and babyhood. We had a fair collection for a lending library for our class. But now I'm back to my usual fare: science, science fiction, short stories, mysteries—a bit of everything. Every now and then I think I should borrow one of the books about preschool activities, but I've never felt I *had* to. I'm sure they have ideas I could use, but I also have quite a clear idea of what the kids like to do.

Our curriculum is tailored to Maine. If you can play outside, you usually play outside—that's first priority. We have vehicles for almost everybody now. Kristin and Matthew brought their trikes over to stay. Heather has a new tricycle, Gabriel rides the old tricycle, Jocie has the plastic shoe. Carmen likes to *sit*, which is a problem. I chase her to exercise. The baby will go in the backpack or the stroller. In summer we have a kiddie pool out back, and that's good for an hour and a half of water therapy in the afternoon.

They like to paint and color, and we have lots of blocks. They like to play with dolls, and be read books. And they like to eat. The ones that are little take naps, and that takes up a day's activities, with variations on a theme. If they are happy, I leave them alone. If they start to fight or run out of ideas, I give them an idea. I try not to take over their game but to spark their imaginations. "Why don't you play fill-in-the-blank?" or "Find the tools Mommy brought. You can play doctor." "Oooh, yes," they say, and all

Group activities complement spontaneous play at the Kahns'.

run and get what they need. In a flash they are lying on the floor poking one another and playing doctor. Children don't need their hands held. They only need ideas sometimes for what to do. With all the other stuff I have to do like catching up on the dishes and figuring out are we going to have popcorn today or not, I wouldn't have time to play with them more. And I don't think they want me to.

The helper has allowed me to split up the group and take the older ones for a long walk. Some of the kids love a walk on the coldest days. Others, like Heather, are super chicken, although I hope this year she'll be better. I'll try to hire a helper more hours this winter. Behind our house is a 440-acre cemetery with a duck pond at the bottom. Among the gravestones are terraces and little hills that are great places for sliding. Kristin and Matthew are outdoorsy kids so I took them sliding last winter. Heather hated it; "There's snow on my face, take me home." When the others are clamoring, "Do it again!" if a helper's along, we can.

One of my favorite parts of doing day care is seeing how different all the children are. For example, Kristin isn't interested in drawing yet. The best drawing she has ever done was one day when Heather was out visiting a friend and every other child was asleep, and I had played with Kristin enough and she had nothing else to do. She sat down and did an excellent intricate drawing. She's capable of it, but it's a last resort. She'd far rather run around outdoors. Heather's been able to write since the day I built the easel. Trying out lines and colors there is the activity that holds her longest.

We have no television; I think it's terrible. Nobody watches *Sesame Street* at *this* house. Down at their grandmother's the girls get their semiannual dose of the tube. Grandma thinks it's good for them, like baby food. And we don't think it will do any permanent damage in *that* dosage.

Providing family day care *is* hard work, but not as bad as you might think. The hardest part isn't taking care of the kids, it's lack of adult companionship. Especially with my wife working weekends. If my kids were older, I'd be finished with child care at five o'clock. Instead I continue all evening and usually weekends, because the weekends Jean is often on. She is here in the morning and then she's gone. Talking to people who are older than six occasionally is vastly pleasing, and I don't do it enough.

As far as I'm concerned I suffer from the typical housewife syndrome. She's home with the kids all day, and she goes crazy. I'm a househusband, but the situation is exactly the same. I get sick of the routine.

Also, the normal household tasks are augmented. I can do all the dishes and the kids eat lunch, and I can do all the dishes again. Every day it's like having a dinner party with all your friends over. Mealtimes I find hard. No matter what time I decide to feed them, they are always hungry a half-hour earlier. It happens automatically, as soon as I go in the kitchen.

How, I wondered, did Barry see their family life evolving?

We are going to stay here for a while. It's nice. Besides which the thought of moving makes me want to die. Of furniture we have almost nothing, but we keep acquiring books. The equipment from all my past professions adds up too. I sold my darkroom equipment because I wouldn't be living anywhere where it could be set up easily. But I still have cameras and lights, plus all my jewelry stuff even though I'm phasing that out. Boxes of tools and findings so when these little beauties say they want to go out and buy earrings, I can say, "You're NOT going to go out and buy them, you'll make them yourselves." Plus junk, baby clothes, winter clothes, old toys, and so forth.

We won't have more children, probably, although part of both of us would love to keep having kids. Jean thinks of it as this interesting roulette because you never know what you are going to get next time. But the logical, sensible part of me says that our kids are finally old enough so that we can leave them with a sitter and Jocie doesn't throw a fit as we go out the door. She'll wave goodbye. We've taken to going out for dinner a couple of times a month. That's our big thrill, to go out and eat Chinese food, whenever we feel we can spend the money, and more often than we can afford. Now we can go out for *two hours*, and not think about the kids! And that's nice to do once in a while, very good for our grown-up psyches. We'd gone to some movies separately, but last Friday night we went to *Raiders of the Lost Ark* together. It was entertaining. It also scared the hell out of both of us. I couldn't believe there were some people there with fairly young children.

I like the ages the kids are now. I've liked the stages since they were born, but this age gives us new freedoms. Jean was saying today at lunch, "Maybe next year we can go camping with them. They'll be old enough to go camping and enjoy it." Next year will be five years that we haven't canoed or camped. We think it would be great to take a trip with some Peace Corps friends of mine, all our kids, and canoe and camp.

But you never know. If we did have another child, I suppose it wouldn't be the end of the world. Financially I don't know how we would survive. Plus Jean's mother probably wouldn't speak to her anymore. Unless we had a boy. That would be different. All the grandchildren on both sides are girls.

I asked Barry if he and Jean felt any tensions over their respective roles.

I'm very happy that she has a career image. We see absolutely no reason why it's any more legitimate for a wife to help a husband with his career than for a husband to help a wife. We can't fathom what people do when they *both* want careers.

The tensions that we do have result from the fact that she is a student during the year. Jean is making up for those poor grades that she got in high school. Even though it's just about impossible with the system of tests they give, she wants to be the best in the class.

So we don't see enough of each other, and that's inevitably a problem. She goes over to school and studies every night of the week. It's hard being a nurse, and the two-year training program is very compressed. The degree is an associate's but she'll be an R.N., taking her boards next summer. The amount of work she does sometimes equals what you would do in medical school.

Jean's schedule makes it rough, and also that we have the other kids here when she's home. It's not just the four of us, except on weekends. Last year, when Jocie was a baby, Jean had classes from eight to eleven or noon, came home for lunch, nursed Jocie to sleep, then took off to the library to study before the afternoon classes. Sometimes she would study in the little alcove off the living room, but as I had more kids this became impossible.

(Very pretty but what is it? An airplane? Good, Heather, can we fly to France? Build a BIGGER one.)

So that to me is our perennial problem. It would be great if we could both take a week's vacation someplace and do nothing on the sand but sunbathe.

It is as hard for Jean as for me. Especially when she comes home for dinner but has to go back to the library afterwards. She is being torn two ways. She has strong family instincts and strong student instincts. Sometimes I just say, "Go study, will you? Give me a break!" During the school year there is an exam almost every week, and the students are always playing catch up. Besides which all her textbooks weigh fifty pounds and are six inches thick! Nursing school is hard, and I'm proud of her for doing so well. But we don't see enough of each other.

Having extra kids here in the house is a burden on the marriage too. Although in most ways I wonder whether it's any harder to take care of six kids than just two. As soon as we hit a weekend, Heather asks me, "When are Kristin and Matthew going to be back?" The day care children are someone to play with, and Heather is *into* playing. Jocie seems to care less. but even Jocie on Sunday likes to run down the list of as many names as she can think of who are coming tomorrow, and she usually gets most of them.

My teaching two or three nights a week whittles away at our free time too. It puts a time pressure on me because I must be out of here at 6:00 to get into town to teach at 6:30. The day care kids are gone at 5:15. To try and make dinner and juggle these other things is g-a-a-a! I might quit my job in the fall, if we can afford it. I'm more or less withdrawing from all my other businesses, just doing day care.

I'm not sure how many *friends* Jean and I even have right now. When she started school, our social life rapidly became zero, and it hasn't recovered. It was already on a steep decline from the time we had kids. Our friends in the crafts business from the time we moved to New Hampshire and I started showing at the Rhinebeck, New York, fair were either single, living with their girl friends, or married but had no children. From the day Heather was born and we became fanatic parents, the people who had no kids didn't *care* that our daughter had toilet trained, or peed on the wall, or any of the other marvelous things that kids can do. It's not their fault, childless people simply can't relate.

Two things I told people when we were teaching home-birth classes that they come back and say, "You were really right" about: (1) that your preparenthood friends are not going to be interested in your baby's antics, and (2) your sex life will drop to zero if it hasn't already during pregnancy. People come back and say, "You know what you told us in the class? I thought you were crazy. Sex only once a week, once every two weeks—I'll never permit it. By God, we're lucky if it's once a month!" These changes are normal among other parents we talk to, but the average friend from before doesn't understand.

Barry elaborated on his and Jean's suitability for their respective roles.

Temperamentally I am now the person better suited to taking care of small children. My tolerance for upsets is much higher than Jean's. First, she has the urge to get her work done. Second, she is unused to the rhythm. I've always admired her as a mother. I think she's a great mother to my kids. But I know she doesn't have the patience that she did.

(You're hungry, Dee-dee? Want some more banana? Want some cheese? What would you like? Tell me what you want and I'll get it for you. [Heather, raptly:] "We want you to GUESS." How about a peanut butter and jelly sandwich? . . . Good!)

I think patience in large measure is a factor of familiarity. Take, for example, when a mother nurses a baby—Jean is still nursing Jocie, not too much but some. When you spend so many hours in contact, you are inevitably attuned to your child. Jean says often she wakes up and turns over and sees Jocie sleeping, and as soon as she turns back Jocie wakes up too to nurse. Like a lot of breastfeeding mothers, Jean actually doesn't know how many times she nurses in the course of the night. "If I'm sore it must have been twelve times, or one twelve-hour stretch," she said once. "Who knows?"

That kind of tuning in between mother and child takes place because of the closeness in nursing. I believe the father who spends a tremendous amount of time with the child tunes in fast too. Being self-employed, I was able to spend a lot of time with my kids. I did it and liked to. The more time you spend the more intimate you are.

When we were presented in home-birth class the idea of convivial nights, "family bed," it sounded strange. But at the same time I was very much in favor of Jean's breastfeeding, and it seemed dumb to put an infant in a crib and then have to get up in the middle of the night to fetch her. So we figured for the first six weeks we would have Heather in bed with us, and not worry about it.

Jean's mother insisted we buy a crib, and gave us the money. Our kids never used it except a few times to play in. If I bring it down now, they will both want to jump in because it is such a novelty—"A new place to play!" Matthew, the seven-year-old, will probably want to pile in too. . . . (I'll have to fight you guys out with sticks!)

Heather was born at 6:05 on a Monday night. Jean and I finally fell asleep about midnight. We lay in bed with this new person between us. There was no question that's where we wanted her to be. I don't even know if we discussed it, except to laugh about how we could ever have considered any other way. She's slept with us ever since. We have two double mattresses on the floor. Up until Jean started working evenings, I slept with Heather on one mattress and Jean with Jocie on the other so she could nurse her. Now that Jocelyn is being weaned, although she doesn't know it—and you wouldn't either if you watched her—Jean sleeps on a single mattress in the living room for much of the night. If Jean lay beside her, Jocie would want to nurse too when she woke up to pee. Then between four and six, Jocie wakes up and *really needs Mommy,* so Jean rejoins us. Afterwards I may stay in the bedroom or go out to the living room, because I have to get up earlier than Jean to prepare for the onslaught. At some point after Jocelyn has weaned, I expect the girls will sleep together.

I think I am more patient than Jean, especially with all the kids, from sheer repetition, because I've had to deal with them for nine months, since September, on a daily basis. I know a lot more tricks for getting the kids off my back for five minutes so that I can finish making lunch than she does. And it's purely a matter of having to do it. It's like learning anything else, having to learn to cope with whatever your problem is. So I'm good at it, and she is less so. She's into being a student. Certainly Jean was incredibly patient when they both were babies. Heather had a strong sucking need. She would suck on my pinky finger. When I managed to pry it out, it would be pale from the sucking. Jean used to lay on the bed and nurse Heather for what seemed hours.

I asked Barry whether he thought he related to young children in a masculine way. Was his approach more directive, more joking, less physical, more distanced than most women's?

Yes, probably, simply because I am a man and grew up in America. I know the way I interact with the kids is certainly masculine. I'm the daddy. Even though Jocie calls me "Mommydaddy" sometimes. Just so she'll get somebody. "Mommydaddy, Mommydaddy!" "Yes, I'm here." The kids have learned there is a limit to how many toys you can bring out, or you can't walk across the floor and punch somebody. I think one of the reasons that I can handle the kids in a group more competently than Jean is masculine team skills. Maybe. But I cuddle with them if I think they need

28

cuddling. And half the day I don't treat my kids as though I'm their father because they are just part of the group. To the extent that men are different from women, my voice is here and Jean's is up there, we are different too as parents. But a different man would interract with the day care kids in his own way.

I commented that not seeing enough positive male models is a problem about growing up in America. Did the day care parents whose children go to Barry appreciate having "something special"? He replied he didn't know for sure how the parents felt, except in the case of Carmen's.

Carmen's father thought it was great. He's a lawyer and her mother works in the planning office at city hall. He took a year off from work so that his wife could go back to her job, feeling hers was the less expendable. They came over to visit, and Carmen's mother said, "Mike thinks it's great that you have a beard the way he does and that it will give continuity because he's been home with Carmen from the time she was six months to two years." He thought it was super that there was going to be another daddy to take care of her.

Once they are over their initial surprise, parents accept that the provider's a man and seem to think nothing of it. I haven't advertised for a long time. When I did, I said, "Licensed family day care"; I didn't include "by a man."

The calls I get now come through either the Department of Human Services or word-of-mouth recommendations. What happens is that people call up and if she's here Jean answers the phone because she's closer to it. She tells them, "It's not me, it's my husband." "Oh can I talk to him?" they say. So the idea isn't so totally outlandish that people won't accept it.

Although friends of mine, more ex-Peace Corps people, who live in New Haven and have two daughters, the older one six, passed on a different story. Ginnie, the mother, is a dance therapist. She got a part-time job, and she and a friend were trying to find a babysitter for their three kids so they could combine the cost. They put an ad in the paper and one of the first calls was from a man. Ginnie said she didn't think twice about it, that there would be anything wrong with a man taking care of Jessica. But her friend was horrified. "Are you kidding? A man taking care of my daughter? A pervert maybe! Never, no way, not in a hundred years."

It never had occurred to me either that people might have reservations about a male provider, but once the idea is put in your head, you can see where the fears come from. Kristin's and Matthew's mother, who is a social worker with child abuse cases, sees many kids who have been sexually abused by parents and foster parents. Recently she went to rescue a girl who, having been sexually abused by her real father, was put in a foster home and the foster father did too. There is hardly a *good* tradition in America of lots of hugs between men and their kids. We have to create it.

I turned to the financial aspects of running a day care service. Did it provide an adequate income for the Kahns?

You could earn a decent amount of money by doing this if you had no kids of your own and you weren't incredibly ambitious. The normal rate when I started last year was $40 a week for full time. That was what I charged. I'm raising my rate to $45 in two weeks, because I figure after a year I deserve a raise—everything else is going up. No one has complained at all. Either they are people with enough money, or they are stuck. The little baby Rachel will pay $50 because babies require more care. She will be the finishing touch to my labor. I might be crazy taking her on, but she's a cute kid and I like babies.

I'll be grossing about $200 a week from day care. I also work part time teaching English to Indochinese refugees two or three nights a week, through the Portland city schools. Actually I am thinking of quitting. It is really a drag when Jean has a night off and I have to teach. Last year we needed the money badly, and I enjoyed it. Now I teach the intermediate class, which is smaller, and find it less exciting to deal with three or four people only. I like the people but don't feel really needed.

We are going into debt like crazy. Our debts are student loans though and feel respectable. We had to be bailed out recently a bit, when a stolen car hit our 1970 VW Bug while I was teaching downtown. The insurance didn't cover it, so the crack-up precipitated buying a car a year in advance. I telephoned my mother, who is the family banker although she doesn't have that much money, just more than anybody else. She loaned us enough to buy a new car. I just made the first payment on it. A compact stationwagon. I can't get used to the idea of a car that you don't have to do things to every week. I was hoping the VW would go through the winter; the new car's an expensive luxury, but we are willing to pay for it. Emotionally it was worth it. There is room for us, the kids, and the groceries now. I'd still like to repair the Bug, though, if I can find the time and the parts.

Fathering and day care providing, Barry's private and work lives, feed into each other.

I'm not just a stay-at-home father, I'm a working stay-at-home father. We need the money. Otherwise I couldn't justify it. The day care justifies the staying home on two accounts. First, financial necessity. We must have the income. In most families nowadays, the husband and wife both have to work unless daddy is a lawyer or an executive. Most of the people we know are working couples. Which is not to say that staying home with the kids isn't work, as I can testify. But unless you are willing to accept a very low standard of living by American standards, you and your wife both bring home the bacon.

But this necessary income also helps my pride. I can tell people I stay at home and take care of kids all day and I'm earning $200 a week. Which again by real-world money is "peanuts," but by what we need to live on is good money. Parkinson's Law explains that expenditures rise to meet and surpass income. It doesn't matter whether you are making $5,000 a year or $50,000, the law applies. You automatically spend 10 percent more than you earn. I hate money; we still need it, but we live on *little*.

(You want to play with your Lite-Brites? Why not? It's a good thing we have a million toys.)

Two hundred dollars a week is enough to live on minus car payments. I can support our family, which means we can pay back old college loans in the bargain. It means we will never have our house in the country and land, but I don't think even if we both went out and worked "real" jobs anymore we could do that without killing ourselves.

It's a question of priorites. My wife and children are my best friends and my greatest source of pleasure, and I don't want to lose that in the pursuit of money. Maybe when Heather and Jocelyn are twelve and ten, when they don't need me at all anymore except to drive them to the library once in a while so they can continue their research or whatever they are doing, I'll say, "Now I might as well go out and start earning our money to buy a house in the country." Will we still want it? It's too far off to worry about, it really is.

People ask me if I want to start a day care center. I honestly don't think it's for me. If I became the director, I'd earn a lot more money, but I'd also have more headaches. And it's frequently a lousy, exploitative business. If you are the director or an upper staff person, your pay's okay, but the help receive a minimum wage and no benefits.

So I do feel happy. I feel that my business—which is what this is now—is solid. So long as I have all the people calling up looking for a babysitter.

For right now I have no career thoughts beyond taking care of kids and getting Jean through. I do, however, have ambitions. The biggest is to reserve more time in the week for myself. I withdraw into books whenever possible. If all the kids are playing with blocks, or hiking around the circle, or in the wading pool, and are super happy, and I'm not too far behind in my housework, I'll grab a book. But it's not relaxing reading because I have to keep my eye on everybody.

My spending many hours working in the cellar on jewelry is something else we fit into our life. Right now I have three wedding rings that are due in less than a month, and because they are for a wedding, they have to be done on time.

What it amounts to is we're overextended, and I'm trying to cut back. Starting next year I'd like to be able to do some cabinetwork. I have some of the tools already. It's only a matter of finding the time. And that will be my new hobby that I'll swear to myself and all the world I will not turn into a profession so I can enjoy it as long as I want. So far all my hobbies—jewelry, photography, even guitar when I was teenage—eventually have become money-making ventures. Which has its good and bad sides.

As far as day care is concerned, I plan to continue. I may burn out in a year or two, but for now it's going smoothly. Among the kids I have no real problems, and all the parents seem happy. The kids don't always leap out the door when their parents come to pick them up.

As my kids grow older, I think it will become easier. For sure, especially since Jocelyn is demanding. Already Heather is a big help. There are two sides, of course, but in many ways I like this for my kids. Aside from the fact that they have instant playmates, they have learned a lot of responsibility. Heather keeps an eye on the others for me. If I am in the kitchen and they are in the living room playing, and somebody prepares to leap off the top of the couch, she comes running. My kids know the rules of what is okay and what isn't. They will help me enforce them just by telling me there is a problem.

I never thought about it, but one of the reasons I will *stay* home is that our *kids* will be home. I'm an advocate of John Holt's home-schooling movement. I have no desire to send the kids to school. I see no benefits and immeasurable harm from formal schooling. People learn things fast when they are interested in them. It can be a fairly painless process provided it's something you want to learn. And if you don't, why bother? To my mind the school system is about how you make people learn things they don't care about, don't understand, and probably never will use, but which they are supposed to learn. As Holt points out in *How Children Learn*,[1] if you pursue any line of knowledge, you can start anywhere and go all through the universe. His students—this was before he got into home schooling—started with, "Where does wool come from? Who first built the loom?" Although they didn't realize it intellectually, the children discovered that

[1]New York: Pitman, 1967.

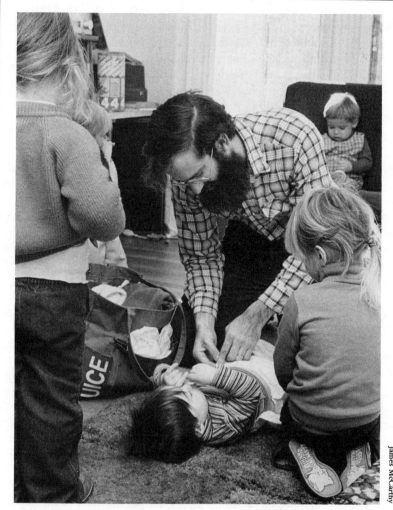

Heather fetches the necessary supplies when Barry needs to change a diaper.

knowledge is interconnected. From wool you can move into history, engineering, math, you name it!

This year Matthew brought here seven to fifteen mimeographed worksheets from first grade a day. Matthew's a smart fellow. In math he could be doing work a lot more challenging than he is given to do. He spends hours on it every day, and the amount of brain he has to use to accomplish the stuff is zilch. If for some reason he had to do the actual learning of it, he could master it in a half hour a day easily. The rest of the time he could be roller-skating, riding his bike, or building things. I *don't* think home schooling is anywhere near as hard as some people say. It *does* help if a parent is available. It's been worked out that my wife is going to hold a job full time outside the home, therefore I won't.

Not only should women get equal pay for equal work, they should get a lot more help with child rearing than they normally do. It would be all right if the husband said, "I'll work a nine-to-five job, and you'll work your nine-to-five with the kids, and the rest of the time we'll divvy up fairly." In the home-birth classes I've heard so many times from working women that this is NOT the way it is. When he comes home, the husband still expects the wife to have supper on the table, the house in order, and the kids under control. Which is beyond being unfair—it's criminal!

(Can you say please, Heather? Shall I put this cushion on top of you and turn you into a sandwich? May I sit on the couch at all? . . . [Heather:] "You can sit on the couch." Thanks, boss . . . It's nice having your life run by little kids.)

Should all men have a turn at staying at home to care for their children as Barry has? Are some men without the "instincts" even if they wanted to do it? In response to these questions, Barry referred once more to the home delivery of Heather and Jocelyn as having sown the seeds of his and Jean's radical stances on child rearing.

Certainly all men *should* take a more nurturing role. One of reasons we became involved in the home-birth movement is this: When a couple is pregnant, particularly with a first child, is one of the few times in their adult lives, for the vast majority, when they are capable of changing set ways of thinking. It is true in any time of crisis, but there aren't many. Particularly in America, eveyone's drive is for security, even though it's an illusion. To me parenting starts with child bearing. From the time you become pregnant, you are in the process of preparing for parenthood. Some people prepare for it great, others not at all. But it's the time when at least the potential exists for people to break loose from whatever bad habits their parents put into them.

Those people who don't read books or take classes or somehow delve into the changes having a family will usher in are willy-nilly going to copy what their parents did, with "genetic variations" on the theme, for better or worse. Or they are going to follow what their peers do—if nobody else is breastfeeding, your chances of breastfeeding are much reduced; if everybody nurses, you wouldn't think of doing anything else. Whereas if people put new ideas into your head then you *consider*.

It is usually the women who think of having a home birth first. Women seem more open to new ideas. Even if later they say, "Forget it," they think about it first. Whether it's home birth or family bed or child-led weaning, on family issues it takes a dynamite explosion to move most men. In the case of the woman, her body is undergoing changes already.

To me the coparenting doesn't have to start with the child's birth, but it would be a natural and pleasant place to start it. Be it home or at the hospital or at a birth center, if there were family-centered childbirth in this country, with all that it implies, then I think it would be easier to share the nurturing later on.

I suppose that you could say it comes down to bonding. Fathers who have half a chance to bond to their children are more likely to take an active part or want to, unbidden. Feminists won't have to force it down their throats.

If the father felt as bad at eight o'clock leaving for work as the kid does when daddy leaves, then maybe these kinds of arrangements that some families make would be made by many more families. And if you are going to talk about the ideal future or one where there is revolutionary pro-family change, if one father in a company of 2,000 says, "I want six months leave of absence," or "I want to work half-time," the boss says, "You either work the full day or you are fired. Forget it." If 500 fathers say, "Look, this is what we want to do," their company will institute it—because they can't replace 500 engineers. It's only a question of will that many people ever be that enlightened?

Five Days from Barry Kahn's Daybook

21 July 1981

Today, in a ceremony which brought tears to my eyes, Heather [four] and Gabriel [three] were married. Heather was "a vision of loveliness" as our landlady is fond of telling her, dressed in diapers. One was a wraparound skirt, a second covered her shoulders like a shawl, and the third hung from her head, held in place by a pink plastic hairband. Gabe's outfit was simpler: one diaper tied at the throat superman style. Chris [summer helper] recited the appropriate verses, and they exchanged rings made of paper. As I watched, impressed by their gay solemnity, I kept thinking that this scene would be repeated before too long. Take your time, Heather, cause Daddy and Mommy aren't ready yet!

22 July 1981

Today, Heather divorced Gabe and married Matthew [seven], who is back from vacation. Matt was very jealous when he learned of the marriage yesterday and followed Heather around for most of the morning trying to bribe her into a change of husband. At last she relented, the diapers were hauled out again, and somewhat perfunctorily, they wedded. Heather has clearly acquired new powers over the boys (I never thought this would begin at age four!) and has no qualms about exercising them. Gabe and Matt were not speaking to each other by the end of the day.

Our neighbors, informed by the kids of the wedding yesterday, were kept up-to-date today. I think Heather's divorce and remarriage shocked them slightly, but as I pointed out, she's right in the modern American tradition.

Attempts to wed Gabriel and Kristin (four) failed. They don't get along too well—very sensible of them to refuse.

1 August 1981

I am living in echo land. (Some people think I am living in cloud cuckoo land.) Jocelyn [two] and Monica and Carmen [both two and a half] have taken to repeating each other's statements—endlessly. If one says, "I got my dolly!" the others instantly shout it, too. It doesn't matter who says it or what they say—I always hear it a minimum of three times. If it tickles their little funny bones, I hear it thirty times. Is it any wonder I'm losing the ability to think and speak like an adult?

Update on the wedding-divorce scene: It's getting on my nerves. Heather walks around bargaining, "I'll marry you, if you let me play with your car." "Okay," says Gabe smiling. Five minutes later she is saying, "Gabe, I'm going to marry Matthew instead cause he's bigger and he can pick me up." Gabe sulks; Matthew struts around. Ten minutes later she's back to Gabe. I should point out that there are no longer any ceremonies involved; Heather just *says* she'll marry this one or that one. The little ones are cuter about it: Carmen and Monica are walking around holding hands shouting, "We're married! We're married!"

36

8 August 1981

Kristin has a new doll named "Baby Wet-and-Care." I tried in vain to get her to give it a more attractive name like Sally or Sue or Something, but she wasn't interested. I should know better. This particular creature came equipped with little bottles, a horrible orange drink mix, disposable diapers, lotion, and a rash on its butt. I was quite content with this new addition to our happy family until, returning to the living room from the kitchen, I found that "Baby" had peed on the sofa. Kristin hadn't noticed, nor had her crew of assistants, and she was flustered when she found out. I got her a towel and encouraged her to change her baby on the floor henceforth.

"On the floor floor or the carpet floor?" asked Heather.

"Either, as long as the towel is under her," I replied.

At that moment Carmen grabbed "Baby" to get a closer look, and Baby, being upright, peed all over the front of Carmen and down the front of the couch. . . . When peace returned, "Baby" was diapered, Baby's bottle was in a high place, and other games were beginning.

26 August 1981

Some days start off with a bang. Out for a walk with the kids early this morning around the campus: Gabriel, crossing the street in front of me on his tricycle, crashes at top speed into the curb, flies over the handlebars, and lands on his face. No harm done aside from a scratched chin and a flood of tears. After he recovered, he said he wouldn't do that again.

I've been pretty fortunate as far as accidents. In the year I've been doing day care: Jocelyn has dislocated her elbow (unknown cause); one little boy fell down about four steps (no injury); Gabe did as above; and Kristin has fallen off, over, bumped, and scraped herself about 5,000 times. As I write this, I am mentally knocking on wood with vigor.

23 September 1981

I wonder if toy manufacturers ever imagine some of the uses to which their products will be put? Cases in point: I bought a Lincoln log set for the kids, it being a toy I remember using a fair amount as a child. Some effort was made to build with it (and Heather did build a cute little building before going to bed last night), but mainly the kids took the roof slats and either used them to stir the "soup" (all the other pieces) or pretended they were chopsticks and tried to pick up the "food" (the other pieces).

Second example: we have a Capsela set which we acquired for four dollars (used, and missing only a few pieces). Yesterday Matthew discovered that if he hooked up just the battery and motor and touched the spinning shaft end against the little Halloween masks I bought, the resulting noise sounded very much like a dentist's drill. This discovery was followed by half an hour of busy medical-dental experimentation.

Final example: what are crayons good for? Well, Jocelyn likes to *peel* them. She will sit, or stand, and peel the paper off crayons for extended periods of time. She would rather peel than color. We now have a shoebox full of naked crayons as a result.

One never knows.

Postscript re: Kristin's doll

I guess it peed all over the place at home, too, because Barbara, Kristin's mother, got her two little *sealed* bottles which contain liquid resembling milk and orange juice. This solves the wetting problem, but now I have kids walking around sucking on little bottles at every opportunity. One thing that drives me crazy is to see children sucking on plastic. Yeech!

3

RELATIVE AS CAREGIVER

By the time the youngest children have learned to keep the place tidy, the oldest grandchildren are on hand to tear it to pieces again.

Christopher Morley

Ismail and Fern Khan have three boys—Yussuf, age ten, Javaid, seven, and Nafees, eighteen months. Ismail is from Pakistan and came to the United States as a university student in 1954. His sons all have Muslim names. Fern Mair Khan was born in Jamaica and came to Chicago in 1958 to study at Roosevelt University, transferring after one year to New York University. She met Ismail at the International Student Center, and they married after a courtship of eight years. "We were friends for a long time," says Fern.

Ismail has worked for the city of New York in the Department of City Planning for eighteen years. He is an energy-planning consultant and has done advanced studies at Columbia University. Fern holds an administrative position at La Guardia Community College, a unit of the City University of New York. When the school opened in 1971, she was hired as director of the paraprofessional teacher education program. She now develops continuing education programs for a variety of adult populations. Between them, the Khans earn over $65,000 per year.

In 1973 the Khans used their savings to buy a brownstone house on West Ninety-second Street. The Khans live on the second and third floors and rent out the first and parlor floors. In addition to being landlord, Ismail handles small repairs in the building and does some renovations himself. When asked why he bought a house in Manhattan, Ismail answered: "We both lived in Manhattan before having children, and we love it. It gives us proximity to friends and an atmosphere we find charming. My childhood memories are of India, but as a young man I was brought up in Karachi. Fern is from Kingston. We are urban-oriented."

Their living quarters are roomy and adequately furnished. The normal disarray of a busy family is not tucked away. The home reverberates with the activities of two working parents, two active sons, and a toddler, but also—remarkable in a metropolitan home—with the informal comings and goings of their many relatives and friends.

The West Side neighborhood where the Khans reside is a melting pot if ever there was one. Blacks, Hispanics, and immigrants from the Indian subcontinent share apartment buildings and streets with nonimmigrant whites, predominately Jews but also Gentiles. Along Riverside Park on the west and Central Park on the east live a large number of upper-middle-class whites. In between, toward Amsterdam Avenue and Broadway, which run downtown, the population becomes more black and Hispanic.

The Khans' brownstone stands directly across from a public school playground. After school and during vacations the playground swarms with ball games, tag, jump rope, and just plain hanging out, young and old alike. The Khans allow their two oldest sons to play there when accompanied by an older person.

Instead of the nearby public school, Javaid and Yussuf attend the Bank Street School, a laboratory school run by the renowned Bank Street College of Education. Tuition for the two amounts to more than $7,000 per year. Why do the Khans send their children to a private elementary school? Fern said, "We wanted them to have the very best educational background at the start." To provide their children with a change from city living, the Khans spend summer weekends and summer vacations in western Massachusetts, where they are transforming an old barn into their country home.

Five blocks from the Khans, Fern's mother Auveril Mair, lives in a one-bedroom apartment in a newish high-rise. The apartment has a sunny southern exposure with a long-vista view of the city, which Mrs. Mair enjoys while sitting reading, talking on the telephone, or preparing food at her big kitchen work table. The large living room is furnished with contemporary furniture and lots of plants. Lining the walls, propped up on bookshelves, in frames on doilied side tables, are dozens of photographs of the children she has cared for over the past nine years.

Here Monday through Friday Mrs. Mair takes care of the toddlers Nafees Khan, Allegra Stewart, and Patrick O'Neil, 8:00 A.M. to 6:00 P.M., and Nafees' two older brothers, 3:00 to 6:00 P.M.. In addition to those five children, two other grandchildren, Tanya and Craig Chin, live with Mrs. Mair Monday through Friday and then go home to the Bronx only on weekends. In her home, then, Mrs. Mair has total care of one family's children five days a week, and daytime care of three other families' children, two of whom go to school and three of whom stay with Mrs. Mair ten hours. Mrs. Mair is the caregiver of an extended family group consisting of two daughters' nuclear families and the children of two other unrelated mothers. For the latter, both of which are single parents and one of whom adopted her little girl, the extended character of Mrs. Mair's caregiving is a big attraction.

The Khans' Commentary

FERN: My father is a retired station master of the railway, in the parish of St. Catherine in Jamaica, West Indies. He worked for the government for many years. In many ways he was my ideal because he was very hard working and a competent person who believed in people being productive and independent. In Jamaica what we have is not a commuter railroad but a long-distance railroad, so he was called a station master, meaning he was in charge of that particular station and had a house to live in provided by the railroad. He worked from very early until whatever time the train came in;

He had to get up and make sure all the signals were in order. He was a wiz at the telegraph.

It's the dream of most Jamaicans to come to New York. My mother had always wanted to come to New York, but when I was growing up it was very difficult for most Jamaicans to come here, because of the McCarran Act and the quota system. She had been trying for years and had no way to get through.

Then a friend of mine invited me here to study when I was seventeen. I decided to come. I went to Chicago and stayed there for about seven months and then transferred to NYU. I finished college and then graduate school in social work and later became a permanent resident. That made a big difference. Then I could send for my mother. Next my sisters came, and my younger brother also. Both Ismail and I are now citizens.

Mama lived with me for three years until I married. My idea was first of all to bring her over here, to America, to help her. After we married, I felt even more what I had felt before, that if I didn't have my mother here to help with the children, probably I would not have children, because I had seen how difficult it was for people to have children. I hadn't thought much about it. It was just there in my mind. Compared to the Jamaican situation, where people live together as an extended family, the American way seemed foreign. In Jamaica, you never thought twice about it. You had cousins or some other relative nearby who would come up and help you. When I came here and saw how difficult providing good child care was, and how the focus was on the nuclear family, I thought, "Gee, I don't think I could manage without my mother's being here." That's how it really began.

My mother came up initially on a vacation, and she liked it here. Also my aunt who lives in Queens is her closest sister. Because we were here and my aunt was here, it was convenient for my mother to stay. She became a permanent resident. She lived with me before we married, but not after.

Ismail and I married, and I was working. My mother worked here for a while as well, but it was not easy for her to find a job she liked and enjoyed. First, her age was against her. She finally got a job at the Children's Aid Society, but it was part time. So when I had the first baby, it was just understood she would take charge. I don't think we talked seriously about it; it was understood. She then stayed home in the daytime and looked after Yussuf; she began to work in the evenings. She stayed with the baby until I arrived home, about six o'clock. Then she went to work, three hours in the evening, four days a week.

Fern described her mother's attitudes about raising children.

My mother doesn't get worried about how the children behave. With the first child, if I called her and said, "How is everything going?" or when I returned home from work asked, "So how was he today?" she answered, "Oh he was fine." Or if he had a temper tantrum when I left him in the morning, when I came home I said, "How was he? Did he cry?" She would say only, "You know how babies are." If he cried, babies are expected to cry. My mother is very easygoing, much more easygoing than I am. For me she is very good that way, because she doesn't become flustered. Certain things are expected of babies and of children, and it's not a surprise when they behave in that way.

I'm sure that my mother will do the proper thing. A lot of my colleagues at work say, "You're so lucky to have your mother take care of your children." I am, especially compared with what's happening with them. They have to be vigilant. The babysitter may not even turn up, or may become sick. All kinds of things can happen. I never have to worry with Mama.

Once she got sick, but it was such a coincidence—that same week I had arranged to take off for a spring vacation. We were going away. We just changed our plans and stayed home. Allegra, Patrick, and the cousins— they all came down to our house in the mornings, and I looked after them. I don't know what other arrangements I would make. I have never used a babysitter, and it's been nearly ten years. I wouldn't even know where to find a babysitter. I have not only my mother but my two sisters are here, and I have some very close friends living nearby—we grew up together in Jamaica—so they will always pitch in if I need someone to keep the children. It's a very extended relationship of family and friends.

My husband comes from a different part of the world but has a similar background in terms of the extended family. The cultural pattern is of being very close to family members and turning to them for a lot of support. So it was a natural arrangement for him too. As a matter of fact, I think he especially liked my family because we were so *many*. It was a contrast because when he came to the United States he was alone. He married a family!

My mother usually handles any problems that come up. There are so few situations that require discipline. Normally she would not hit a child. Only when one of the big boys does something bad, and she doesn't know what to do other than to spank him, she asks his father. She wouldn't *want* to spank him. She's very peacefully oriented. I remember times when I said, "It's up to you, he's your grandchild. You handle him." Once when she did spank Yussuf, she told us with evident regret, "I had to beat him." I said, "So you did what you should," but she continued to feel badly and concerned. It may be she feels the strong compunction because the boys are older. She spanks my niece and nephew when they're deserving.

As long as Mama is here and there is a need for her to take care of them, even when they are big boys in high school, I wouldn't even think twice about it. It's very good for the children having two homes, although recently Yussuf has been telling me, "All those children at school have teenagers that look after them. I have to go to my grandma." I have to say to him, "Do you know how lucky you are? How many of those children would love to have a grandma look after them—and you're complaining." It's just now that they want to be like other people who have babysitters. Now that they are older, they do a lot by themselves and with their friends. They visit them. If there is an arrangement for Yussuf to go somewhere else, as long as we know where we give permission. If someone phones and invites him at school, he phones my mother first and tells her. But they do prefer to bring their friends here to our home, because all their toys are here and it's just different. We make a point now that the boys are older to pick them up earlier, by 5:30.

My mother doesn't try to do the educational kinds of things. When Yussuf was one, the only grandchild, she would. But after a while it became too much. Now there are not only my three children but my sister's two children and the two other children, so it's impossible. Because she has so many children there, it would be difficult for her to supervise work. Since Tanya and Craig live with her during the week, sometimes she says, "Tanya, you ought to have your work ready for tomorrow." So she keeps an eye on them more. With our children she knows we will see that they get their homework done.

Mama expects the children to have the imagination to play by themselves. I'm like that too. It has something to do with the Jamaican expectations of children although I dare say it runs through a lot of cultures. We weren't into structured activities for children. We grew up in open spaces. Nearly every house had a yard. Even if it wasn't a garden, it had grass and shrubbery and rocks. Children were free to go outside the minute they were up in the morning. It was a routine: you took your bath, went outside, and played—all day. The woman in the house was busy doing her cleaning or sewing. I don't recall any play with my mother or the adults in the family. We were always involved with them in talking, or if they were talking with neighbors we were right in there listening to everything. We were exposed to grown-up discussions very early. If they felt a child shouldn't be there, they said, "Go somewhere else." I think Mama is the same way now, and I feel I'm the same way. My big son will accuse me, "So-and-so plays with her children and you never play with me." Then I feel bad and think maybe I should play a bit more with him, but I do not always follow through. Often I say, "Get your friends to play with you!" although sometimes I will play Monopoly or some other game.

If the children are bored, my mother uses television, especially cartoons, to entertain them. In the summertime she takes them all downstairs to play behind the building. She spins the rope for the children to jump and gives them chalk to draw. But in the house she's busy with feeding them. It seems it never ends. They're fed, and they take a nap. That's her day. They provide the amusement for one another.

Because of the relaxed atmosphere and because they are exposed to so many children, within a short time you can see the difference in the children who come to my mother's. They become more outgoing. That's one of the most valuable aspects of their coming to the house. When they came they were all only children—Patrick, Allegra, and the others before them. They gained a big family. When I look on, I think, "These children are really lucky! They become part of our whole group. All the children call my husband, Uncle Ismail. He comes in, and they run to him. He lifts them up and plays with them. They get a lot of attention from him. He loves little girls anyway!

The Khans' view of family responsibilities underlies their child caring arrangement. Fern described her feelings about the roles of family members.

I guess because I'm the oldest I have always felt that my mother was my responsibility. It may not be true in reality, but it's something emotional which I feel. If anything should happen, I am there. In Jamaica, people place a higher value on daughters because girls tend to stay with their families, and especially with their mothers, more than boys do. Boys, when they marry, move into the girl's family. A mother can rely on her daughter for whatever help she needs. It could be emotional sustenance of physically being nearby or for financial support. Whatever it is, her mother can count on that bond between them. It's unspoken but it is there. It's a girl-oriented society. I've always seen the women as very strong; I can't remember a weak Jamaican woman. My memories are of women who are self-assured even if they had frailties and faults. If they felt insecure, they rarely showed it. On the outside they were hard working and independent. Even my ideal of women physically is big—you had to have some meat on you to look strong.

So when we got Mama the apartment across from us in a new building, I took care of everything. Before coming here, my sister Phillipa had married Maurice Chin, a Chinese-Jamaican. After she had her children, we decided to split the responsibility for Mama's upkeep. We do not feel that we are paying her. My husband and I know that if we had no children, we would still look after my mother.

We give her the rent. We combine both amounts, and the middle sister, who used to live with her, then writes the check. Because my mother doesn't handle checks, she need not worry at all about the finances of living in the city. So far it has worked out nicely.

My sister's situation is different from ours. She lives in the Bronx and works in Manhattan. Consequently, her children stay with Mama from Monday through Friday. On weekends they go to their parents in the Bronx. They have gone to Mama's from the day they were born. The Chins lived in Queens before they went to the Bronx, and at one point Maurice decided to look for someone nearer to them to take care of the children. So they found a woman who lived in the same building, and Maurice hired her on the spot.

My mother was distraught. She said, "Those children will not be looked after properly. Who's going to care for them?" What happened was the first morning that my sister took them to the babysitter, the woman said, "The children must not run around the house, and you have to be here by 5:30 exactly, not a minute later." There were so many rules and restrictions. We weren't used to this at all! So Phillipa went home in tears that evening. The next morning she said to her husband, "You take them." So he did. Apparently when Maurice saw what happened at the sitter's, he took the children right back to my mother's. That was the only time any of our children has been anywhere else, and it was such a negative experience! My mother feels it's more than her duty, it's love, it's also her *right* to look after her grandchildren. Why should somebody else interfere?

Yet having the grandmother play this role is a very individual situation. I know many families where the grandmother and the children don't get along, and it wouldn't work even if they tried. Or where there is tension between the grandmother and the daughter, which passes tension on to the children as well. Disagreements occur about how they should raise the children. It's a coincidence that in our family it doesn't work that way. Because I am seven years older than my first sister, Phillipa, and I've been in America the longest, I really am the *big* sister in many ways. We have a very good relationship. I wouldn't say our experience is for everyone. It may not be practical for other families or may not work. However, there are alternative child care approaches utilizing older adults who are doing nothing and feeling useless. They enjoy becoming involved with children who may not be their own.

Auveril Mair in her apartment with her daughters and grandchildren: (clockwise) Fern Khan holding Nafees, Javaid Khan, Phillipa Chin, Craig Chin, Tanya Chin, Mrs. Mair, Hope Spence, and Yussuf Khan.

I asked Fern if she thought being in the house always with the children suited Mrs. Mair. Did her daughter feel that more contacts during the day with adults would make her mother's time more vital?

Staying at home is hard for any of us. I empathize and don't know how she does it. At times I feel strongly she should be out more, and that it would be better if she had a job on the outside. She's worked part time in the Children's Aid Society, and she really liked it. She gets along very well with people, she has a therapeutic effect on them, and they like having her around. She listens. She's not at all a judgmental person, so people find it easy to talk to her. I'm amazed at the number of neighbors who talk to her about their problems.

One of my jobs at La Guardia College is to develop programs for different adult populations. For years I'd been doing that. Suddenly one day it hit me that my mother was sitting there, and she should be going back to school too. I had been telling all the other adults who came in and never told her. We began talking about going back to school, she discussed with a friend who had gone there to a high school equivalency program at the college, and Mama went. At first she was scared. She thought she would not do well, and she had been out of school so long. The usual fears but for her they were more intense because she was coming from a completely different culture, a contrasting system of learning. So she was worried and hesitant, but our teachers are very special, and she did well when she took the test—just a few points below the passing, not bad for someone who had been out of school for years. But she was so disappointed. I had to be there saying, "But Ma, that's very good for somebody that hasn't been to school in over forty years. You did very well. Some young students we have wouldn't score as highly as you did." It was in the science area that she encountered difficulty. She would still like to earn the high school diploma. She is still talking about going back.

My mother continues to have numerous friends, and people gravitate to her. She is extremely supportive with them all, and sometimes I warn her, because a person like her can be taken advantage of. You could go in with a story and tell it, and she would feel so sorry for you. That's why she has all those children there. My mother has a very soft heart. If someone comes to her and says, "I'm in a pinch and need help, I can't find anybody to babysit," even though she knows that she should say no, she says yes.

It has created some troubles—we're all discussing this—because sometimes I feel it's too much for her. There was a time when she took on an older girl, a pre-teenager, who was very difficult. She wanted to roam outside on her own, and she didn't mind my mother. I told Mama that she couldn't keep her. After a while she said, "But I feel so sorry for the poor woman, who has no one to look after her daughter." She was very concerned. She wanted to do whatever she could. But she stopped it because her health was getting bad and she was having attacks. Then the mother came back to her and asked, and she started again. But when Mama took

48

the girl back, she got sick again! I said, "This is it! You're not keeping her again." Then she told the mother she really couldn't. Usually I ask her how much she plans to charge. Usually "threateningly," because she'll do it for nothing.

Are the Khan children tri-cultural or do they identify only with their American surroundings?

They feel they are Americans. They feel that they are also of both parents' cultures. They have been to Jamaica once three years ago. They talk a lot about, "How come we haven't been to Pakistan? You promised to take us to Pakistan and you haven't." They talk often about their grandfather in Pakistan who has passed away since. Ismail tells more stories about his culture than the rest of us put together! He teaches the children some Urdu words.

They know a lot about Jamaica because of what they hear in passing, but not because we consciously tell them stories. Now and then I say, "Oh when I was a little girl I used to have a tree swing or sing that song." And the nonverbal legacy is Mama's cooking. She cooks only Jamaican dinners. The only dishes that weren't in our background are spaghetti and meatballs, and macaroni and cheese. Jamaicans when I was growing up hardly ate a sandwich. We had beef patties for lunch or ate a full meal. She cooks a full meal at lunchtime, and the children share whatever she makes. Patrick's mother is a vegetarian so she doesn't want him to eat meat. Every morning she brings fruit and vegetables for him. When mother cooks, she doesn't give Patrick the meat, but the meat juices are all right, and the rice and peas and other Jamaican dishes. All her foods are highly seasoned so they take a long time to cook, and when they're cooked, you really taste the flavor. If she is going to cook chicken, she doesn't just sprinkle on salt and pepper and start cooking. The meat is seasoned from early morning and stays in the bowl and marinates. Even if she cooks American steak, she seasons it all morning and leaves it to absorb all the seasoning, and *then* she cooks. It is a very Jamaican way of cooking, and of course what with chopping onions and soaking beans, she is very tied to the kitchen.

Seeing her husband in the doorway, Fern Khan said, "My husband wanted to listen to see if I'm telling the truth. He said that my side would be very biased since I'm a daughter talking about a mother." Joining us briefly, Ismail spoke about the contrasts between the growing-up process he remembers from his Indian (before-Partition) childhood and in American today. He retains a detached foreigner's eye more than his wife does, with regard to his children's lives.

49

ISMAIL: I always am fascinated by how children learn so quickly in this country. We sometimes feel if Jean Piaget were doing his research here in the United States, he would have to rewrite all his theories. I watch my own children and their friends and see their perceptions and understanding are quicker at an earlier age than what the textbooks tell. This fascinates all of us from other parts of the world. It is something peculiar to American culture that the child is a human being—he doesn't have to be childlike—and he grows so very fast. I am overwhelmed by it!

FERN: This is a subject we talk about informally, especially my sisters when we are all together. In Jamaica children grow up on proverbs. When I was growing up I heard proverbs like "A penny saved is a penny earned." There was no "psychology." We didn't rely on the educational psychologists. We grew up on folk wisdom and stories. That is one of the striking contrasts here. The children hear the proverbs but only occasionally. If I were misbehaving, my father or mother looked at me, one look, and I stopped immediately. I may try the same measure with Yussuf, our biggest son, and he doesn't even know what the look means. Even if I say, "Now Yussuf, when I look like this it means 'Children should be seen and not heard,' " it has no meaning. My mother cannot look at them sternly either, but then they are not rude to her!

We're raising the children Muslim, because although I don't want to convert, I believe in a religious foundation for children. My mother went to Anglican Church in Jamaica. As she's grown older, she's more sensitive to religion. But except for grace, she doesn't usually use the religious quotations to raise children. Instead of bringing up God or Christ, she uses admonition and aphorisms. Examples of these are "Children should obey their parents" and "Blood is thicker than water." That has to do with family relationships, and staying close to your family members regardless. Or she quotes, "A new broom sweeps clean, old broom knows all the corners," which has to do with long-term relationships. The person you have known the longest you should rely on and be friendly with, not the new person who seems so attractive. She hardly ever gives explanations as are given in American society. She finds proverbs faster and more effective.

My father used to have his own little phrases too. When I helped him with his books, balancing the tickets of the day, if I made a mistake I might say, "I'm sure I'm right." He answered, "Figures don't lie but liars figure." He would never say, "Now you go back over that, and check it."

There's a phenomenon that when you leave your own culture and live somewhere else you hold earlier values much more precious because you are not around them. For my husband, values he experienced when young are now very forceful, and he says how he misses them. They are uppermost in his mind now that he has children. He would like to transfer some of these values to his children, but the culture around him doesn't allow for that very easily. Even if he has Muslim friends, it's not the same. They are going through the same problem. They wish to convey some of the past to their children, and yet they know they never can. There's a wistfulness or longing. All of us feel it. Some people are more sentimental than others. Ismail feels it more deeply than I do. I'm more practically oriented.

My mother doesn't know anything about Islam and doesn't understand it. Sometimes we have little discussions. She listens, but she doesn't hear me. She says, "But!" We do the *akiko* ceremony, which is like a christening to boyhood, and celebrate certain Muslim holidays, such as Idd. The part of our family life, though, which is probably most consonant with my husband's Muslim upbringing is the extension of our family to include grandma, sisters and brothers, the cousins. All the cousins get along very well. There are no rivalries so far. The only girl, Tanya, stands out and gets along wonderfully well with all the children at Mama's place. We socialize very much. Phillipa gives dinners, and her husband cooks Chinese food and invites many guests.

ISMAIL: Also we enjoy a cultural custom which doesn't seem to be an American one. Both in Pakistan and Jamaica we visit friends and relatives often unannounced. The friends or relatives can come to our house, and they are always welcome. And we can visit them and feel welcome. In addition to the socializing that is planned is the socializing that is unplanned. And the unplanned is more prominent. Generally when we come back from Massachusetts, we stop by my sister-in-law's. If they are cooking, we eat. It's a cultural habit. It's never thought you aren't supposed to drop by. It's the same way in Pakistan.

FERN: What's missing in our situation compared with other parents is we don't have the level of anxiety about raising children. I'm not anxious at work. I don't even remember them until I'm home. And my mother is comfortable with them, not tense over what happened during the day. I advise her for her *own good,* for example, to get out more, not in terms of the children. We're mother and daughter, but she's also like a sister.

Auveril Mair's Commentary

I came to New York in 1968 from Jamaica, West Indies. I came here from Kingston but was born in Westmoreland in 1921. I came because I have two sisters here, and they wanted me to come. But I didn't until Fern, my first daughter, was graduated from New York University.

When I arrived in New York, I thought it was very hard. But then I got into it. If I go back to Jamaica, I still think about being back in New York. New York is very interesting, and now I have so many ties.

When I came to New York, I hadn't any idea what I would do. The years when my children were growing up, I managed a dry cleaner's, for about ten years. I came to see my oldest daughter on a vacation from my job. I was to return to Jamaica. But when I came, my daughter and my sister in Queens said, "Why not stay?" So I decided to get my papers and get my permanent visa. My boss was very upset that I didn't come back, but I didn't miss it. After I came here, I met a Jamaican woman who had a dry cleaner's, and I worked with her for about two years.

At first I lived with Fern in the building where Ruth Stewart, the mother of one of my day children, lives. We lived there for about two years. Then I moved over here. She didn't have children then. A year later, she married. Two years after, she had her first one, a son. Then I started to look after him. She was living in her apartment, and I was here. After she had the second child, she bought the house on Ninety-second Street. So Yussuf this year will be ten, Javaid is seven, and Nafees is a year and a half.

All the grandchildren, I have taken care of them since they were small. Fern went back to work three months [after her children were born]; Phillipa, the same. She has two, Tanya and Craig, but they are going to school now. They come after school and stay with me for the week and go home on the weekends. Their home is in the Bronx. Tanya and Craig's father, Maurice Chin, works for the Long Island Railway.

The children of Fern who are school age take the 104 [bus] from Bank Street [School] every day to my house. Tanya is eight. She goes to P.S. 75 and comes home with a friend, Shirley. Craig goes to North Meadow School. I take him to the bus at nine o'clock in the morning, and he returns at about 2:10 in the afternoon.

In Jamaica bringing up children is different. People live more like a family, and they live together until they are of good age. Here people don't stay very long together. In Jamaica we might all have been living together or very near, and you could get a full-time maid to take care. The grand-mother can do it, but usually not while they are babies.

I also care now for two others: Allegra Stewart and Patrick O'Neill. Judith Rodgers, whose child used to come to me, recommended me to Mrs. Stewart, who is an executive at the New York Public Library. They both live in the same building. Then Allegra's mother recommended me to Patrick's mother—they live in the same building.

Since I have been here, I have looked after many children. (*We look at*

Mrs. Mair's loving care of Patrick and Allegra means so much to their working mothers.

the photographs.) I cared for this little boy three days a week. . . . Here is another little boy, Damion, that I used to keep. . . . This little girl used to live with her mother on the second floor. Her name is Nadine. I used to help her also. She is a big girl now. Her mother moved to the Bronx. I have cared for others, but never over two besides my own. They all call me Grandma. The children who aren't in the family pay me weekly or every two weeks. I charge them one rate.

Nafees comes at nine until six. My daughter brings him nearly every morning, unless she has to go to work a little early, then my son-in-law brings him. In the afternoon at three o'clock all seven children are here.

But sometimes Yussuf and Javaid don't come because they have after school programs or visit their schoolmates. Maybe twice in a week they don't come, but generally they do.

The children play together—they enjoy one another's company, and they learn from each other. They get along well. For instance, the little ones see the bigger ones going to the bathroom, so it's easy to train them.

When the weather is good, I take them to a playground in the back. We go to the park in Park West Village if the weather is fine. I haven't taken Nafees, the smallest, yet to Central Park, but he can go behind the building for the slides and benches and climbing things he likes. We start to go to Central Park in June.

They really don't give me that much trouble. Of course, sometimes the children give a little trouble, but it passes fast. Maybe I don't feel the taking care is hard because they are either my own, or they are nice understanding children that I get. Even if sometimes they give a little trouble, they always have respect.

When they give me trouble I say, "Don't do that, that's not right." I never like to hit them. There was only once, when Yussuf and Javaid were fighting all the time, that they wouldn't mind at all. I told their father, and he said, "Take the strap and give them a beating." I never like to hit children. Although they were my own, I didn't want to. But with the bigger one I had to take the strap and give him two licks. He knew and after he behaved.

But look at Allegra! She doesn't give me any trouble. The other problem was between two brothers, bigger boys, and the father said to make them change we had to do something. Allegra is very interesting, and she learns so fast. Everybody who comes in contact with her finds her interesting. She is a wonderful, very intelligent child.

With my own grandchildren, I can tell the parents any trouble. Sometimes they become rude and hit one another. They play, but they play rough. I complained to their mother that Yussuf and Javaid today gave me trouble hitting each other—"It's not nice. They don't have to hit so hard or play so rough." She said, "You know what to do!" My daughters know me so well that they don't have to ask me what I do. They know that I'll take good care and that I understand the children because I have dealt with them so long.

How does a typical day flow?

In the morning I get up at around six and clean up the living room. Then I make breakfast for myself and sit and read my Bible and some Daily Words that I have. Then I go in the bedroom and wake up Tanya at a quarter to eight, because she has to go to school. I get her breakfast and comb her hair. I get her clothes, and she gets ready and leaves for school. When Nafees arrives at 8:30 with his mother or father, Craig wakes up. I get him dressed and give him his breakfast and take him to the bus for school. Then I come back and Allegra comes at a little after nine, with Patrick, and they play with Nafees. Sometimes they watch *Sesame Street*. After that I go in the kitchen and look about their dinner. They have an early lunch, often cereal, cornmeal or oats. Then they sit and play for half an hour more before their naps.

Around three o'clock I have dinner. They like spaghetti or soup. Sometimes I cook for the children rice and red peas—kidney beans—or the pigeon peas with rice and coconut milk. Another dish I cook is stew peas and rice. You stew the peas with meat. When the meat is cooked, you drop some dumplings in it. The broth turns to a sauce and you eat it with rice. The children can make eggs for themselves. Tanya and Yussuf make soup from a can. I'm trying to get Nafees off his bottle now. He's starting to use a mug. All of us have dinner together. Patrick, the vegetarian, has his salad, potatoes, and vegetable soup.

After dinner we go out, and they stay out for two or two and a half hours. When they come back, I have a little juice for them, and then their parents arrive for them. The day is finished by 6:30. Except that my two grandchildren from Phillipa stay the night.

Once or twice in the week Phillipa comes and stays with Tanya and Craig here, to help Tanya with her homework. She stays for two nights. Then Friday evening they come from school at three o'clock, and she comes from work at five—she is a secretary at Booz, Allen, & Hamilton— and they go home. They don't mind it. In the summertime when evenings are longer they sometimes go home. But in the wintertime they usually stay for the week. Phillipa works in Manhattan, Maurice in Long Island, and if the children went to school in the Bronx, they wouldn't have anybody to stay with them when they come home. It would be very difficult for them to have the children there. Maybe when Tanya grows big and she can travel, they may change and have her go home to the Bronx after school.

The day changes as the children go to school. Allegra will be at Riverside Nursery [School] next year. Her mother, a library administrator, could have her stay all evening, but she decided no, for her to come back at three o'clock. The day would be too long. And then on Fridays school lasts only a half-day. Her mother will have someone bring her to me.

It is not different bringing up these children from my own so much in how I am but how they are. My children were raised in Jamaica, and that's a different atmosphere. Children there live in a house and have a yard and a big veranda. They can go out and play when they like. The seasons of the year are also different. We only have one season to deal with. Here you have four. The American children seem harder to raise. You have to be doing things more for them, and they live in the house more.

Children in America—it's really hard and it's expensive. For instance, no one in Jamaica will pay you any money, or very little, for the care of their children. Further, they would get you as a full-time person, to stay in the house. In Jamaica I wouldn't do the taking care and have someone pay me. In Jamaica most of the time a person would come and ask you if you will be home today and will let a child stay with you. People you know come and say, "I'm running out. Would you let this child stay with you until I come back?" But here nobody would ask that.

Basically I do the same thing as with my children. I comb their hair, clean them, bathe them, brush their teeth, and put on their clothes. The big difference is their being indoors from the Jamaican children's being outdoors. Maybe this is why they go to school from three, in Jamaica not until five. The children here grow faster. They grow much faster than in other countries, I think. They grow faster in body. I wonder is it the food that they eat here that makes the difference? The other difference I see is that children here are so crazy over toys. Toys mean a lot to them. Jamaican children don't use many toys.

On the weekends I have the time for myself. I can go shopping. Sometimes I visit them! This weekend I was in the Bronx for a cookout, because Phillipa has a backyard. I stayed the weekend.

Just two years ago I decided to go back to school. I took my high school equivalency, but I failed one subject, science. I took it twice and I failed twice! I do the studying here and go to La Guardia from nine to one Saturday mornings. Last year I didn't do it, but I'm going back. Because it keeps me concentrating and not forgetting, and knowing more about America, the history and the civics. It only takes me about fifteen minutes on the number seven train from Times Square. Being mostly with little children, this makes a good difference in my life.

Do the children ever rebel, I wondered, despite their grandmother's easy ways?

Each of the children has different ways and thinks differently. They cooperate. The older ones come faithfully after school, and they never rebel. Only Craig sometimes because he knows he is going home on Friday afternoon. If his father stays away a little longer, he says, "Why does daddy stay so long? It's time for me to go home." So sometimes he is mad if his father is late.

We Jamaicans are accustomed to kin helping kin. I don't know whether it is love or what it is. My daughters trust because they know the children will be protected and will get good care. They are at work, but they are at peace. If anything happens, I can help myself. If the children are sick, I can help them. It's the same with Ruth Stewart. She has that trust. She doesn't even call me, only if Allegra is feeling a little sick, she calls and says, "How is she?" She trusts me and has confidence that everything will be all right.

Children are different in this age. You have to know how to deal with them. You have to give them certain privileges because they are born in an age when everything is open and there is so much for them to know. Especially when they begin school, they get into everything and know everything. They are *not* going to sit by and take things. You have to treat them with a certain respect, and they give it back to you. It's the same the world over, you might say, but American children are the fastest now to grow up. I have always said that the roofs, the bridges, the whole design, everything made in the United States is so different from in other countries. So many things educate children in this country. Even different ways of city traveling are so exciting to them. Four years ago I visited a nephew in London, and I toured, drove, rode on trains a lot. I still say America is a great place!

What are the financial arrangements with her daughters?

Anything I want they give it to me. They pay the rent. They don't give me money. If the television goes out for repairs, they pay it. I don't charge money for taking care of their children. They do what they think is right.

My daughters aren't doing what I did, staying home, but I don't see they are missing out. Phillipa stayed home three months with her second baby. Both breastfed each child for several months. I don't see that they have regrets or that they should. When they get vacations, they always want to stay home with the children. As a matter of fact, Phillipa last year was away from work for about six months, and she stayed with her children at home. They treat the children well, and they think of their welfare. From what I see nowadays, professional people can't stay home with their children. The cost of living today means a family can't make it with one person's paycheck only, especially if they have a house. My daughters have to go out and work, and this way it's easy for them to work it out.

NANNY

"Well, Ida," says the Consul, "I have been thinking it over: you took care of us all, and when little Johann gets a bit older—he still has the monthly nurse now, and after that he will still need a day-nurse, I suppose—but will you be willing to move over to us when the time comes?"

"Yes, indeed, Herr Consul, if your wife is satisfied."

"Gerda is content to have it so, and thus it is settled."

Thomas Mann, *Buddenbrooks*

George and Nancy White are a successful two-income family that relocated from the United States to Ottawa, Canada, eight years ago. George, 40, is the son of an engineering professor at Northwestern University. He is as easygoing as he is tall and hefty. His mother-in-law describes him lovingly as looking forever like an "unmade bed." He enjoys his job as an accountant for a large engineering firm and enjoys even more the fruits of his career and marriage—a comfortable house, a vintage Mercedes Benz, sailing, community affairs, an active social life, a lovely wife.

The woman who thrives with this affectionate man is stunningly attractive. This is a person who cares about the details of dress and physical appearance. She is vivacious, high-strung, self-conscious yet candid, and very good at her job as director of a large social welfare service. Because of evening events such as meetings with city officials, she puts in a long work week.

The Whites' bilevel house is located in a cul-de-sac in a quiet neighborhood that took over farm land about fifteen years ago. The Whites bought the house before it was built. They altered the plans to make showers and stairway clearances high enough to accommodate 6'4" George, and to enlarge the den. The house is handsomely furnished. The living room is reserved for adult entertainment. The kitchen has an eating counter. The first floor also has an office for George and the large den where Robbie, four, plays. This room is a child's delight. In addition to shelves of books, drawers of blocks and trucks, and musical instruments enough for a small band, the room has a large platform that George built to support a Lego erector set. In this den, Robbie has spent a great proportion of his play time. Only recently has he shown much interest in outdoor play.

Myra Dalrumple, the Whites' nanny, is a fairy godmother with an Ontario accent. For most of her life she was a housewife. Only in her fifties, after a bad second marriage, did she go to work as a child caregiver. The experience of having raised three children of her own is the crucial background to her relationship with Robbie. She is low key enough to find great personal satisfaction in taking care of Robbie. She loves him as a grandmother or aunt would. She likes to be her own woman. She lives alone and relishes time off from her nanny chores.

Myra is not one to sit around all day. She *likes* to do householdry such as cleaning, ironing, simple cooking, and sewing. Days pass quickly, and evenings are welcome. Amazing to the Whites and telling of Myra's poise and self-understanding is that she departs from an eight-hour day with Robbie as fresh as when she arrived. Myra did not drop from heaven, but the Whites bless the day they hired her, a rock of good sense and cheerful spirit in the midst of a busy two-professional family.

The Whites' Commentary

Where did the idea of having a nanny come from? "Guilt, absolute guilt!"
Nancy White answered, making that grim bolus of the working mother
seem as melt-in-your-mouth as a peppermint pattie.

NANCY: As a psychotherapist, a person who does a lot of work with parenting and education, the thought of delegating child rearing was abhorrent to me. On the other hand, I had just taken my present job. They hadn't had a woman in the position for sixteen years. At the time I was hired they were very concerned whether I might become pregnant. No, I told them, we didn't know whether we could even have children. Which was the truth, except I was pregnant at the time! So four months after taking the job I had to announce that I'd be leaving to have a baby. So then we thought, "Well, what's the best way in terms of a child?"

My preference was someone who would come here and make a long-term commitment, but not live in. When I come home at night, I'm tired. I've had a long day immersed in the lives of many people. I don't want to have to think of anyone else but George and Robbie.

So that's how we got started. I contacted the nanny training program at our local community college and found that they only had five graduating and each of them had a job. The college is comparable to a sophisticated trade school in America, and very responsive to the job market. At that point not many nannies were being turned out, they were being snapped up rapidly, and anyway they were young. My preference was for somebody mature. I called nanny placement services, I was offered one lady with a family of six who had to come on the bus, and then she smoked and would have had, moreover, to get home to her family of six. Because I often had to stay late that wasn't appealing.

When I mentioned to my receptionist that I was looking, she suggested her mother. Myra at that point was staying with teenage children in well-to-do families when the parents went on vacation. So I asked my receptionist if her mother would be interested in a full-time job. I knew anybody who raised my receptionist and her sister would probably do a fine job. Lo and behold, Myra said she would be interested. She came out while I was pregnant, and she agreed to come and try it. When Robbie was six weeks old, she arrived, and we were off and running. Financially we were committed to my continuing work. Also professionally I felt I had a commitment. I would have hated myself to bail out at that point.

Fortunately because Myra has her own place and is on her own, she can come anytime we need her, and she babysits for Robbie if we have to go out in the evening. So she is virtually the only one who has ever cared for him outside of his mother and father. He's never had another babysitter—which is good and not so good.

GEORGE: I think there was that sense of keeping Nancy's career going. We had just bought this house and had a healthy second mortgage, and like most people when they buy a house, we stretched it to the limit. Nancy had already built a career in the ten years since graduate school. Continuing it just seemed the natural thing to do.

NANCY: We didn't talk to or know anyone else who had a nanny, it was our own idea. First of all, I thought it important if Robbie had to be left at all that at least he be in familiar surroundings. At least here he had his own bed, toys, and food. Also, there was a selfish consideration that I would not have to bundle him up every morning and transport him someplace, and repeat the whole procedure at the end of the day. By the time the baby was born I was weary, and for the first year and a half he was never a good sleeper. A steady person who came to us meant one fewer complication I would have to contend with. Also, if he were ill what would happen to the day care? So this solution seemed better. We didn't know people with small children at that point, except casually in the neighborhood, to compare notes with.

GEORGE: Four years ago we didn't hear of as many people doing this as we do now. It is a recent phenomenon. Four years ago Nancy was the only working mother in the area; no longer. Some of the people with a similar need seem now to have looked at us and decided it works. In the neighborhood the reaction is, even if you have to work, the atmosphere for your child is wholesome because—"It's wonderful that you have Myra." Everybody now feels, including Nancy's family and my family—everybody who was prepared to be censurious initially—that Robbie is not getting a raw deal, that he is okay and we are not neglecting him or traumatizing him. That was quite something to accomplish!

Did they still have pangs of guilt?

NANCY: Oh yes!

GEORGE: She does, I don't. I was more open to day care, but I recognized that it would be more her choice. It was an adjustment for me to realize that I was going to have a working wife no matter what. I don't know where we crossed that threshold, of my realizing that Nancy was more than a second income, she had a career of her own. Certainly in the environment where I was raised, the wife stays home. That's what was familiar, and I was a pretty decent male chauvinist pig. Yet I don't remember having any anguish about discarding the old idea.

NANCY: No, you quickly got used to a second income!

GEORGE: My parents are 500 miles away so we see them maybe twice a year. My mother experienced a lot of interference from her mother-in-law, so she is making sure it doesn't happen to her daughter-in-law. She's being very cautious about judging by her own past. My brother and sister-in-law have been using a day care center. With both of them going to school, they haven't had the luxury of choice. We did.

Having somebody come in each day is the most expensive alternative. It's cheaper to have the person live in. We have to pay Myra enough to pay her rent, transportation, and everything else. Whereas if you have a house already, especially one the size of this, it is a lot less expensive either to redo the existing basement or put her in an existing bedroom. The idea of a live-in didn't bother me, but the way I looked at it was that Nancy's salary was paying for it. If she felt strongly against a live-in, there was no point in making an issue of it.

For her part Myra was firm on what she wanted. And I of course wanted less. She was looking at how much she needs to live on. We probably started out a little under $600 a month. Nancy works every Thursday night, so the original hours were 8:15 to 5:15 and on Thursdays noon to nine, five days a week. Then we found Nancy was having evening engagements, speeches, or board meetings, and that by working a full day Thursday she could take Monday off. Then Myra could take Monday off, so she was working just four days. At the start we payed her at nominal babysitting rates, a dollar or $1.50 an hour for evening babysitting, the same it would have cost with a sitter. When we cut the daytime hours, she agreed to do the babysitting free. That's the way it goes.

And Myra's flexible. For example, Nancy had to go to Toronto yesterday so Myra worked Monday and she'll take Friday off. She lives eight miles away and drives her own car. She drives Robbie to nursery school and picks him up. Nancy used to drop him off, but Robbie preferred to have Myra drive him, so she comes and picks him up, takes him to school, comes back, does the laundry, and drives back for him.

Based on my own childhood, I would say it makes some difference having a nanny. She becomes a third parent, a third set of standards. That's a complication. More so on Nancy's part than mine there's a sense of guilt that she's not at home so we tend to be more lenient when we *are* home than we might otherwise be. Certainly it's great having all my shirts ironed! We hired Myra on the assumption that she would take care of Robbie and that was her sole job. But she was willing to do the laundry and the ironing. She's one of those people who loves to iron. She at first even pressed my undershorts until I told her it wasn't necessary. So she'll iron anything. It's her habit. She sweeps. She doesn't do any heavy housework. She doesn't garden—which is unfortunate because neither one of us does either. The understanding was oral, no contract, that Robbie came first, and anything else was bonus. But Myra very much takes the responsibility, she's that sort of person. So she feels very obligated to get the laundry done. That leaves Nancy only what accumulates over the weekend. Myra obviously cooks Robbie's meals when she is here. Often she takes him to her apartment in the afternoon, more by his choice. She started that in the last year, when we bought her the car seat so she could take him.

Myra has defined her own place in the Whites' lives. What picture did they have of this person before finding and hiring her?

NANCY: We were looking for a loving person. All I knew at first was Myra was my receptionist's mother. And I knew what kind of person my receptionist was, and she had talked about her own growing up. I knew about the other daughter in the family too, and how she had turned out and was raising her children. I felt that this person had done a good job, and would probably do the same with Robbie. So really we were very lucky. If I hadn't found someone through the network, it would have been difficult. The best luck people in the neighborhood have had is not through the agency but through the newspaper: they advertise in the newspaper for what they want. You have to do a lot of screening yourself, but everyone I know has found someone they are satisfied with. Agencies prove less satisfactory. Especially if you hire a nanny from abroad, there seems to be a year's period that they're with you, then they learn English and move on.

In the interview you try to find out to the extent that you can what their approach to child rearing is. I wanted Robbie to be loved. I said to her, "I don't want the best-mannered child in the neighborhood. I just want him to be loved and secure." Myra turned out to be firmer than my wishes. Especially when he was a little baby, if she had done everything that she knew to do and he was still crying, she could crank up his mobile and walk away from the crib. I couldn't do that, and at the time that gave me pangs. On the other hand, she was probably more realistic because where I was worn to a frazzle trying to meet every demand, she paced herself. And at the end of the day she was fresh as a daisy, even when he was an infant and toddler. In that way I suspect she was wiser than I. She sets the limits and has been consistent with them. But she's very loving. She adores him.

An interview question like "What is your approach to raising children?" gives some information. Broaching concrete situations gives more. Such as, "If you've fed, if you've diapered, and the baby still cries, what would you do?" I had a friend who hired someone as a daily kind of nanny, and at the end of the first day my friend realized that the woman was a disaster. It was evident that her child had been neglected during the day, yet the caregiver was oblivious. I doubt she could have answered that question sensitively.

Certainly discipline is a key issue. I asked, "How do you think children should be disciplined?" and "What did you do when your children misbehaved?" Anyone who used corporal punishment wouldn't have lasted five minutes with me. Fortunately, Myra's approach and ours match. She's *not* a person who resorts to corporal punishment. If there were a discrepancy on an issue like this, maybe the parents could lay down their law. They could say, "No corporal punishment. If the child cries, pick him up. If he doesn't eat his dinner, he can't play with his toys." And so forth. But I think if you ask the person to do something that is too different and foreign, she'll sabotage it. Even if she tries to implement your way, it won't work because she doesn't believe in it, and is going to be resentful.

GEORGE: You're going to be challenged when you're tired or feeling under the weather or he's crying the most. That's when your instincts or nature come out. You need someone who has a similar approach to yours. Where it matters is when you act on your "instincts." Making sure that you have a common philosophy is much more important than codifying rules to be done or laying out a routine to be followed.

NANCY: In social work I have often asked myself, "Why do so many people who don't like children become teachers?" The primary requirements for anyone who is in a nanny position is to like children. I mean really like them, like the way a child thinks, like playing, think every coo and gurgle is adorable. That kind of person is going to roll with the punches more than somebody like myself. I would not be good as a full-time mother. I'm too tense and get too jittery. My nerves start to shred, and I get irritable. Whereas Myra is so accepting. Anything Robbie and we do is fine. That she has had children of her own is a strong advantage.

The other side of it is that his nursery school teachers, who are young and don't have children, are wonderful. So I think temperament is paramount. Certainly though, if you have had children, you are better able to cope with situations that come along, the decisions you have to make on the spur of the moment.

At the same time, I'm not sure that if we had just the nanny and couldn't put Robbie in nursery school that we'd be as content. It depends on the nanny. Our only problem now is that Myra isn't oriented to getting him out and involved in the community and with other children. As a result of his personality and her personality, he tends to be a very isolated child. And he's perfectly happy with that. Now he might have been that way even without her because I wouldn't have been running him around much either, visiting with the neighbors. For that reason we felt that it was vital for him to be in nursery school, to get the peer exposure and try to develop some social skills. We tried him in a program last year and it was disastrous. He was very young in his reaction to it. It was a strict Montessori school with twenty-eight children in the class with two teachers. He's now in a Montessori school in a woman's home, and there are sixteen children and two teachers and always a student aide. The system is more flexible. They use other materials as well as Montessori materials. It's much better. But it was dreadful last year.

Nancy cast her mind back four years to recall the specifics of the interview with Robbie's nanny-to-be.

NANCY: I asked my receptionist to ask her mother if she might be interested in this kind of job. Bernice came back and said her mother would. I called Myra and arranged to go out to her place to pick her up. I wanted to see her standards of cleanliness and organization—that sort of thing. On the phone at that point we clarified salary range. When I went out, it was a mutual interviewing process. I was very impressed with her place, with her appearance, her bearing, her manner. I said I want you to see the house, see what it will be like, see if you like us, and then you can tell me if you are still interested. I brought her out, and George sort of alienated her. Because his stress was on discipline and how much housework was she going to do. She was not taking this job to do housework, she replied—although of course in reality she likes to, beautifully irons everything, to take a prime example. So that sort of thing from George put her off, but she said she liked me at that point so she was willing to do it.

I'm a person who likes to delegate. If I have confidence in people, I'm not going to get in there and supervise them to death. So I said, "When you are here you will be in charge. It will be your decision what he eats, what he wears, what you do, if he needs medicine. You're in charge." Myra liked that because it gave her a great deal of autonomy. She is not a person who likes working with a lot of people. Here she could run her own show. With us she has as much or as little contact as she wants. If she wants to stay around and chat to have a little contact above the one-year-old, she can. If she doesn't want to, she can go right home to her own place. She has said that this is one of the nicest points for her, that as much as she loves him, she can go home at the end of the day and recharge *her* batteries, and go home on the weekend.

Even the excellent permanent relationship between parents and caregiver has snags at first. Despite her training in psychology and joy at her baby's development, Nancy felt vulnerable to Myra's criticism. Caution on both sides colored the early relationship.

NANCY: When Myra started to work, I came home for a while at lunch and early after work, to check on how things were going. She was jittery about the job initially. She had been through a bad time herself, and she wondered if she could cope with the responsibility. So we were all figuring it out. Because I felt we were entrusting the most precious possession in the world to Myra, I wanted to monitor the care as well as I could. Initially she smoked, but very little and not around Robbie. Then she gave it up. Neither George nor I smokes.

Not too long after she came, Myra got phlebitis. I thought, "Oh my gosh what am I going to do?" because I had no back-up system. She was out for a few days then, and one of the part-time people from my office filled in. That threw me: Would she be sick frequently? But she isn't.

The only doubt that went through my mind was the first week or so when Myra said two or three times, "He's a nervous baby, isn't he?" I would get all upset and say to George, "She thinks he is a nervous baby, what does that mean? Does that mean she doesn't like him? And if she doesn't like him, she's going to be terrible, and what will I do?" That's something that bothered me at the beginning. Not merely that her judgment was critical of me, but if she didn't like Robbie, what would she be transmitting to him?

GEORGE: I don't recall having any concerns.

NANCY: George is always very reassuring. George is optimistic, and that's good for a person like me. Usually he is right, too! Except, really, the first two and a half years of Robbie's life were very hard on us as a couple because George could not buy my approach to child rearing. He kept saying, "When do we start disciplining him?" And I said, "Look, it's not saying no that makes you a good parent. It's teaching him how to behave in the right way." George was skeptical. And he has said since this arose from his uncertainty. He didn't know whether by our leniency we were making a terrible mistake. And so he was extremely critical of me. Meanwhile I was having a hard enough time from the lack of sleep and the pressure of having to spread myself. It was very trying. Now the last year we feel we have done "all right," and between George and me is much better along with the rest.

GEORGE (laughing): In spite of you! . . . Rifts occurred by dint of our backgrounds. I come from a more authoritarian mode and my approach is too. Nancy has been very good about *teaching* Robbie. My approach is more of a structured environment. The other source of differences is I'm much more patient than she is.

NANCY: Yes, when I'm fatigued. Myra is between both of us. She can be firmer than I am, but she is more relaxed than George. Also, she is secure on how she relates to children. I don't think she agonizes about it. How Myra fits in is that with her I am able to come home even at the end of a hard day and enjoy seeing Robbie. Without her I would be a basket case at five o'clock. And the quality of mothering he would have at the end of the day would not be too terrific. So I think he is better off because we share caregiving.

Food probably now is our greatest area of difference. What she eats and what she feeds him departs from my ideal diet form. I feel that is one area where I can be flexible. If she wants to give Robbie cookies and candy and everything else, that is only one meal of the day, and we can fill him up on fruit and vegetables the rest of the time. In the long run it will even out.

How did the Whites and how do they try to monitor? Mother and father take a break from amplifying each other's comments to view the matter differently.

GEORGE: Nowadays you are pretty lousy about it!

NANCY: George monitors better than I do. Myra is good at saying, "We had a good day" or "We went to my house" or "This is what he had for lunch" or "He napped (or didn't)." If she doesn't volunteer, I say, "How was school today?" or "What did he have for lunch?" so I know what to feed him for dinner. If I feel Robbie is borderline sick, I'll either call during the day and we confer about whether to give him aspirin, or stop by home. When I return at night, I say, "How was he? Was he cranky or tired? Did he seem hot?"

GEORGE: But often you come in and she goes out, and neither one of you says much at all.

NANCY: Oh we always chat, but he's always running around.

GEORGE: Oh you always chat, but you never talk about him. Because I'll ask you, "Did he have a nap today?" and you reply, "I don't know, call Myra."

NANCY: Yes, George's concern is whether Robbie's had a nap because if he has then he's good till midnight. That's not my big concern so I don't ask about naps. She tells me if something is wrong.

GEORGE: There's a complete trust. A little story here is that one day Myra was talking to her grandson and said, "You're my boy." Todd was five. And Todd said, "No I'm not. That boy that you take care of, *he's* your boy." And literally she loves him I think almost more than her own grandchildren.

NANCY: That's why we didn't ask too much at the start. The first day Myra came to take care of Robbie she brought him a little stuffed dog. Very soon she was buying him blocks and other lovely things. Robbie has 500 blocks now, of which she's bought him perhaps half. He was in the book-of-the-day club for a while. So we could *see* how she felt about him. And I saw how he responded to her even as a very small baby. If I had seen him being tense or her being tense or seen her wanting to rush away or getting here late or taking a lot of sick days, then I would have felt something was amiss.

GEORGE: Myra was pretty open about her personal problems. Her first husband died. A friend of her husband married her on the rebound. It was a total mistake, and he took her for a ride. What didn't come out until later was that her son has had troubles, too.

NANCY: We knew this beforehand, in the large. But to me how a son goes is often more related to his relationship to his father. Very soon after she came, a matter of weeks or two months, she began to say—when I said, "We're so grateful to you and feel so fortunate"—"Well it's good for all of us" and "I really didn't have much to live for before I came to you, and he has given me a reason to live." So it was mutually beneficial.

With their nanny the Whites do not mandate, they request. How do they conceive the relationship?

NANCY: It's an employee/employer relationship, but she has become a family member. In many ways she is more like his grandmother than his real grandmothers. Because they live far away and he doesn't see them. Just the way I wouldn't order my mother to do something, I won't order Myra. I say, "I'd like it if he could do this or that. How do you feel about it?" Or if I feel that she has reservations then I say, "How else could we do it?" Or I try to think how we could do it to take the pressure off her regarding something she doesn't really believe in.

GEORGE: I approve of Nancy's management, more or less. I was in the navy, which is the opposite of this relationship. But what I realized was that every time I pulled rank to get a job done, to me it was an admission that I was doing it the wrong way. A good human relationship is founded on mutual respect. I think we have it here. Myra is not afraid to voice her opinion.

NANCY: That has come gradually.

GEORGE: She is more likely to complain to Nancy than to me. She is still intimidated.

NANCY: Even so she does it gently. She worked at one point for the wealthiest family in town when the wife had had a mastectomy and the husband asked Myra to come in and run the household, but her place was blatantly "downstairs." One day in the dining room the light was dim and she switched a napkin ring. And he said, "Mrs. Dalrumple, you gave me my *wife's* napkin ring." And she said, "I resigned that day because he treated me like a servant." Myra does not want to be a servant. That we treat her like one of the family is a proud feeling for her.

GEORGE: Yet when on occasion we have suggested we go out to dinner together or some such she hasn't wanted to.

NANCY: No, but the last time my parents visited from Newport [Rhode Island] she was willing to socialize. We went out to dinner and she took care of Robbie, and when we got home, she sat and visited with them in the living room. That was the "closest" we have ever gotten. I don't think it is that important. For Robbie's birthday she stayed for dinner a couple of times. It wouldn't bother her to eat with the two of us. But anything beyond that would make her too jittery. Especially if my parents or George's parents were around.

GEORGE: When I first gave Myra the keys, I said, "Here is the key to the

69

front door, here is the key to the back," and maybe handed her the back first. She said, "Do you want me to use the back door?" And I said, "Oh, no, no, no!" Ironically, she comes in the front door, and we use the back door. I'd say both of us have felt strongly about treating Myra with respect as a person.

NANCY: When she began as nanny, I wouldn't call her by her first name because I felt she was a professional in her own right. I didn't want to demean her. After a while she said, "Won't you please call me Myra?" And I said, "Well if you don't mind." She called me quite quickly, "Nancy." Of course George is "George" to everybody in the world so he established that.

We're very aware that in order to keep her we pay her well, extremely well, and people are appalled. She has never asked for a raise. We give it to her. When I get a raise, she gets a raise, the same percentage or this time a little bit more. At Christmas we try to give her as nice a gift as we can afford, which in the last three years has been Royal Doulton figurines. About a $150 gift. And we send her flowers on Mother's Day.

GEORGE: We do?

NANCY: Yes. And birthday presents. And if we go on a trip we bring her something. So we try to demonstrate consistently how much we value her service.

GEORGE: There has still been some concern in her mind, will we want to keep her when Robbie goes to school? One thing we find is that it is very important as with any employee to think about the future. We've made up our mind that yes, even when he goes to school, that we would keep her as a housekeeper. We are in a situation where we can afford her, and we are used to her, and also we feel a sense of responsibility. But it didn't dawn on us until just recently that, gee, she had been concerned. The worst thing that could have come out of it is she might have thought, "Well, Robbie's getting towards that age. I'd better start looking for another job." What I told her is we want her on whatever terms she wants. If she wants to continue full time, barring something unusual, we will keep her full time. If when Robbie is in school, she wants to cut back to half time, that is perfectly amenable too. Realizing that she does need enough to live, she doesn't have much else to go by, what we are saying is we want to make you feel secure with what you're doing.

The only misgiving I have is about the health situation. We can't afford to pay sick leave, and what do we do if she becomes sick? At Myra's age, fifty-nine, there could be a serious long-term sickness. She is overweight and has a circulation problem in her legs. Our arrangement with her is that if she is sick and we have to call in somebody else, then we deduct it from her pay. She in effect has no sick leave.

NANCY: Except that last year when she had an operation on her leg and was off six working days, I stayed home. I took vacation days. My job gives me the flexibility to do that. Some women couldn't.

GEORGE: The time Myra had a bad cold we told her to stay home. When she had stomach trouble and came, having been vomiting, we told her to go home. We appreciate that on days when other people would have stayed home, she has come.

Probably it would make sense to have a contract, but we have never felt it necessary. We are happy with the relationship. It's quite possible she might misinterpret it, too. She might be threatened by it.

NANCY: A nanny doesn't always work out so neatly. One woman social worker I know had a nanny with active syphilis. This woman was up from the islands, on her own, and needed a job. Again she came during the day. There are other horror stories, some of which make your blood run cold. I have another friend whose oldest child is a year younger than Robbie and she has had her child in about eight different day care arrangements, from nannies to day care center. Even with the day care centers it hasn't been stable because the first center took them from infants to three, then she had to change. But then at that point she had a new infant. So then it was two different day care centers. With all the factors considered, we feel that we do come out ahead in terms of the alternatives.

Used now to being a triangle of parents, were the Whites still against the idea of a nanny who would live in?

GEORGE: A family across the street has a live-in, so do some friends down the road. The ones down the road think she is super.

NANCY: But they have only had her two months. And the ones across the road had theirs three weeks and her mother developed terminal cancer, so she left and they had to find somebody else. In the first place, I wouldn't want it because I don't want someone extra in the house. I can tolerate George, but anyone beyond that no! Sharing the kitchen, the bathroom . . .

GEORGE: Nancy is the kind of person who wants to work in the kitchen alone. She can tolerate my being out there. But her mother or sister or especially my mother, that's unacceptable.

NANCY: Never to be alone, not to be able to fight even. The feeling that you would have to go into the bedroom and shut the door and whisper while you fought would be very difficult. Also, fortunately for us, Myra likes her privacy. She likes having a life away from us, apart from her job, having that independence and autonomy. So for us it is better this way. There really is no alternative. I would go crazy if I had somebody living in.

GEORGE: I could tolerate it. I'm from a big family.

NANCY: The people across the street who now find it is all right are also from big families. I was from a small family so I am not used to a lot of confusion and action. Maybe that is one variable. Also, if you are more easygoing, it is easier to have somebody living in.

GEORGE: I personally think it would be nice if we had a live-in and she came in right now and took Robbie up to bed.

NANCY: I know, but that would mean even less contact for you and me, and I don't like that idea. I think that he has us few enough hours of the day that I wouldn't want to see that diminished.

GEORGE: When we come home in the evening, he is greatly stimulated.

NANCY: Robbie gets all wound up when George comes home and wants to do things with him. With Myra he plays for very long stretches by himself. But once George is here he wants to be playing with George. I can often go lie down and read or turn to something else and Robbie tolerates it so long as he has George to play with. And George is very much the playing parent. If Robbie wants to be read to or cuddled, he comes to me. In terms of playing, it's Daddy he wants.

He stays up late, evidently because his part of the day with us started in the early evening. We could put him in bed at eight o'clock, and he would still be awake at 11 or 11:30 if he slept in the late afternoon. His normal bedtime is 10 to 10:30. Even as a little baby he didn't go to sleep until 10 and then he was up a lot in the night. So sleep has never been one of his big things even though he is not that active a child. He simply doesn't care about sleeping.

The Whites and Myra have worked to make the "changing of the guards" occur naturally and smoothly. Nevertheless, Robbie lets his parents know that being left is not the sweetest feeling.

NANCY: Robbie gets up, and most days stays in his night clothes until Myra arrives. For a while I took him to nursery school because I didn't want to put that burden on her, but he decided he would rather have her take him, so I said, "Myra are you willing to do that?" It's up a little hill and in snowy weather I worry about her falling or having problems. But she said yes, that she was willing to do it. So she dresses Robbie, and because he doesn't want to eat right away when he wakes up, feeds him breakfast. Then she drives him to nursery school, and when nursery school is over, she picks him up. Usually at that point she has done the wash and straightened up. Then they usually go to her house. They have lunch at her house and play for the afternoon. Then she brings him home in the late afternoon. I get home about 5:15, we have the changing of the guards, and she tells me what has happened. We try to plan whatever is on for the next day.

The interesting thing is that even though Robbie has had Myra virtually every day since he was six weeks old, he's had a lot of separation anxiety. Every day that I left until very recently is was, "Mommy don't go, Mommy don't go, please Mommy." He would try to push Myra out the door, even though he loves her, and that was really hard on her. Now in the morning we have a fifteen-minute overlap so when she comes I don't go right away. With a period of adjustment, not being rushed, Robbie responds much better. He's at the point that he gives me his "R2D2," and as long as the toy goes with me, he can separate comfortably. But that is a recent phenomenon. It has amazed me that he takes the parting so hard. I would have thought that with her coming into his life so early and being such a consistent figure, there wouldn't be so much distress as there has been.

GEORGE: When I come home first, Robbie is glad to see me, and it's "Go home, Myra," and that is just how he views it.

I think part of the reason Robbie had trouble separating in the morning was the way we handled it. Because initially separations were so difficult, Nancy had a tendency to sneak out. I could be wrong, but I think that reinforced the negative feeling, instead of quickly from the stairs saying, "Goodbye, I'm not going to be long. I'll be coming back."

NANCY: Possibly. The other factors was I had to be away so much; my schedule is not predictable. I'm out at least two nights a week, often more, and I think he felt that any time he had me out of his sight I might be gone again. That made him more insecure.

73

GEORGE: Nowadays we explain to him that Mommy has to go to a meeting, or—it happens to a lesser degree—that I do. If we tell him in advance, he accepts it.

NANCY: He says, "Take R2!" And as long as we take R2, that's all right.

GEORGE: In retrospect I think that if we had consciously mentioned the separation and not tried to downplay it, said it was there, and it became a fact of life, I don't think his anxiety would be as strong as it is.

NANCY: We go on vacations without Myra, of course, and he doesn't miss her. He seems to have her in a special niche. She is not family. Even with my parents he says that he wants them to come and visit or he misses them, but with Myra it's not that way.

As Robbie scooted around the corner, George asked him, "Is Myra sort of like Grandma?" Robbie: "No, she isn't." Nancy: "What is Myra's job?" Robbie: "Myra's job is to take care of me."

NANCY: A year ago Robbie said, "Myra's another mommy." He says, "Myra is a mommy too." She calls herself in recent months a babysitter. Recently Robbie and I were talking about babysitters, and I said, "Myra's not just a babysitter. She's a very special babysitter because she takes care of you only. She loves you much the way Mommy and Daddy love you." So when last week Myra said something about being a babysitter, he piped up and remarked, "No, no! You're a very *special* babysitter."

GEORGE: That's an interesting point. We haven't called her a nanny. She sometimes refers to herself as a housekeeper, sometimes as the babysitter. It's a matter we never have resolved. It hasn't been worrisome, but it has been ambiguous. Robbie is starting to play the two of us against the other but not Myra.

NANCY: That may be because, mostly out of luck, there's so little conflict in how we approach and handle things, and in how we react.

An area where we are fortunate is that Myra doesn't watch too much television. Robbie doesn't like it. He goes and turns it off. She had one soap opera that she may still watch. The television is on for a half hour. If she tries putting *Sesame Street* or one of the other good children's programs on during the morning, sometimes he watches and sometimes not. He has been big on books, not television. Before he ever went to nursery school Myra was a marvel that way. She started reading to him at eight months. She read to him a minimum of two hours during the day, and I read

G.D. Brown

Although it was Nancy who suggested reading to Robbie when he was only eight months old, his enthusiastic response made Myra a champion of early reading experiences. She began reading to him a minimum of two hours a day.

to him two hours during the evening. That was his favorite activity from that age on. He really got into it at a year. But when other children were pushing trucks around and riding their tricycles, he wanted to be read to, and she was very ready to do that.

GEORGE: Now she just reads to him a little during the day and we read him two stories at night. And he is more interested in the Legos or drawing.

NANCY: Back in college I said I'd never delegate my child rearing to someone with less education than I. Well, Myra had to leave school after ninth grade because of family pressures: her mother had died and she had to take over. So in terms of formal education she doesn't have much. But in terms of wisdom she has an enormous amount. She likes books, and has encouraged him in that. The encouragement of learning that she has given Robbie has been incomparable. She has stimulated him to do things that I wouldn't have done. So our experience really blew my myth about what you need to have to be a good parent or even a good-parent surrogate.

We have tried to have neighborhood kids come over from time to time while she is here. That doesn't work too well. She isn't thrilled with that. It's the extra commotion and responsibility that make her balk. That is what we are working on now. We said that this spring we want him to be more with other children.

GEORGE: I've sailed some comments to her and. . . .

NANCY: Yes, she became upset that George didn't approve of what she was doing, so we are still talking about that.

GEORGE: Not consciously, but I suppose I come on as the heavy.

NANCY: Right! And I smooth over, reassure.

GEORGE: I intimidate Myra. I don't try to. Partly it's my size, and maybe I can be a little short.

NANCY: Yes, Myra thought George was grumpy for about a year at one point. She said it to me a couple of times. That was another problem, because I felt in the middle, and that made my stomach go in knots. When Robbie was about two, we bought her the car seat so she could take him places like the local park where they have ducks. After he left Montessori school last year, I signed him up for a couple of programs at the library and she took him to those. She was reluctant, though, and uncomfortable. She felt older than the other people; "They are young mothers, and I am more like a grandmother." Then in the next series I enrolled him at a time I could take him. Myra takes Robbie shopping with her and out to lunch.

GEORGE: But basically she doesn't. She prefers to keep him here or in her house. She has been very reluctant to mix with the neighbors. And she doesn't want to stay outside with Robbie when it's cold. She feels she has to stay outside with him. So he hasn't been out playing even though four other boys live within five houses in each direction, all his age. She has kept him inside.

NANCY: We have said just in the last week when the weather gets warm we want him to play outside. He has become interested in hockey now, and has a hockey stick. She said, "Well, I would have to stay out with him," and I answered, "I think you could let him go out by himself." My feeling is I'd rather have her watch out the window. She doesn't need to be by his side, yet I'm not confident about a four-year-old being aware of the traffic and the dangers. Most of the other children are out alone, but I'm jittery about that. And the neighbor's girl disappeared for over an hour yesterday, one of his peers. I prefer that Myra is monitoring somehow.

The Whites summarized how a nanny fits into their expectations for Robbie.

NANCY: She is working along well in giving us a stable life. He is not in and out of all these child-care arrangements that can be devastating to other children. She's one more person to love him. Because we are really a nuclear family, oh, about 350 days of the year. Myra gives him a little extension of that family. She takes him to her daughter's house, and he sees her grandchildren and all. That is nice for him.

GEORGE: As far as intellectual stimulation is concerned, she is adequate and good. The one place where she falls down is on the peer exposure, which relates to his social maturity. Robbie will attend public school if it works out. If he went to private school, we would be spending $13,000 a year in today's dollars for child care and education.

NANCY: We hope he will be able to get along in public school, but he may not. I'm concerned about the quality of the public schools. So we'll just see. If we lost Myra tomorrow, I'd kill myself! Seriously, what I think I would do would be to investigate the nanny program at the local college. They now are turning out many more graduates, who are highly respected. And now it wouldn't bother me so much that he had a young person. No one caregiver can be everything.

Myra Dalrumple's Commentary

I had done a few similar jobs before, looking after older children when their parents went away for holidays. One family lives on a big estate and also has a hacienda in Mexico. When the parents went south in the wintertime, they had me come in to look after the two teenage children for a couple of months. A friend of mine had been contacted, and she wasn't interested. She asked me if I would be. I said, "Oh I'll try it." I needed money, eh? And so I worked there for two or three years in the winter when they went away.

Then another family heard about me. They had three children. The youngest, eight, a boy in high school, and another boy out working. If they went skiing or on trips, they had me in.

Those are really the only times in my life I'd ever worked. Then one day my oldest daughter told me that the head of the agency where she works was expecting, and looking for someone to watch the baby when it came along. Would I be interested? I said, "I don't know. It's been quite a while since I've looked after babies. But I'm willing to give it a try."

It started with an interview before the baby was born. Nancy came and brought me here and introduced me to George, and we got to know one another. They promised to let me know after the baby was born when they would need me. When they were ready for me, I came here and have looked after Robbie ever since. It has worked out fine. They seem happy, and I'm certainly happy.

At the interview they seemed satisfied with me and didn't ask a great many questions. I suppose knowing my daughter helped. Nancy said the main thing was for me to look after the baby and do his washing. But later when I began, I found that when the baby was asleep, I'd rather keep busy. So I vacuum and find other things that need doing. And while I was doing his washing, I figured I might as well do all the washing and ironing.

It had been thirty-some years since I had taken care of a baby, but I do have grandchildren although I don't look after them steady. It wasn't as though I hadn't handled children for all those years. But even the first day I don't think anything was hard. Because I've never felt I had someone standing over me saying, "You must do this and you must do that." As long as I looked after Robbie and kept him happy that was all that they asked of me. Anything else that I have done they appreciate, but I don't feel that I have to. It's like having a second home. I feel at home here. I can do what I want.

He hasn't been any problem. He's a good little boy. He amuses himself with his toys. I can go upstairs and iron and he'll play around here. Of course when he was younger he couldn't do that. But then I did housework while he slept.

As I told George the other day, I think that if more women my age did something like this, they would be a lot happier. After my first husband died, I had a bad second marriage. I was depressed, eh? I spent too much time alone thinking about what happened in the past. This way I'm out every day—I'm with him. Especially now that he's older, he's such a joy to be with, and he makes me feel so happy. And then I'm glad to get home to my place in the evening. Before I thought, "Well, I'm no good to myself and I'm no good to anybody else." I felt useless. Now I don't. I feel there's a place for me. And I love him and he loves me back. I couldn't think more of him if he was my grandson. I don't know how many times a day it comes out of me, "Oh I love you, Robbie!" And so often he'll answer, "I love you too, Myra." So we have that bond.

I asked Myra about Robbie's problems in separating from his mother.

Nancy felt torn for a while when Robbie cried as she left. But usually as soon as she left he was all right. Very seldom would he carry on after she went. I tried to get his mind on something else. If he was having a particularly bad day, I'd let him cry for a while and then talk to him about something else, or ask him, "Shall we read a story?"

This morning when Nancy left, Robbie was still asleep. I think he must have heard her car go out. So he started to cry. I was downstairs, and I heard him upstairs. He was in on his mother's bed, he had gone out of his room and in there, and he was crying. When I went in to go to him, he said, "No, no, go away!" and so I stayed away from him for a few minutes. Then I said something about "Did you see it was snowing outside?" He said, "I saw that." I said, "Do you want to come look out the window?" So he went to look out the window and said something like, "I'll have to get a new mummy robot." And I said, "Oh Robbie, your mummy's so good to you, you don't mean that! Mummy went in and kissed you good-bye, but you were asleep and didn't know anything about it." Then he turned around with his arms to me, and I hugged him. I was sitting on the edge of the bed so I fell back on the bed with him, and hugged him again. He gave me "big bear hugs," and he was fine—no more trouble.

A person in my position has to realize that a child will reject you. Why, he'll even reject his own parents at times. Children don't always give out love. It helps to have been a parent, but a person who is intelligent and has warm feelings for children would understand Robbie's rejection just the same. When I was younger, I had never been around children. When I went babysitting, I found it very awkward because I didn't know how to relate to a child. On the other hand, there is a girl who babysits around here who was raised with a bunch of brothers and sisters, and she is very good with children. It's something you have to learn when you have your own children, unless you have been raised in a large family.

The nanny or the parents—who makes the decisions?

Of course raising Robbie is *not* the same as raising my own children. I don't have all the say of raising Robbie. Nancy makes the big decisions. She tells me, and I follow her orders, eh? She was the one that suggested we start reading to Robbie before he was a year old. Of course, we never did that with our children, and I thought, "This is ridiculous. He can't understand what I am reading." But I did it. And she did it too. And he'd sit there and listen, and he enjoyed it. He learned a lot, and now he loves books. Even yet I read to him every day. Now I can see I was wrong, she was right. She's had the schooling, eh, and she knows. I have bought him books, and they have bought him others. Even as a baby Robbie sat there listening as though he was understanding. I think being read to taught him to love books.

But Nancy didn't tell me, "This is how the day should be." It was never stated that he had to have a nap, although usually he would. If he was tired, he went to sleep. Now our trouble is to prevent a nap, or else he doesn't want to go to bed at night. What it is, he's away from his parents all day. When they come home, he's so glad to see them he thinks he doesn't want to go to bed. His father doesn't want him up until midnight. Naps I handle the way I would do whether Nancy were in charge or not.

With meals she doesn't tell me what to do because he's one of these who eats what he wants and nothing else. Luckily he likes vegetables, and he is doing all right. Nancy, when he was smaller, used to cook up foods and put them in the freezer, so all I had to do was put them in the microwave and use what was already cooked—meat patties and stuff like that. Usually now he wants to come to my place. I pick him up from the nursery school, and we go to my house for lunch.

Nancy decided when he would get off the bottle, but we didn't have any problem there either. Toilet-training has been more difficult. He was good for a while, and now, for some reason or the other, he doesn't want to go on the toilet. Just in the last few weeks. I don't know why, but Nancy says she's read where this happens quite often so we're not going to fret about it. I toilet-trained him in the daytime, she did at night. I was less strict than with my own children because Nancy said, "Don't worry about it." We didn't *have* to have him trained. A lot of this is more relaxed than when I raised children. Then we thought we had to do this and that at certain times, where that was ridiculous. Just because somebody might say, "Why is your child not toilet-trained?"

I took Robbie to my place once or twice to fix him lunch there. I don't know why he likes it so much now. Maybe because it's an apartment, maybe because it's a change of scenery. We eat. Then we usually read a few stories. Today we took his motorcycle men and his motorcycles. Sometimes he doesn't even play with them. He dumps them out of the bag and leaves them on the floor. But they're *there*. And of course he has to take Whitey, his blanket, wherever he goes. One of my grandchildren had a toy dog like that, that was a disgrace, and she wouldn't part with it. Another had a bear. They still have these things even though one of them is a teenager, the other, twelve. If Robbie likes it, and Whitey means so much to him, why take it away? It's almost like a person.

The questions about bringing up another mother's child caused Myra to review her own mothering of thirty years before.

If I were to raise my children again now, it might be different. Instead I only have Robbie. My three children were born close together. When the

80

youngest was three months old, my husband went overseas to fight in the war. When the three children and I were there by ourselves, it was great. I spent time with them during the daytime. If I couldn't get the work done, I had the evenings when they were in bed. Then my husband came home from overseas, and he was a man who wanted his meals on the dot, and it didn't matter if the child needed attention or not, he came first. Soon he started to remodel our home. He had his brothers over helping him. It was bedlam. Living in a house and trying to remodel it, and a bunch of people around. At first we'd be living in the front of the house, and then in the basement for a while. When the brothers helped, of course you had to give them meals. And then trying to raise the children at the same time. So I can't compare that to what I have here, eh?

After the war, I kept on raising the children. I never worked outside the home. I had to drop out of school at fourteen to look after my mother who was bedridden three years before she died. After her death, I stayed home and looked after my father and brother until I married. Then my husband died fourteen years ago yesterday. He was on his way out to work one morning and dropped dead on the sidewalk of a heart attack. Finding myself all alone—my children were grown and married—I guess I was frightened. A fellow I'd met through my husband made himself very available. He was going to teach me to drive. He was so nice. Being scared I relied on him, and we got married. All he wanted was everything he could get. I owned a boat, a motor, and a car. I made a big mistake. But it's too late to do anything about that now. For a while it was pretty bad.

My two daughters live nearby, and I'm quite close to them. I was at one of their place's last night for dinner. The other one lives near me, and she and her husband have been great.

What is Myra's daily routine?

I usually come to the Whites in the morning and get Robbie dressed, take him to nursery school, come back, and if there's washing to do, I wash and iron, clean up, straighten, clean the kitchen. Usually Thursdays I clean upstairs, Fridays downstairs while he's at school. We go to my house when I pick him up, then we come back here somewhere around four o'clock. I leave here at ten after five, when Nancy comes back. He's glad to see her. I'm not taking her place. I wouldn't want to do that. As long as he's happy with me during the day, why would I try to be a mother figure with him?

I wondered how he would be after they went to Florida for a week this winter. When I came, he seemed glad to see me and tell me what happened. And I was glad to see him. I enjoyed having a week off. Anybody does, eh? But the time goes by faster with a job like this. I don't work

Mondays, and usually have Saturday through Monday off, unless they want to go somewhere. The weeks just fly.

On a day off either I stay home and clean my apartment, maybe do crossword puzzles, or read a book, or else my daughter who lives close by and I go shopping. On Sundays they invite me over for Sunday dinner. My son has two young children, one a little older than Robbie and a younger one, but I don't see much of them. My son is a different story.

Robbie went with me over to my daughter's a couple of years ago in the summer, and we had a picnic lunch outside. Sometimes I bring my grandchildren to the White's, the two that live close, the girl who is now twelve, and the boy, eight or nine. He knows who they are, but Robbie doesn't mix with other children much yet. He will. I suppose it is because he has been with us grown-ups so much. Part of it I guess is my fault. I don't particularly like standing outside while he plays with other children. And he won't play out by himself. He'll get over it. This is what we have to work on now.

A few times I have invited other children in the neighborhood over here. I should do it more often. I had a little feller from next door over a few weeks ago in the afternoon. Well, at that age they don't play together, so you feel like you are trying to entertain both of them.

He doesn't expect me to do something with him most of the time. Today he didn't go to nursery school because he was too late waking up. I gave him his breakfast and got him dressed. He came in the living room and played with his toys. I worked around doing the cleaning: the vacuuming, some washing, and a bit of ironing.

I don't watch television. When he was younger, there was a program that I liked to watch in the afternoon, one of the soap operas that I had been interested in. Usually he napped, and I watched my soap opera. Now that he's older and not napping, I thought he didn't like me to sit and watch television. It doesn't mean that much so I don't bother with it.

I don't make him pick up. The room is usually a mess. This is his room, and we don't fuss about it. He's got lots of time, eh? to start picking up—he's only four. *They* don't make him pick up. They say, "This is his room, don't worry about it." Sometimes I pick up anyway. If I tell Robbie to pick up things and can't get it through to him—he just ignores me—I just pick up myself, which I guess I shouldn't do. But I don't see that *they* make him pick up things either, so I go ahead.

Sometimes I yell at him, naturally, but it never lasts. He knows it doesn't. Sometimes I get exasperated. I know I shouldn't yell at him, but I'm human too.

They don't worry if he makes a mess. It's not my place to correct him. Like, they give him paint to paint with, and he goes painting the kitchen windows and the doors to the dining room and that. They don't care. It washes off, eh? And when you stop and think about it, he's not doing any harm.

If something doesn't seem right, we usually talk it out. One time I said how I thought I should be able to give him a spanking if I thought he needed it. If I was going to be looking after him, he would have to know that he had to mind me. But their idea is no physical abuse. Well, that's okay.

How does Myra think Robbie reflects her? In what way is he different because she has had a major part in raising him?

Maybe he's quieter. I notice some of the neighborhood kids and they run here and run there. Sometimes I think it's a good thing that Robbie is not like that because I'm too old to run after him like that. But my husband used to say I had one speed and that was slow. I'm easygoing.

Myra explained how she fits into the Whites' family scheme and what her job caring for Robbie has meant to her personally.

They treat me like one of the family. I'm not treated as a servant. I banged the back end of my car a few weeks ago, and I said, "George, would you mind, I banged the fender, do you think you could take your rubber mallet and take the dent out of it?" He went out one evening and did it. He's told me, "If you want something done, just let me know." They're good that way. I feel this is my second home.

The great part of it is that this job is not live in. Everybody likes to spend some time in their own house. When I looked after the Phillipson children, it was live in because the parents were away. This was a big estate, and I had the servant's quarters. I missed my place being away from it so long. It's nice at night to be able to go home. You can always relax better there.

A lot of people want someone to live in because they have an extra room and think that when they want someone she'll be there and available at all hours and what have you. And because we are giving her her own room and food then we don't have to pay her very much. I would rather be paid well and have my own place. I'm paid *very* well. I doubt if there is another babysitter in Ottawa who is making what I am making. But then she says I'm more than a babysitter because I do some work too. I've never asked for a raise, but I've had one every year since I've been here.

If the Whites left Ottawa tomorrow, I would have to find a new job. The only security I have is the money that I got when I sold my house. And I'm getting alimony from my second husband, but he's liable to retire at any time. When he was first ordered to pay me, he wouldn't pay me. We were in and out of court. Then they passed a new law where they could take it right from his wages, so this is what the state is doing. If he retires, then they won't be able to take it from his wages, and I don't know where that leaves me. The portion of my money that I have invested I'm trying to build up as security for when I can no longer work. I figure if I can build up enough, then with the interest from that money and in five years my old-age pension, then maybe I can manage. I'll be sixty in August. For me it's not just the White family. This is the way I'd spend my time no matter who. I'm not trained for anything else. And I have certainly enjoyed being here. They have told me that I'll have a job with them as long as I want it.

Never even for a day did I consider quitting. There was a time after my second marriage broke up I was left so desolate—not only with the trauma of the divorce but also my worsened financial situation. Because if I said something to him about how fast the money was going, he said, "What are you worrying about? I'm going to look after you for the rest of your life." And the marriage didn't even last two and a half years. Then I was left wondering however I would manage. If it hadn't been for my younger daughter and her husband, I think I would have had a nervous breakdown. But they had me over every day for a while. My daughter came for me, because I had no car, took me to her place, then took me home at night. They were very good to me. But there was a long time when I didn't even feel like listening to music, I didn't feel like singing. Now I find I'm always singing, I'm happy. So it's been good.

I've got to like Robbie more all the time. What can a baby do? I love babies, but now I find him entertaining, funny, and cute. A lot of women my age sit home and think the way I did, feeling sorry for themselves and that they could use a little extra money. But I suppose they are afraid to go out and try something like this. If you haven't done it, it makes you nervous. But to be around a little one, it does something for you. They're happy, then you're happy, eh?

5

PLAYGROUP

Until the rate of human turnover is substantially slowed, education must help people to accept the absence of deep friendships, to accept loneliness and mistrust—or it must find new ways to accelerate friendship formation.

Alvin Toffler, *Future Shock*

Typically a new mother discounts playgroups, believing that playmates for her tyke will just show up. For a year or so she builds a little palace for her child at home, replete with tropical fish, block corner, and bucket of bath toys. Can mother and child make it right through to kindergarten without that playgroup "nonsense"? She hopes so, equating playgroups with boredom, chaos, and carpet stains.

Yet, as her child approaches one and a half, this same mother may find the palace walls crumbling, and herself urgently looking for a playgroup. Towards the middle of the second year occurs what Louise J. Kaplan, author of *Oneness and Separateness*,[1] calls the second birth. Activity for activity's sake no longer preoccupies the child. Children are ready to cross-pollinate and to develop language and motor skills in a wider social world.

The second birth at fifteen to eighteen months impels children to share all their movements and discoveries with another person, usually the mother. Pleasure in sharing with mother generalizes to a new interest in others. Eighteen-month-olds tend to be *friendly* creatures. They also have a social appetite that mothers and siblings can scarcely satisfy. Playgroups are an excellent way to provide for early social desire, extending a child's trust in the most gradual way.

Via the playgroup, mothers can eliminate isolation of themselves *as* mothers as well as of their children. Many mothers say the playgroup is first and foremost a support for *them*. Working women turned mothers tend to be out of touch with the child rearing community. "Playgroup? I thought it was a theatrical troupe," commented one Bostonian mother. An ex-chemist said, "This has been my sanity, my therapy. Everything might be coming down on my head, but I always manage to get it together for playgroup."

A free lance children's book illustrator, Rita, lives on a farm in rural Pennsylvania. Doing her own work and helping her husband's antique automobile refurbishing business by sewing upholstery leave little leisure for spontaneous visits (requiring drives) to neighbors. Rita talked about her playgroup as a main getaway from the farm and an emotional link with other families. "Out in the country where children can't walk next door, it takes more parental effort, but the need is great. Now that my son is in nursery school and his best friend from playgroup goes to the same nursery school, the longtime contact with other children is especially nice. Playgroup definitely helped acclimate him."

[1](New York: Simon and Schuster, 1978), p. 188.

Dropping by Debbie's

The weekend's over and, effectively, coparenting till Saturday next. Howard, a free lance court stenographer, Israeli-born and a naturalized United States citizen, left for a downtown New York City court at 8:10. By 8:30 the Chaim boys, ages two, four, and five, have their noses pressed against the bay window. Their eyes are pleading to go outdoors. And it looks like rain. Debbie, mid-thirties, dimple-cheeked with long pale blond hair combed flat down her back, makes a phone call for Clearwater, the Hudson River reclamation group, while removing the breakfast dishes. A light smile passes over her face. Not a touch of the Monday blues! Debbie and five other mothers who live nearby in southern Westchester are thinking, "Thank God, it's Monday!"—and time for their weekly get-together with the playgroup.

Clearwater is only one of the volunteer organizations for which Debbie, daughter of a liberal activist Unitarian minister, works. From the maxi-size Rolodex that she relies on, Debbie extracts the telephone numbers of several women who can explain playgroup.

The mothers speak to me of different priorities. Two are keen on playmates for their children. A third, the youngest, mentions the helpfulness of connecting with women who know more than she about baby food, shoes, and stages of child development. The Japanese mother finds the playgroup has opened a whole social and language world. Nuclear family self-reliance, states the last, is not her ideal image of parenting young children. "Playgroup is the place where we acknowledge our need for help."

Debbie's playgroups seem to stay forever young. The playgroup of Adam, her oldest, has dispersed and been replaced by the playgroup of Benjamin, her two-year-old. Karen Trepp, a White Plains mother from a prior incarnation of the cell, looked back on why she joined and her experience. "I cast around and saw that other playgroups were the kind where children were dropped off. But I wanted playmates for my child without sending him off to nursery school. Everyone at Debbie's playgroup was so animated and relaxed. It was informal, almost like an extended family, and it was regular. Playgroup was a continuity for both of us, but looking back I think it was more for me."

A career woman, Karen had assumed that she would place Richard in day care and return to work. "But having arrived at motherhood I decided it was too precious," Karen said. She didn't care to juggle lives and felt returning to her old job would take a lot of maneuvering and loss on the home front.

Karen believes that via Debbie's playgroups, mothers try to recreate the old-fashioned neighborhood. "I yearn for neighborhoods more as they used to be," she sighed, "with mothers home more instead of children at nursery school by three years old, day camp from the next summer. I wish there were more spontaneous in-and-out-the-back-door visits, where kids could leave, cut through a hedge here, and in back of a garage there. A mother may long for that, but in this neighborhood and many others you walk through and wonder, 'Where have all the people gone?' A playgroup is not as spontaneous as an old time neighborhood, but it is the closest substitute."

When to Start

By the age of two, most children not only have playmates, they like to talk about them to mommy. Developmentally, age one and a half cruising into two is the natural time for first friendships to crystallize. Dr. Spock says a child should be with children his or her size and age at least two periods a week by the second birthday. Some mothers, though, who feel the need for themselves to gather with other women can pave the way for the child's need, which comes a little later. "Some of us couldn't walk yet because of the stitches," one mother said of her playgroup, that continued until her child was three and a half. A playgroup can be beneficial to a child before two even though the play that occurs is hardly definable as "group" play. For a very young age group, parallel play can be a warm companionable *association* and a caring *bond*. The children of a few months old crow, giggle, and rock at one another. When they can crawl, like infant gymnasts they roll and tumble over together and try to follow the leader.

Earlier too, a mother may have an easier time entering into the acquaintanceships from which the playgroup grows. A mother with an infant in a baby carriage is more prone to stop and chat with other strange mothers who are equally new, than she is later on. If she's thinking playgroup already—as a parenting workshop and information network— she can begin to collect her group.

A playgroup of one-year-olds is relatively tranquil and affords mothers time to get to know one another. When tots are engaged in rhythm bands, hammering at toy workbenches, and shouting it out, adult communication becomes harder. When it's every mother's first child, there's especially much to share about early behavior, from feeding schedules to sleeping habits. Mothers of infants get emotional support at a time when they need it most. By two, children clearly look forward to the playgroup event as well.

A rule of thumb for age spread is that the children should be within four or five months of one another if younger than two and a half, while for children of three, a six-month difference is acceptable.

How to Start

Two or three women meet or get together, then the group grows by word-of-mouth referrals. A sympathetic pediatrician is often a broker for a playgroup, so a mother should express an interest to both doctor and receptionist. A doorman may cue a mother in to the presence of other tinies in an apartment building. Other places to flag down families with a child the appropriate age are a church or synagogue nursery, the line at the supermarket, the sandbox in the park. Debbie Chaim related, "I picked up two in a parking lot. I see somebody, and I make overtures."

The group should be no larger than the smallest playroom can accommodate. Certainly any mother, before impetuously inviting in a new family, should consult other mothers. A group of eight children may work well when everybody meets outside in clement weather, but that means an unwieldly sixteen persons indoors come winter or a rainy day. A group of four or five mothers with an equal number of tots leaves leeway for natural expansion—a second tier of children who may, if the playgroup endures, tag along with big brothers and sisters sometime hence.

A playgroup is a sorority of sorts, but usually not a sisterhood of child rearing. In Debbie's playgroup several mothers breastfeed, while one bottle feeds; one insists her child mind his P's and Q's, while another mom is more laissez-faire. The social need for drawing together rather than ideological or attitudinal comradery motivates the formation of the play-group. "We had real differences in terms of our ideas on child rearing," said one mother, a psychiatric social worker. "From the mother who worked three days a week and bottle fed to the mother who nursed her baby until he was ready to carry her up the stairs. Despite her rather rigid view of mothers who work, the second mother tolerated the first."

A mother asking around the neighborhood for a peer group for her child must take risks. She calls up a mother she may not know, makes a social commitment for the future for herself and her child. If the children get along with each other, she could be seeing a lot of a mother who is not a kindred spirit, over the next months or years. Even if she is bored or irked sometimes, she will probably decide that it is the child's playgroup, not her coffee klatsch, and put up. This is a good initiation to one of the motherly virtues—tolerance when a child is choosing friends all on his or her own.

Social class, education, money, material goods, space indoors or out—

these elements matter little in choosing playgroup families. What counts is a common child-centeredness. A mother should share a delight in children other than her own, too. Essentially she is looking for aunts for her children. Like a familial tie, the shared commitment to the children should rise above differences of opinion and occasional discord and hold the group together.

According to Honey Dickson, a schoolteacher in Rockland County, New York, seeing their children a little apart makes playgroup moms more receptive to the ideas and experiences of other parents. "We influence one another's approaches to day-to-day push/pulls when away from the group as well as when we're there." Talking to other mothers can help an unsure or unhappy mother diffuse her anger and marshal positive responses. Compelled to discipline her child in the playgroup milieu, any mother can see her measures more objectively and often "key them down" emotionally. Said Honey, "No one took the stand, 'Let them fight it out themselves.' No one felt it was okay to haul off and hit another child. Yet nobody felt it was cause for a spanking or hand slapping."

Frequently mothers do find they have landed quite astonishingly with mothers who have matching backgrounds and interests. A Croton-on-Hudson, New York, bookbinder and mother of two, Sylvia Anderle, said, "All five of us married late, had similar educations, were professional people, reacted to children in much the same way. And ours is a varied community! At thirty-one I was nervous I'd only meet twenty-one-year-olds, but we ran the gamut from twenty-seven to thirty-seven, with our philosophies the same. Now I've met other mothers and see I took this for granted, never realizing how similar deep down in approach we were." Sylvia's playgroup came together by happenstance. "I met a woman at the obstetrician's; do you mind if I invite her?" Then two dropped out and others filled in. Affinities within the group contributed to the long term success.

Playgroup Patterns

There are three basic types of playgroups: (1) where the mother and child gather, (2) babysitting services where mothers rotate child care, and (3) proto-nursery school programs where the children meet periodically outside the home.

Where mothers rotate care, sometimes they double up, so that, for example, two mothers take charge of six children. This is a higher ratio of adults to children than required of licensed day care programs. However, a one-to-three ratio is advisable because the day care center is geared to toddlers and has very few hazards for them around.

Sometimes a scheme is worked out whereby a mother has one day each week "on" and is freed four other days (morning or afternoon). The chief advantage of this type of playgroup is that it allows women who cannot pay for or locate appropriate babysitters to get some time off from mothering, either to recreate or to work part time. The playgroup need not be less exciting as it becomes more routine for the children. Mothers often discover that being an adult in charge is as much fun as being "released." Nevertheless, five days together each week is a lot of socializing for young children, and a better, though more complex, schedule can be worked out monthly for this type of playgroup two or three times a week. A nice compromise is for mothers to all remain with the children every third, fourth, or fifth session.

Mother-and-child gatherings are less strenuous than babysitting cooperatives to organize and keep afloat, and it is hard to convert the former to the latter. As one mother said, "We had the idea of two moms on, two off, but nothing came of it. It was not a problem of separating from our children. Something in the mom group jelled."

Whereas in the mother-and-child type, organization is minimal and evolves according to the mothers' and children's needs, in the playgroup that is also a babysitting pool the ground rules must be established in detail before the playgroup starts. There must be agreement, for instance, about drop off and pick up hours, whether clothes and diapering supplies come with the child, what happens on holidays. Rotating playgroups tend to see the mother-and-child counterparts as inefficient and a party for moms, while the mothers in the latter may regard the babysitting arrangement as a dumping ground of lesser educational value. Both types, of course, are great for those who need and desire them. In either case the children thrive on the friendships and different settings they experience.

My neighbor Carol Brown's playgroup was organized as the babysitting type: twice a week, four mothers, each on once every two weeks. The first go is etched in her memory. Christin's house was the place. "Don't worry, it will be fine," said Christin's playgroup-experienced mother. So two mothers left, but a third decided more cautiously on that first day to stay. Carol described her return two hours later: "Walking up the hill to the house we heard everyone screaming. They were huddled miserably on the stairs for the entire two hours. Thank goodness, the one mother had stayed. One child's crying had set off a chain reaction."

In Carol Brown's playgroup, the mothers found that while their children were in the fifteen to twenty-two month range, leaving them with one mother didn't work. Two hours away spelled abandonment and wreaked havoc, so they decided to take it more gradually. "For a month we all remained. Later we left for forty-five minutes. Most of that year the mothers stayed twenty minutes at the start. By June when the children were reaching two we were leaving them two hours, and no pangs." Still, two hours, in Carol's experience is maximum in a playgroup without mommy for twos. "At that age they often cried when the mothers came back, even after a fun time. Whereas from a few months older they were all smiles."

A version of the playgroup, a third type, a kind of proto-nursery school, is gaining popularity. Sometimes called Mothers Morning Out, it meets weekly in a church, Y, or town civic center. The charge is as low as 50¢ an hour, and covers materials and a pittance for (in general nonmother) teachers. The curriculum is usually *play*. The mothers either leave or stay in another room in the building to discuss pertinent subjects. Everyone seems pleased.

Every big church in Charlotte, North Carolina, has a Mothers Morning Out, and these programs have seeded others. The programs serve best a transient population. "A lot of folks are more ready to come to a church than a babysitting service when they are new to the area," said Hilda Rutherford, who runs the Mothers Morning Out at Charlotte's Carmel Presbyterian Church. "From what I understand, people comment on the friendliness here, and for young families, church members or not, a part of it is these formal playgroups."

Twelve children between the ages of fifteen months and three years come four hours a week, one half day. Hilda stresses that hers is not a teaching program, but a service offering a variety of play experiences. "The goal is a safe and happy place where very young children can be comfortable while mother's gone away." Every day the children do a simple arts and crafts project, such as fashioning caterpillars out of egg cartons or pasting precut leaves and stems on paper baking cups to make flowers. Hilda brought in a kite in March and everybody flew it; then the children made kites to take home. Making something at playgroup to take home is exciting for children. Hilda added, "Even at such young ages, they paste and color in distinctive ways. And when it's time to go home, they recognize their own work."

Playgroup ingredients can be successfully mixed. An example of a hybrid flourishes at the Village Church in Wellesley, Massachusetts. It was established in 1970, and by now, reported one mother, the "kinks are worked out." It has groups for younger twos and older twos, and additional groups for threes and fours. The littlest come one morning for two hours, the oldest on three mornings for three hours. The church provides the facilities, and the mothers supply materials and labor.

Each playgroup day three mothers of the older twos group (eight children) are "on," and one is a "floater" waiting in the wings in case an "on" mother is sick or to help with a field trip. The crew is broken down to a "boss" who arrives early with snacks and sets up; a second mother in charge of the project; a third who does the story, music, and game. The mothers rally to the balance between routine and spontaneity.

Hosting a Playgroup

Ordinarily, the mother-and-child playgroup pattern begins at 9:30 and lasts two-and-a-half to three hours. It tends to stretch longer as the children grow and cut out one of the day's naps. A morning playgroup for the eighteen-month-olds may take in lunchtime, too, by the time the children are two, and later spill over into the afternoon. "I never would have believed it at first because I'm not a joiner," said Ellen Sternlieb, a Yonkers mother, "but Debbie's playgroup started at 9:30 and went until 3:00 in the afternoon." An astonishing number of playgroups *do* evolve into daylong fiestas. There must be emotional and physical space to which a mother and child can retreat as well as a room where mattresses and blankets can be spread for babies' naps.

Although rotation among homes is the usual practice, it may suit one mother best to host the playgroup more frequently. Debbie Chaim has a great swing set, a sandbox, a log playhouse, and a roomy home. The other members of her playgroup have one child each and live in apartments. Every Monday the Chaims' kitchen looks like a little food fair, with salads, bowls of unsalted popcorn, carrot cake, and a rainbow of juices, which the five mothers have brought for the all-day playgroup. Before they leave, the mothers make an effort to pick up the house, and sweep and vacuum. They keep an eye on garage and rummage sale announcements and chip in for equipment for the playgroup. Because Raggedy Ann has become a kind of leitmotif for the group, one mother is sewing, one by one, starting with Beloved Belindy, big dolls of all the main characters in the story.

Some mothers swear by the purely spontaneous flow of events during playgroup sessions whereas other playgroups fall into predictable patterns of storytime, arts and crafts, indoor and outdoor play, and eating. Generally speaking, at each home it is a good idea for the host mother to be responsible for some group activity. It could be as simple as watering pansies in the garden or as complex as cutting out gingerbread shapes. The other mothers can be supportive from the sidelines. The day before, the host mother should think through the equipment and materials required. That evening she should bring out selected toys for the day, but the playroom should not be set up to display every toy her child owns. As much free space as is possible is important.

Children in Debby Chaim's playgroup gather for crisp apple slices at snack-time.

Fingerpainting, stringing macaroni, pasting collages—super, but a mother shouldn't begin them too soon just to entertain a playgroup. If her child isn't into dolls and dollhouses yet, neither will the other children be, but they might find paper bag puppets interesting. For a two-year-old to sit in a group for ten minutes and string beads or play a clapping game is a big learning experience. The threes may pass half a morning rummaging in a box of old clothes, hats, and shoes, and dressing up. All mothers have times the little plan fails. Mothers should be careful not to compete.

In one Connecticut playgroup of three-year-olds, the five mothers capitalize on their respective talents and develop them as ways of relating to the children. The artistic parent always initiates an art project when playgroup is at her house. The handyperson has the children saw, nail, and build. The gourmet cook, who happens to be very patient, does simple cooking like three-step cakes, vegetable soup, and pizza with "everything." A fourth focuses on singing games and singalong because she plays the guitar. "I have no talent," moaned the fifth mother, who has ended up always *taking* the children somewhere. Hers turns out to be a favorite "house"!

"We didn't do much any one day different from any other before the children were two and a half," said schoolteacher Honey. "Even then when we cooked, one child's whole activity might be to mash the butter in a cup, wait his turn, then add it to the mix in the bowl. By the time we did special activities, we were very comfortable together. A mother could say, 'This happened that was crazy last night, and I don't have a special thing.' And that was okay." For the twos, the big happening that structures that day's playgroup may be as simple as blowing bubbles outdoors or parading to a marching record with a complement of pots, spoons, and rattles. Mothers like Honey who are models of planning and forethought learn a measure of social spontaneity from their children.

When the weather permits, even twenty minutes outdoors merits getting coats and gear on. Children whose sights have been enlarged by views of skys, and whose senses have been quickened by the touch of the earth, are more apt to share playthings when they return inside.

The host mother should not pick up as the children play. Nor should she say it's okay when they pour apple juice in her toaster. She should expect her child to have the hardest time when on home turf.

Benefits to the Children

"Oh, they too have a kitchen, a bathroom, a dog. Jennifer's toys are *upstairs,* and she has a brother." Playgroups provide opportunities for children to observe similarities and differences. They can compare and contrast in a fruitful way, house versus apartment, single versus two-parent families, or a family unit including a grandparent, for example.

In a playgroup children show one another the way to wean to the cup or even to toilet train—much as goes on in a day care center—effortlessly. The timid child dares go down the slide in line with the others. Threes begin to assign and pick roles to play firefighting, wedding, or *Three Little Pigs*. Even the child of four is wild to see the new toys at somebody else's house. Playthings are less likely to lose their luster when there's a play-group.

Even though it is a mother-and-child gathering, mothers ought not be roped into staying unremittingly. They should schedule an appointment, do an errand, or just garner some free time if that is what would lift their spirits. Often the difficult or fearful child will do better, will get over a hump, if alone without mother for a session. A prime example is the excessively picky eater who dives into the communal meal of bean-sprout-and-ham sandwiches. Accomplishing some of what Kaplan means by the second birth, the child "finds the distance that allows him to be part of his mother's space while keeping his own space inviolate."[2]

Children go through a "That's mine" stage when possession, it is said, is ten-tenths of the law. The playgroup is a marvelously moderating influence. With peers children must work out give and take. They see that throwing a tantrum gets them on the hobbyhorse no faster and maybe that a make-believe ride on the plumber's helper can be as much fun as mounting the beast itself. "There are periods when children behave outrageously, will NOT share, then days when they move in orchestral harmony," said Sylvia Anderle, the self-employed bookbinder. Mothers will reach out to the mother whose child is upset and establish support. Sylvia said, "Some mild trust allows a lot more to happen within the group."

A playgroup answers a child's companionability, but parents should not view it as a *sine qua non* for learning cooperation. Ones and twos play solo or side by side, enjoying the closeness but not really communicating game plans, theorists on child development say. At the next, associative stage, children will decide to play with the same toys but are still absorbed by their own ideas. True cooperative play follows sometime between the ages of four and six. Jeanette Stone, director of the Early Childhood Center at Sarah Lawrence College, said: "We tend to expect kids to play cooperatively long before they are able. Cooperation should not be foisted on kids. Preschoolers are egocentric by growth and development. If you scold

[2]Kaplan, *Oneness and Separateness*, p. 191.

a child for not giving up half the Legos to another, the child knows he's been bad but can't understand why. It's like making a child walk when he still needs to crawl. He has to comprehend ownership before cooperation."

No child should get away with biting, pinching, or hitting another child in the playgroup, but mothers shouldn't expect them to play like a team. Often conflict can be averted and dissolved. If Legos are popular, a playgroup should have lots of Legos. It is important to guide the children into solutions other than anger when they are frustrated. Do not be a punctilious arbiter of playgroup members' individual rights—someone will flare angrier!

Some playgroups are more structured, some more free flowing, and few do many trips to the zoo or amusement park. Being in the home seems to be the main thing. The rest may be better left for weekends and done *en famille*.

The Mothers' Benefits

A Manhattan feminists' playgroup, after the children were used to one another, began to do things for themselves: poetry readings, eurhythmics, and so forth. Yet a mother shouldn't expect to have heart to heart or stimulating conversation every time a playgroup gathers. Mingling with young children often takes up most of the attention. Honey Dickson explained it: "I might talk to Sally ten minutes, five to Martha. Or my child and Denise's might get into interaction so we can talk twenty minutes. I've visited playgroups where mothers sit at the dining table and treat children as a distraction. Those playgroups had a lot more fighting and confusion."

By interacting with several mothers, a child learns to trust people outside the family. One child brings his mother a book, and maybe to get her attention, says, "Read." She reads it to her child, and other children sidle up on the other knee. This is how the transfer of trust happens.

Sometimes trading off and letting a different mother cope has good results. "If Paul was having a hard time sharing, it wasn't always me who worked it out," Honey noted. "It might be Denise or Martha who helped him through. As soon as Paul 'got' language he was calling all the mothers by their first names. 'Leslie, give me puzzle.' Once he spoke to them, they felt that when he grabbed the truck away they could say, 'Angus had that first you know, Paul.' There were times when as mothers we talked; we needed it. If the kids got a little wild, it didn't matter. But that wasn't the norm. I really never knew on Tuesdays—we never expected to know—what the other families had done on the weekend."

Inviting the parents to dinner? Apparently this occurs rarely with playgroups. Surprising? Not to those who think with their "young-mother caps." Families with small children find it hard to keep up with their pre-established friendship circles in terms of entertaining. They are relieved not to feel pressure from the playgroup to exchange a flurry of invitations to adult parties. Debbie Chaim's playgroup finds that one superduper Fourth of July picnic works well. That way the fathers can see the much heralded playgroup in action. On the other hand, one or two lasting, close friendships often emerge from the group of mothers.

At times a child will have an awful playgroup day. Inevitably the mother wonders, "What am I doing here?" Usually the wearing times come at the start. Sylvia Anderle recalled, "Laura went off the wall at first. She was a year old and still toddling. I'd leave at the end of the session with a lump in my throat and conclude she couldn't cope. But the next week we'd be there again. Then one day I left Laura on her own, and she had a wonderful time. Maybe the playgroup was noisy for her, all the babbling and talking so different from home. But when she didn't have me to retreat to, she began to enjoy herself and get into the act."

A playgroup shouldn't be judged on one or two experiences. The unpredictable and irritating behavior—it may be called regression—is but a muddled response to complex stimulae. The child *will* sort things out! Remarked a seasoned mom: "Two days everybody gets along great, the next session they are pummeling one another. Was the moon in a funny phase or did everybody have a touch of the same bug? Who knows!"

As a peer group, playgroup mothers provide vital reinforcement and encouragement. "For new ways to handle a child, it is more important to be supported by peer culture than a family," said Suzanne Salzinger, a child psychologist at the New York State Psychiatric Institute. "The playgroup provides mothers with a less restrictive environment. Everyone improves while the therapist monitors, but mothers who don't have peers usually go *back* to old, negative-reinforcing behavior. The therapist may teach a parent strategies for dealing with a hyperactive child, or an eight-year-old who says no all the time. But the technique takes hold best if the mother relates to peers regularly." Being open to change means listening to different ideas, and playgroup moms are not too proud to be receptive.

Four of the mothers of the playgroup to which Ginny Abramson and her son Brian, two, belong know one another from childbirth class or La Leche League. The fifth adopted her child at age six months. Because nursing and delivering were the common bond initially, in the first few weeks of the playgroup the "natural" mothers tended to "get off" on subjects in those areas. But the group had the sensitivity to see that the fifth mother was being left out, and passed on to other areas of common interests. Now the adoptive mother is comfortable and, with the support of the playgroup moms, is going to try to nurse the second child she and her husband will adopt.

Bringing the Curtain Down

It is a shame for a playgroup to peter out. When several of the children are in nursery school or reach kindergarten age, the playgroup can be considered to have run its course. When the lifeline changes to an obligation, instead of having the playgroup collapse slowly, why not have everybody say—as Sylvia Anderle's did—"This is it."

The happily-ever-after is that from the days of a playgroup on, a mother has a guest list for a birthday party of truly close friends who shared her child's first steppings into the world.

A playgroup will save a mother hours and hours of making arrangements for her toddler to have playmates, as well as enable her to grow as a mother with other mothers. "I feel their children are like my children, and we will always care about one another," said the psychiatric social worker in Debbie's first playgroup. "Now that our needs are less, our differences are more important, but week in and week out the playgroup more than met our daytime social needs, during a very formative period of our children and our families."

CIRCUS OF SITTERS

The author who talks about his own books is almost as bad as the mother who talks about her own children.

Benjamin Disraeli

Unless you are their mother and have the ever-ready recourse of nursing them at the breast, caring for infant twins solo is an inordinate challenge. A few times before they were six months old, I stepped out to the movies, reviving a pastime of childless years. A baby bundled in each arm, my husband Chris waved me off reassuringly. I chose short movies, for three hours was the limit of time that I felt physically and emotionally comfortable separated from the twins.

After the show I called to see how urgently my husband needed me back. Depending on his response, I took a taxi or a bus home. Usually it went swimmingly, and his face was wreathed in proud, relaxed paternal smiles. Other times he counted the minutes—time to be endured with two inconsolable charges, neither of whom, until Emma weaned quite suddenly at six months, would have any congress with pacifier or bottle. Now it seems incredible that the mother-child attachment was so fierce that more than three hours apart from the twins bordered on abandonment. But such was the bond of the breast.

The first nine months of Emma's and Burton's lives we lived in Manhattan in tight quarters but old splendor in Columbia University's Butler Hall. Two apartments down from us lived a frail, very elderly lady with an honorable academic past. She took her main meal at the Terrace, the several-star gourmet restaurant that iced the fifteen-layer residence hotel "cake"—as accessible to us graduate students as Lutéce or the Four Seasons. Mrs. Beale was companioned by a practical nurse who was her true friend. Sometimes the nurse, Anna, wheeled her along Morningside Drive. In the worst weather they sat by the potted plants and fountain in the lobby, watching the life pass in and out the revolving doors.

Anna had exchanged pleasantries with us in the lobby and elevator since we moved into the hall. On our trips up and down after the twins were born we heard both gentle advice and gratifying compliments. She became the twins' first babysitter. She came for half what she received at her usual posts because there was no agency's fee involved. We realized she was, all the same, beyond our means in terms of the pattern we were initiating, but the need was infrequent. Also, we felt the traffic and organization of caring for two ambulant babes required more than a willing amateur from nearby Barnard College. Infant care takes special knowledge. I wanted my children always to experience "being sat" as special fun. For a stage when it took the most knowledge, in an urban milieu where we had no family or *doula*[1] support person, we were grateful for the most professional help.

[1]*Doula* is the old Greek term for the woman who comes and helps the new mother. Dana Raphael, author of *The Tender Gift: Breastfeeding* (New York: Schocken, 1976),

Anna's care of the twins the dozen times she came formed our ideal standard of concerned, smiling babysitting. A matronly woman with an ample figure and spiffy sports clothes, she always stationed herself on the floor with the children as soon as she arrived. At the end of the dark hall, laughter issued from the door to greet my return. As the children passed infancy, we would expect less training in a sitter but recognized the same spirit of competency and mood of pleasure-taking in a child's nature.

The arrangement suited Anna too. She could come at the end of her regular work, or after a turn of shopping, and still take her bus across 125th Street and home before night. She liked the change from being with oldest to being with youngest, especially since her own children were now teenagers. Formerly, Anna had been a day nurse for new mothers for the first month or two after a baby's birth. When a family tried to persuade her to remain longer, she never would because the attachment became too great. I can well imagine the help she gave in a practical way and the model her unhurriedness and light, sure touch supplied.

Of course, the perfect security came at a price—a full $5 an hour in 1978–79 in order to quit the apartment *sans* kids. For other than a "command" engagement, it would have felt extravagant.

Our neighbor's apartment, when she once had me in, seemed so astonishingly spacious and refined. She slept and led most of her life in one small room and contained her Duncan Phyfe and other early American furniture and antique silver heirlooms in the other. What a contrast our similarly-sized apartment had to hers. When the twins were born, we transformed our bedroom into their nursery. In the big, many-windowed living room, the pull-open, Marimekko-covered sofa became both our new bed and the twins' preferred playground. We screwed the musical mobile into the pine-board rim. A hand-me-down, it had grown motion sensitive. Sometimes in the middle of the night it started spontaneously, circling its barnyard creatures over our slumbering heads, and playing its nursery tune.

Another overloaded circuit of activity was the kitchenette. It had standing room for one. When we moved in, being a far more efficient if less inventive cook than I, Chris assumed permanently the short-order cook's apron. We were now alarmed to discover that its half-size refrigerator had standing room for half-size baby bottles only. What luck I chose to breast-feed! Eventually, though, we knew we would have to move. By the nature

---

identified the phrase and behavior. Matresence, the period of becoming a mother, Dr. Raphael emphasizes, should be unstressful and exciting. A woman's *doula*—usually another woman but it can be her husband—supports the mother so she can be free to breastfeed and transit to her new role.

of Manhattan real estate, this meant a classic trek to the suburbs, not to a multi-bedroom apartment.

Getting the Acts Together

How could we afford child care when the house begged for a new roof? Didn't other women writers forego sleep, and write in the off-duty wee hours while their children were little? Wasn't Chris more cheerfully ready to do his share than most husbands? In our case, we didn't canvas for a sitter, she showed up at our doorstep. Our suburban babysitting arrangements began almost in spite of me.

When we bought our Victorian Dutch Colonial house, we knew we would have to take a roomer on the third floor to meet expenses. During the school year the intense demand for off-campus housing at Sarah Lawrence made this no problem. The summers would have been a different story, but the former owners put their babysitter in touch with us. She had just graduated from Sarah Lawrence as a psychology major, and had a job lined up there in the laboratory nursery school for the summer.

Cindy moved in. Since the "apartment" shares a staircase and front entrance with us, she was eager to maintain the separateness of lives. It was not until mid-summer that we and the children ventured onto more intimate friendship than "bye-byes" and excited hi's with our lodger. By this time I wished to have some hours free each day and wanted to see how the children would respond. Our toddler geminis turned one in June. Families who knew Cindy at the nursery school loved her, but I could not accept her offer to sit occasionally free, yet couldn't pay her either—we were still reeling from the expenses inevitable in acquiring an old house. Fortunately Cindy was short on cash, and instead of paying us rent in August babysat three hours a day.

I wonder now, if her need hadn't pushed me, how long would I have done without? For the stay-at-home mother babysitters can be The Answer, making her a stranger to the ills most young-mothers say are chronic: monotony, fatigue, and the doldrums of a one-dimensional self-image. Would I have remained one of the many mothers who deny themselves their separate lives because they view babysitters as an extravagance?

The appeal of babysitting day care was threefold. First, it was traditional, a compromise of the children's being entrusted much of the day to another's care but at home. As a free lance writer I could do much of my job at home. I was encouraged by a report from the Bureau of Labor Statistics citing 1.9 million self-employed women in 1979 *not* to go into public relations or join the staff of a magazine, natural directions for my writing career to take. I was impressed by what the poet Anne Sexton's daughter Linda Gray Sexton said of her mother, that even if she was in her study working when the children came home from school, her presence in the house gladdened.[2] My sitters have observed that Emma and Burton felt a measure of this reassurance from my physical proximity.

Working in our bedroom/office on the second floor of the house while a sitter is with the children downstairs is *not* the same as wrenching separations that occur when mother first leaves for the full day. The sitter punched in while the twins were still napping, at abut 3:00 P.M. I often hung around until Burton was awake. Later he and the sitter trod upstairs to fetch Emma. "Mommy's working," he told his sister (one of his first sentences), and she tripped or backed (in the early toddler period) down after him. Only a few handful of hundreds of times sat have the twins asked to come in and stay with me. At age two-ish they would often try the door and then descend directly downstairs. Later they would, again rarely, have something urgent to share like an art project completed or first braids. But they never came with the desire simply to interrupt, nothing like the "more juice" delay tactic used at bedtime. They have respected faithfully Mommy's need to do some of her work, part of each day, alone.

In addition to permitting me to work yet be available, the babysitting "system" was appealing because of its flexibility in terms of expenditures. "Fat" months or months when my assignments were heavier, I could expand the number of hours we hired sitters. Holiday times or after an assignment was finished, I could reduce the sitting quota. Either way I won. It is great to tackle writing in a concentrated way, a few hours in the morning plus three again in the afternoon. By the same token, I enjoyed letting up on the routine and having stretches of more time with the children—in good weather, at holiday times, to visit a friend at some distance. It was not a question of daylong units of time with the children or without. Since the children continued their afternoon nap, our usual adventures and outings were half-day sized. Rather, the flexibility came into play in nice, scarcely perceptible changes. The end of day can be a raggedy time. When the children seemed to "need Mommy," sitters were instructed to have them rap at the master bedroom (and study) door. When Chris, usually an athletic and bouncy type of guy, showed signs of fatigue, I

[2]Deborah Trustman, "Linda Gray Sexton: Defining the World," *Harvard Magazine*, January-February 1980, p. 91.

asked sitters to stay a half hour longer several days running, so he could shower and rest his bones after returning from work.

Finally, I chose our babysitting arrangement because I *like* teenagers and college-aged youth. I was willing to give up experience for youth. I felt the twins should have "grown-up children" around, not just adults.

We did look into alternatives. I visited a reputable day care center in a bordering town. The rate was very low. I admired their science curriculum and the abundance of puzzles. But I decided no when I walked in the door. Unlike some of the super day care facilities I'd visited in the city, it was set up for six-year-olds, with its holiday and subject displays and the predominance of its tables and chairs. Surely not right for exploring tots. I visited a playgroup where the several mothers took turns caring for the group of offspring in their homes. Here the children were happily doing what I thought children should be doing, playing, but one wore a sling, another's forefinger had to be swathed in a bandage, and the driveway the tricycles were pounding down ended on the edge of an embankment. I almost hired a regular older woman who finished at 2:30 at another house. But she spoke so critically of the family where she worked that I cringed.

I also tried for two seasons the informal moms-and-tots playgroup that is the most typical prenursery school peer exposure in our suburban community. Their homes were curried and decorated, but I noticed we were always hurried to the nursery where we squatted on kiddie chairs for the two or so hours. The other women didn't care to discuss politics, whether global or local, or books of any type. My not making a fourth at bridge or golf undoubtedly reduced my usefulness to the group. Their "I'm going out of my mind; we haven't had a ski weekend all month" or "Oh drat, I have to pick up those tickets to Curaçao" eventually grated on my nerves.

People say, "You're lucky, you can work at home." I acknowledge a half-truth. I'm not a chemist or flight attendant or banker. My career has taken shape because I chose to be available to my children. Farther away from the communications hub of New York City, I might still be performing with our marionette troupe or be cat breeding or college teaching. It would be nice to take on assignments requiring travel or just more assignments and augment the family budget more than just keeping the sitter's envelope filled and paying for extras. But I am a *committed* part-time professional, and (as Edith Piaf sang) *"Je ne regrette rien."*

Among the stay-at-home moms I meet at nursery school are many who when they hear I work part-time at home say wistfully, "If only. . . ." Even if they don't choose to work now, they sigh with envy at the idea of a sitter some daytime hours a day or week. Then they could go out and volunteer, or get to the museums or the shops, or recap their pleasure in togetherness with their tot.

It's a matter of priority. Chris and I can't afford the annual vacation we would like to take. Our old clunker of a car *has* to last. In the summer for family fun we take the twins to pizza and pinball parlors and the amusement park, or we wade in a shore town's beach in early evening when it's open to us. To add a verse to Woody Guthrie's song, "We want our good times, and we want them NOW." That child rearing be exhilarating, not wearing, and that we address our own work interests are how we see the good times. Our sitters are what allows us to have these interests. *We believe in paying for services*. We find it makes sense. I see in families with good incomes tired and frustrated mothers to whom paying a sitter anytime except a going-out at night is uncouth.

I say, share the caregiving role now—you and your children will enjoy one another more. I recommend getting a sitter just to relax, to be one's own person, and see how those hours apart bear fruit. Wouldn't mom like to brush up on her Russian, lay out a dress pattern, have intimacy with her husband before the clock strikes ten? If a child is a late sleeper, a mother can steal some peaceable early morning hours. They're good for writing a letter or washing a kitchen floor—but Balzac? Not all activities that give fullness to the days can be done with young children. Passions wither when not practiced. Alone, parents can try out the *weekend afternoon,* reaffirm the prechild bond and quicken the romance that having children has enhanced but also batters. And are small children ever glad to see mommy and daddy come back.

After Cindy left at the end of summer, I had a hard time finding regular, reliable sitters. The high school published a list of dozens of names of girls and boys, thirteen to seventeen, who offered to do everything from address envelopes to wash windows and babysit days, evenings, and overnight. But name after name was intensely involved in fall sports and was trying out for winter sports. I applauded these girls and reflected on how times have changed. But weekday afternoons were tough to schedule.

October passed. My need to be spelled grew. Chris suggested I telephone the guidance department at a large Yonkers high school. A senior with a light schedule, access to the family car, and experience as a mother's helper was enlisted immediately. Rena never failed me. When her friends came, she was especially good. She was gregarious and would bring a girlfriend or boyfriend from school. The den was transformed into a picnic area, and the children watched wide-eyed.

In addition to Rena, I began gradually to employ other sitters as the children continued to respond with delight and enthusiasm to the young women they chose to call "visitors." A plan evolved of using a different sitter each day, and that seemed to suit us on so many counts. As newcomers to town, we wanted to meet people at the two colleges, and our neighbors. Here was a way. We anticipated each sitter would have special strengths, her own manner with the twins. We knew that the most interesting young people might have no more than part of one day to give and they would be more faithful if the burden on each of their schedules was less. Finally, we weren't sure how much babysitting we could afford, or desired.

The twins were two years old before we left them, *sans* either parent, for a whole day. It felt like stepping off the edge of the world. Six hours: would Burton, not yet weaned, "make it"? Chris and I went to lunch and a movie but skipped a third plan, returning with little gifts and beseeching eyes for everyone.

David Bliwas

Monday through Friday's babysitters get together for the first and last time—on Sunday for a group portrait with Emma and Burton.

As the children moved towards three, I began to hire *two* sitters in one day, someone for a few hours in the morning, someone for another two-and-a-half to three in the afternoon. I then instituted an "open door policy" during one half of the day. Either I work in a room on the first floor where the action is, or the door can be opened. They bob in; they never stay. The message is that Mommy's working but accessible to communiqués. Somehow it is crucial today that *Mommy* tie the sneaker or buckle the sandal, or a child wants support—even the words—to ask the sitter to push the doll Carly in her stroller.

Three hours seemed like a *long* time apart when the children were two. About the time Burton weaned, at thirty-one months, I began to go to the city occasionally for a whole day. Thereafter, five hours of babysitting (divided by lunch and naptime) did not seem inordinate.

Our "luxury sit" became an institution by accident. What with working in a hospital laboratory and going to graduate school, our second school-year roomer in the house had a very busy spring semester. Instead of doing the agreed-upon afternoon of sitting as a quarter of her rent during the week, she asked to do it in a block of time her only free day, Sunday. For the children before the ages of two-and-a-half, it was the icing on many family weekends. For the parents it was sometimes a time to catch up on business, sometimes to sleep, sometimes to turn to projects we most desired to do. You could hear a paper clip fall in the room: this was quiet free time in an undisturbed stretch that the rest of life simply could not afford.

At first I didn't tell the sitters how many they were. As they and I gained confidence, I did. I used group notices like "Sitter: Empty potty if used," "RETURN all 24 pieces to this puzzle," and "Record player's a manual: TURN OFF." Actually, by knowing they fit into the scheme, the sitters are impelled to perform well. It's a *job*. The sitters must understand that the commitment is not casual. I let them know that sitting for my children is not a popularity contest between, say "Tuesday" and "Thursday." All the sitters are important in the family picture!

I remember as a teenage sitter the color television, the cookie jar, the plush, more contemporary furniture than at home or in my dorm, the relief sometimes of not waiting for "him" to call, the giddy cutoffness from my familiar world. Pyjamaed children waved from the stairs to the second floor, or sat and listened raptly to my stories before plunging into deep sleep. Furthermore, earlier in my life, when I was being babysat, I recall college girl sitters who logged time with their most boring textbooks they couldn't hack on campus. They *sat*, and my brother Tom and I played hushedly and got them ginger ale. Our twins' sitters, the ones who continue, are far more engaged in nurturing and work harder than that soft-lit, quiescent image would suggest.

Highlighting the Performers

When the twins were approaching three, I decided to talk over with our five current long-term babysitters the babysitter-family relationship. Successively, I took each of them out to a local Italian café for a neutral place to chat. The first verity these occasions spotlit was how different the young women were.

Susannah, a Sarah Lawrence College literature student and horsewoman from Paraguay, met me wearing her typical costumey, thrift-shop threads, dressed up with magnificent cordovan riding boots. A burntcolored rouge highlighted the cheekbones of her befreckled face. She smoked the cigarettes we forbid *chez nous*, and lent to our corner of the café an air of cabaret.

Chantal, our French Canadian roomer (she is a part-time waitress, not an *au pair*, but babysits as part of the rooming arrangement) looked equally right in the café. But the time and setting change from Berlin in the twenties to the Champs-Elysées in some recent decade *après la guerre*. Country Quebec is a social world pleasantly unsynchronized with Paris or any other metropolis and its trappings of sophistication. Clearly her mother tailored her cap-sleeved raspberry blouse and eggshell white full skirt. She sparkled with pleasure to be in a café reminiscent of French culture at home. Chantal has the grace, natural elegance, and trace of primness of a heroine in one of the Harlequin romances that she reads *en traduction*.

The student from a Lutheran college at the far side of town, Becky, had never heard of cappuccino or espresso or the anise-flavored liqueur. The first two being in the coffee family and the third alcoholic, her order was hot chocolate. I invited Becky in the nick of time before she left for a job counseling at a survival camp for the summer.

Olive, our Nigerian sitter, Sarah Lawrence pre-law, had of this group worked for us the longest, once a week faithfully during the two academic years since she had come to America for her studies. As usual, she was as unreadable and cautious in my presence as she was forthcoming and warm with the children. I vote Olive of all the sitters "Most Self-Possessed." She is the sitter whom I tapped for the doubled-up sitting of my children and a neighbor's one morning a week. I am honored for the rapport with her and sense a mutual respect. Like Becky, she did *not* want to round out the event by having a look at the poker game in the back room.

My pretty poker-faced companion with red hair and mint-green eyes, shifting her shoulders and feet in a stylized shyness was our high school sitter, Amy. Her pose of being on the bench before the high school principal no longer fooled me. There is neither adolescent daze nor trucu- lence in her character. Amy is a listener and watcher just now, not a talker. Terribly serious about going into commercial art, with a cartoonist's eye, she took in and organized impressions of the new ambiance into her visual reserves. Amy chose a serpentine cruller because it looked "weird." She had something to say about the twins and said it, and after drew me into a nearly wordless, observing mood.

My regular helps in child care, these young women and the other five long-term sitters who preceded or followed them, are a younger generation that slips right between me and my children in age. In another generation or milieu they might have been the mothers, and I, the grandmother, of my children. Sometimes while I sit against oversized pillows and beneath a patchwork quilt in bed, a book or notepad or lunch tray propped up in front of me, I hear the sitter romp in a thousand giggles with the twins down- stairs.

At the Caffè Dolce Vita, our Québecoise sitter countered my question about her experience with the twins with another question that darted to the heart of our family's babysitting mode. "Do you think it's better, so many people who help instead of one?" I supposed, I said slowly, as most parents suppose, that we are on some level doing "best," and that for me as mother and for the children our "circus" at any rate provided color and fun.

Chantal went on to tell me about working during her sixteenth and seventeenth summers for a family of four in Toronto when the children were nine months and two years, then one and a half and three. The baby in particular turned to his mother surrogate, the au pair, as favored caregiver. "I changed him, fed him, and mothered him. When I left on my day off, he cried, but in the morning when his mother left he was fine."

Chantal's question made me realize that whatever you do to fill out the child care picture *is* a matter of philosophical choice. As I resumed my free-lance writing life, it had seemed happenstance building from one sitter to a complement of five, by the time the children were two. But actually in my quest to fill five half-day, weekday, child care slots I had rejected (1) the services of a tot drop, (2) the offer of a saintly neighbor to add my two to her brood free of charge, and (3) the recommendation by a family who had employed her of an elderly woman available daily. I didn't want the intimacy of a mother substitute, the competition of her value system with mine, or the responsibility for her well-being. I did want the variety of energetic young people susceptible to my direction and spirited participants in the children's play.

Why do they stay with the job? Here are the answers that the five sitters, none of them ingratiating, gave:

BECKY: It's a chance to get away from college life and pressures. It's also fun. I shouldn't say this, but I would do it for nothing.

AMY: I get along easily with kids. In ways I'm still a kid myself. I play around a lot. They end up taking advantage of me sometimes. When I finally get serious, they don't believe me. [Amy stressed she was not an authority figure but just another kid to the twins.] I don't like being a leader, ordering people around. And hanging around after school these days would bore me. Even most of the other seniors seem so immature.

CHANTAL: At first the exchange of sitting for my lodging was first in my mind. Later the attachment grew very strong. I felt free; they did too. I invited them upstairs to where I live. I made them crêpes the way Quebec people do, and taught them to sing "La Capucine." Emma knows speaking French is how to make me feel good. I'm involved with the children, but before I wasn't.

OLIVE: People in my country, Nigeria, love children. I felt cut off from children's lives when I started my freshman year. When I think of coming to this job, I think of two interesting little people.

SUSANNAH: They give me a lot of love, love I have always wanted and haven't had myself. I never got it when I was little. I feel parents should spend time with their children. . . . I talk to them. I tell them I'm unhappy. They say, "Mommy's upstairs so we're happy." In my mind they are growing up with me.

The sitters create different moods. Becky's visits are a constant celebration, a romper room. Amy comes through the front door silently and pulls a book out of her bookbag. When the twins need her, she's there, but she is not one to pull out the playdough. Olives bathes the afternoon in calm by speaking to the children in a soft, intimate, British-accented voice. She does storytimes and hears the children's news. Susannah's arrival is predictable, but after that anything might happen. Her eyes may brim with tears over some literary or personal sadness, or she may have just had the most wonderful Spanish class. One day she brings a gerbil, another a new dance exercise that the children will try too. Once she arrived with a bag of yesterday's fashions from the hospital thrift shop—"Would you believe it, Mrs. Filstrup? Five dollars for the pile!"—that made the afternoon a

111

At first Chantal babysat for Emma and Burton in partial exchange for her lodging. Later the attachment grew to mutual love.

toddlers' dress-up ball. What mesmerized me about our first regular sitter, Rena, was the teenybop atmosphere that she created with her food, bubblegum, music, nail polishing. Because they have such an array of inventive caregivers coming to the house, toys do not mean so much to the twins.

Gradually the sitters began to take the children places. Before they were two, unless one was ready to carry over 35 pounds the way back, there was a three- or four-block periphery beyond which it was injudicious to roam. But because they were not competing for a parent, the twins were more willing to let the tired sibling be helped by the sitter and continue walking than when they walked with me. Amy has taken them to see her cats at her house. Becky has babysat for them in her dorm room. The most glorious trivia they picked up was that Becky and her roommate too had stuffed animals on their beds. Chantal walks the children all the way to the branch library, half a mile away, except in the worst weather. Sarah, a regular sitter except in their second year (she took her junior year abroad) practices *silat,* an Indonesian martial art, and is very aware of correct and economical body movement. Leapfrog and rolling in a leaf pile are special fun with Sarah.

Keeping the Show Running

I dust, fold laundry, or address envelopes when the sitters first arrive. If they wish, we talk about their lives and my day. With a weekly sitter I make an effort for this to happen no less than once a month. It has been fun to play at being the older sister I never was. Seeing how attractive our sitters are, my husband, who works in a library that employs college student pages, has collaborated with me in playing Cupid. Two lasting relationships have developed of our sitters with bachelor friends in the course of the twins' lives, and no one has been offended when we *tried.*

The help the babysitters frequently ask for relates to jobs—rarely boyfriends, or mothers, or school work. I can write them reference letters, recommend them for other sitting in the area, and counsel about summer jobs and career preparation. We bought a book called *Exploring Careers Through Part-time and Summer Employment,* by Charlotte Lobb,[3] which has been duly passed around. These *are* girls who need to earn money and who tend to be dissatisfied with "just school."

But there are requests for other kinds of advice. One sitter had an assignment to write a satirical essay, and we mapped one out. Another was browsing through my reference shelves when it was time to go. "Do you know anything about abortions?" She needed, and we found, a *poem* about abortion. Another's boyfriend was making suicide attempts: what should she do? Where do you take your folks when they visit for Sunday dinner? Is there a store for stylish secondhand clothes? Part of the isolation of a mother of small children is feeling handicapped at being a normally helpful member of the community. Employing sitters brings some of this dimension of sociability automatically into every week.

Sitters feel differently about whether a modicum of housework goes with the job. My general instructions are to return the house to the state it was in when they arrived, but leave the dishes. One must be reminded to take her *own* gear home and to *dispose* of her yogurt cups. Another orders the toys on the shelves by size, function, and color, and washes and sweeps up the kitchen. How many directions of any sort I give depends upon the

[3]New York: Richard Rosen Press, 1977.

ability of the girl to keep them in her head, too. Girls who have worked as waitresses can be asked to cook the slow-cooking noodles for the children's dinner, and have their faces washed and clean clothes on by the time Daddy comes home. For Becky the children will at least try anything! Days when she sits I'm likely to put a food they are just learning to like on the menu. With another girl I may simply point out current thoughts on safety, "Burton is keen on the hammer today. Be sure he uses it as a tool, not a weapon."

Scheduling takes organization skill, a knack for detail. Even so you may slip up. Twice a sitter called and canceled when I didn't know she was coming. Another day Amy arrived at three and sat in the living room quietly where I discovered her a half hour later. The kids, she thought, were napping. In actuality they were off at a birthday party: my mistake.

In a sitter, I say look for a teenager or college student who (1) has a younger brother or sister—not for experience in handling children but for savvy, tolerance, and no delusions that caring for little ones is a cushy, idle job; (2) has a career or summer-job interest related to child care—the best of all approaches isn't "I like kids" but "Kids interest me" or "I'd better understand kids if I'm going to teach them swimming"; (3) in the interview is excited by the prospect of *playing* with little kids—she or he must have a flair for *passing time* with her charges; (4) lives close by—plot the teenagers from the school sitters list (many high schools issue one) in concentric circles of how near they are to your home. Especially in the winter this counts. It is best not to get into the habit of chauffeuring, the bane of suburbanite parents.

Important also is determining who is most likely to stay with the job. Two high school students wanted to fill the Wednesday slot. Both were cheerful and experienced. I took the poor one! Chances were she would be more reliable and stay with us longer. Several of our sitters—an English-speaking Canadian, a Nigerian, a Quebécoise—applied to babysit because they had student visas and no social security card. All three have babysat for us going on two years, no longer weekly but still upon occasion. With a babysitter one must keep in mind the obvious, that the principal reinforcement is financial reward. Therefore, it is wise to pay at the top of the rates for sitters in the area. This attracts older and more experienced girls or boys. Better fewer hours and more commitment!

Maybe after a reasonable period a child's temperament and a sitter's don't jibe. One sitter whom I liked because she arrived on time, came at the drop of a hat, thought our rates were tops, and was very well-mannered gave the twins the willies. At eighteen months, they rose from their nap and, upon seeing her, backed right up the stairs into bed. That told me something. With reluctance, I tapered her employment to termination.

Another time I complained to Chris about a sitter's coldness to the children. "If she weren't so convenient, you'd fire her," he replied. I was about to defend myself and expound on her good qualities when I saw how undeniably right he was. His remark made me aware that being good with the kids was not enough. A mother's convenience counts. This sitter came at a time and day no one else could. She *was* convenient, so be it! In the mix of wild Susannah and cuddly Becky, a few hours of aloof Rachel was tolerable.

Most important, when bonding does occur between the sitter and my children, I do my best to *keep* her. I give her a raise, discuss the situation with her to see if any improvements can be made to increase her comfort and satisfaction. Amy had babysat over a year when I asked her this. She is quiet, but she knows her mind. *Immediately* she blurted out, "Leave the door open!" Instead of ringing, and sometimes waking somebody, she wanted simply to walk in. What might not work in every neighborhood does in ours. Another's sitter's request: Could we sometimes buy vanilla yogurt please, instead of coffee?

Before I recommend a babysitter to a friend, I consider whether there are any caveats to mention. Does this person sometimes cancel at the last moment or break a lot of dishware? I may not object that a boyfriend is part of the package, but my friend should know. Recommending a good sitter can be a great favor to someone, but I don't let generosity run away with prudence. If I know a sitter is already helping me to the maximum of her free time, why set up a situation where another family and I will be competing, and where neither can ever be sure whether she will be available?

One principle that hasn't changed: five is the limit of the number of sitters that I can juggle, to whom we can feel close. Each has her day, and a day she can fill in. Whether a family needs as many sitters as five, or fewer, I would avoid hiring the sitter who has only the one or two unengaged sequences of time in a week. Inevitably, this person will become still busier and will have to cancel.

Troubles Under the Big Top

Sometimes I wonder if our babysitting arrangement might be topped by more professional care, but essentially I discern it can't. It's my contention that children should lead, adults follow in their activities. Our children know where the art supplies cupboard is, and the records and record player are, as well as the sitters. For the sitter to be stretched out on the chaise longue reading *Mademoiselle* while the children are absorbed in transferring water from their red wagon to the sandbox is, if an unstable state of affairs, an exquisitely happy one. To be partner to it, the sitter must be *good*.

The number of our family is set at four. Therefore, our preschool period is flying fast. I often ache at the pretty hand-me-down dresses I forgot to put on Emma before she outgrew them, or at having neglected to keep a sentimental record of the twins' "firsts." Having the fleet of babysitters accentuates this feeling that combining family responsibilities with a career, even one home based, *is* a compromise.

I miss their moods, even that tempo of boredom and recovery from boredom, of a day that meanders where it wilt. Someone else walks the children to story hour at the library, watches them return to consciousness from an afternoon nap. But of course being away sharpens my delight taking when we come together. The days when I now act like a commuting mom and take the 8:05 to Manhattan for the day, I wake the children early, and we sit in bed and read and cuddle before it's time to dress and wave goodbye. This is what full-time, out-of-house working women value as "quality time."

More pragmatically, having sitters rather than a sitter or more formal day care means considerable scheduling. The routine is sensitive to school vacations. Sunday night as I shore up the child care schedule for the coming week I sometimes hold my breath. Will Olive be leaving early for the holidays? Will I be able to meet such-and-such deadline, keep such-and-such appointment?

Yet the sitters we have employed have been remarkably faithful. One reason I didn't want to hire a retired person, or in fact any individual singly, was the problem of what to do when the caretaker was sick. Our sitters have proved an exceptionally healthy lot. Because they *are* plural, if one is racked with cramps or flu chills and cancels, someone else "knows her lines"! Because they attend three different schools—Sarah Lawrence and Concordia colleges and the public high school—their school vacations are different. In the summer we rent the third floor in exchange for sitting. I try the roomer first for the 8:00 a.m.'s. If she doesn't show I can telephone up and say, "Quick, put on your bathrobe, I must run."

In this circus, the acts *change*. This fact is sad and troublesome for me, but, to all appearances, the children adjust easily. We make an effort to stay in touch with former sitters when the bonding was strong, so they don't altogether vanish from the children's lives. Moreover, change in caregiving is as slow as the flowering of a summer garden. And many of the blossoms are perennials. A girl who graduates and goes off to college returns and babysits the winter and spring holidays. A girl who finds a better-paying job still comes and babysits once in a while. Sarah spent her junior year abroad in Paris after babysitting for us when the twins were one year old.

Susan, also from Sarah Lawrence, left for a year at Temple University to study radio communications. This year the children are three and have these beloved friends back.

Babysitters are in general trained only in so much as you train them. The child care they give is ad hoc. Only thrice has this been the cause of distress. When the twins began to curse, I traced the influence to a babysitter who had subbed for her friend one day two weeks before. They had even adopted her Bronx accent! Another sitter let the children know she would rather not change diapers. She realized this confused them, when we had a chat. I agonized when I heard a sitter mimic Burton's stammering in excitement one day, but he does not stutter, and the jest was not one I think she often repeated.

Our big failure was, regrettably, our only boy sitter. Arthur fell asleep. The children apparently *put* Arthur asleep. One day they sauntered down the drive, onto the sidewalk, and around the bend, alone. When returned to me by a neighbor walking his dog, the twins had that pleased-guilty-dazed-scared look every mother remembers the awful time it happened to her. Admitted the neighbor later, "What I couldn't figure out, it didn't seem to faze you you'd lost your kids." I didn't hiss at Arthur in public, though my anger burned, but I surveyed him the next summer morning he came and sat. By gosh, he dozed off again within an hour of arrival. That was his *last* sit. We offered him a job scraping paint, and so eased him out of our family's life.

Finally, a real drawback to our system: Tax rulings make it impossible to count the expenditure as an income-tax deduction unless a sitter's income is reported. Babysitters who work for a family full time usually don't report their income, au pairs seldom do, and certainly to register five sitters as employees and to report their income would be unmanageable.[4]

At first I let the children pay the sitters. Shouldn't they understand that the sitters like Mommy had a job? But then I decided they should be sheltered from the financial basis of the relationship because that tangible reason for the friends' sitting was one true factor but not all. The *gardiennes*, as the French call them, gave their affection and commitment. So I decided the "bottom line" should be writ small. By two and a half, Emma and Burton were out of the game. Instead, I put money in an envelope prepaid, and only if I napped or had a long-distance phone call and came down a half-hour later than expected, would I fiddle with the cash before the kids.

[4]Under the present tax law, enacted in 1982, the credit that working parents may claim for child care expenses is on a sliding scale and depends on a family's income. The employer must issue salary receipts, and the caregiver must report the earnings on a W2 form.

I've had pangs, flashes to the year 2010 and one of my children on the analyst's couch with a voice enraged saying, "I thought only money could buy trust!" We do pay for our extended family, or if they are roomers, we accept their babysitting in partial fulfillment of their rent. But since I took to slipping envelopes in knapsacks and purses or on a table by the front door, the children have lost interest in the financial basis of the network.

Cindy's Commentary

When Cindy came down from New Haven at Easter, she, our family, and a mutual friend met at the Metropolitan Museum of Art in New York City. I asked her to stretch her memory back nearly a year to describe as the other babysitters had, any strong impressions of being with the children. The conversation topic didn't blend with ancient Korean art; she wrote me instead.

As a student of child development in the spring of 1979, I found the prospect of babysitting for one-year-old twins alluring and appealing for different reasons.

My exposure to children on a regular basis had been limited to groups of children between the ages of three and five in nursery school settings. Infancy and toddlerhood were a mystery to me, and therefore a period of childhood I sought to discover.

The notion of working with twins was also a fascination in itself. I thought that I could learn a lot about sibling relations, peer relations, and differences between the genders.

I lived and worked with the twins for two different periods of their lives: from the ages of twelve to fifteen months and twenty-four to twenty-six months. I have seen them at the breast, crawling along floors, in diapers, uttering undistinguisable sounds . . . and I have heard them speak, seen them eat and drink with proper utensils, flush away their pee in a toilet, literally walk miles.

Our experience together the first summer consisted largely of napping (them, not me!), changing diapers, administering snack. Different from the routine at nursery school, part of snack was spilling juice down the front. Some of it they sucked in using their newly developing lip muscles, most of it was absorbed by the thick towel wrapped around the neck. There was some time spent roaming and exploring. From timid babies, Emma and Burton were gradually reckoning their way into the world of dimensions.

I remember finding Burton afloat in a pool of hot tea on top of the dining room table, having discovered a newer plateau above and beyond the footstool that had led him there. This occurred when Burton was about

118

13 months old. Emma had a similarly traumatic experience. Fascinated herself by the very footstool that led her brother astray, she worked her body under it so completely that she could not back out.

For children this age, the problems and challenges of exploration and discovery are what fill the time for them. Their learning and pleasures are experienced through these movements as much as through their interactions with each other and the significant adults around them. A favorite respite time for the three of us would be to take a good old-fashioned stroll in the heat and humidity of July, languishing in the Bronxville landscape, nodding off (them again!) into a mid-afternoon nap, gently bouncing along in the double stroller, down and around the curvy, bumpy roads.

When Burton and Emma were two, they were capable of new experiences, ready for new discoveries. The family who owned the Filstrups' house before, when they heard I wanted to come back to Bronxville another summer, offered me a place to stay over their garage in exchange for simply watering houseplants in their absence. But I decided—see how quickly these attachments form—that babysitting for the twins (combined with my summer job) would make the summer livelier. So I moved my gear in again.

The stimulation I may have provided for them was as simple as needing to go to the market or to the shoe repair store. They invented errands too. Cans that had been turned over sideways they placed upright, generally tidying the place up. In the shoe repair store they got lost in the big chairs with reclining backs, getting on and off the chairs, pushing and pulling the backs of the chairs to watch the movement they could feel when they were seated.

Once we went to visit a friend whose house was a few blocks away but atop a long flight of stairs. Tony played the guitar. We sang a few songs and then returned home.

The friend who lived with me the second summer sometimes cared for the twins, and sometimes accompanied me when I was with them. One day as we headed for the market Marta had the thought to stop in at the pizza place. Why not? We stopped in at Gino's, lost the children in the big wooden chairs, and gorged them with Sicilian pizza. The greatest! They thought so too.

A diverse array of shoes on the front porch—the Filstrups tried to keep shoes out of the house—might provide the stimulus. For 30 minutes one day Emma and Burton tried on sandals, clogs, and boots belonging to three different adults—a vast assortment.

Occasionally the weather decided for us. I remember both summers heavy rainstorms being an attraction, especially for me. There was a thrill for us all in going onto the wide porch to watch the rain come down so heavily. To be outside and so near it, but also safe from it, was very exciting. I sat with my knees up against my chest. Emma and Burton ran to the edge to reach out and touch it.

When it was too hot for clothes, Emma and Burton needed to take theirs off. One day I had them do this. I gave them a hose and some buckets and gradually they filled up their pool. Mostly they made a swamp of their backyard, but they splashed in their wading pool too. The day and the moment determined this event. And it was a real success.

Emma and Burton would often like to go for walks. Sometimes that meant stopping to behold each flower along the way, or sitting on each rock large enough for sitting. Again, they found a "lesson" as it were in their world. Clearly it was never necessary to entertain these children by indulging them with flashiness or contrived activities. The sidewalks were their gameboard (not to make them sound like waifs or streetfighters). Their environment was stimulus enough. They loved life and they loved learning, and that was a thrill and a joy to witness and participate in.

All of these events and experiences were combined to make a song created one balmy afternoon as Emma sat in the sandbox complacently and Burton tore down the driveway and around the corner on his trike. Marta, my roommate, had the music, and a refrain. While she strummed it on her guitar, I filled in with some spontaneous verse, and it happened to work, we felt, as a song.

Twice as Nice

REFRAIN: Emma and Burton,
                Two little mice;
                Emma and Burton,
                Twice as nice;
                Twice as nice
                as one little baby all alone.
STANZAS: Emma likes to play with sand.
                She pours it in and out of her hand.
                She fills the truck and she dumps it out.
                Emma's learning what sand's all about.

                Burton likes to ride his bike.
                He takes his bike on a bike hike.
                He rides around the corner, then into the street,
                So I go chasing him on my feet. Hey, Burton!

Emma and Burton go for walks.
We walk around from block to block.
We walk down the street at an easy pace
And then stop in at the pizza place.

Burton really likes to dance;
He moves his arms and he shakes his pants.
Emma likes to sing along,
And so we've written them a song.

7

BABYSITTING COOPERATIVE

In playing the piano all ten fingers are in motion; it won't do to move some fingers only and not others. But if all ten fingers press down at once, there is no melody. To produce good music, the ten fingers should move rhythmically and in coordination.

Mao Tse-tung

Like many Californians, Rodger and Justine Ball hail from the East. Born and raised in Buffalo, New York, Rodger and Justine were high school sweethearts. They began in different colleges, but they both graduated from the University of Buffalo, where they met again and married. In 1966, Rodger joined the navy. The navy stationed him at Alameda Naval Air Station and other California naval bases, and after he left the Navy, the Balls remained in the Bay Area. As easterners, the Balls see themselves as culturally different from native Californians, but they never considered returning to the East Coast.

Seven years ago, soon after Rodger left the navy, the Balls moved from an apartment in Oakland to Castro Valley, a small suburban community nestled in the East Bay Hills. This town is an unincorporated area of approximately 42,000 people. Most of the population has moved here in the last fifteen years, often in search of affordable housing. The Bay Area real estate boom has pushed the price of a modest two- or three-bedroom, split-level house to well over $120,000. Castro Valley is solidly middle class, with few blacks or Chicanos. Like most Castro Valleyans, the Balls earn their income in the San Francisco–Oakland metropolis to the north.

When the Balls bought their house in 1972, Castro Valley was surrounded by uninhabited fields and hills. Deer frequently wandered into their yard. Although the street and its houses now extend farther up the hill, the Balls have a backyard large by Bay Area standards and spacious enough to accommodate their two children, Monica and Geoffrey, and others from their babysitting cooperative. The Balls have furnished their house modestly, preferring to spend extra money on travel. They own two cars.

After leaving the navy, Rodger went to work for a shipping firm. Justine has worked thirteen years in the reservations department of United Airlines. Several years ago, she earned a library degree by going part-time to library school at San Jose State University. But she has not changed jobs, partly because public library budgets have been constricting for several years, and partly because the Balls enjoy the benefits of heavily discounted airline tickets. They travel to Hawaii almost once a year. Although they have no extended family in the immediate area, they have parents in Arkansas and Arizona whom they visit once a year. This summer they are also traveling to upstate New York to visit Justine's sister.

The Balls' Commentary

RODGER: Justine and I went to high school together in Buffalo, New York. We married in 1966 and moved to the Bay Area in 1970 when the navy transferred me. We moved to Castro Valley in 1972, and Monica was born in 1973. We had been living in apartments in Oakland and did a lot of research before moving to Castro Valley. Since housing is dense, lots are small, and there are few trees. I was looking for something similar to where I grew up back East. But I wanted it here. So we researched the whole Bay Area, considering where we were working, house prices, major highways. We decided on Castro Valley on that basis. At that time there were homes with large back yards, some were small farms actually. They were places we, being easterners, could feel comfortable with.

JUSTINE: There were two other reasons. The first was the consumers cooperative store. This was the only one south of Berkeley. The consumer cooperative is owned by the people on a profit-sharing basis. I was very impressed by their merchandise, or lack of it, I should say. They're honest and straightforward, their specials are high-protein, life-line foods, they don't push or even carry junk foods. It wouldn't be here unless the people of Castro Valley were attuned to this issue. We're not active in the politics of the co-op. I have enough other concerns—working, school, mothering. The other factor was to be close to the lake. I love passing by the lake on my way to and from work.

RODGER: Most of our friends are easterners who have moved out here. Only a few are natives. The Bay Area has tripled in size in the last twenty years, and most of the newcomers are from east of the Rockies. It took us a long time to feel comfortable out here. Folks here speak a slightly different language. It's English, but their assumptions are different. Family ties are stretched a little thinner. It's more open. You find people able to be themselves. There is a lot more tolerance of different lifestyles. Where we grew up, there would be a lot of gossip if you did something out of the ordinary. Several unmarried couples have bought houses on the street. A couple of fellows had a home across the street. This is the land of the cowboys and rugged individualists. The status quo doesn't try to change the nonconformist that much. That is important to us and perhaps a little special to the Bay Area, where we plan to spend the rest of our lives.

The existence of a well-organized babysitting cooperative in Castro Valley was a great asset for the Balls.

JUSTINE: I first heard about the babysitting co-op by reading an ad in the local dollar saver. Monica was six months old. I had gone back to work when she was three months old. With both of us working, we had a child care problem. We solved it for a while when my sister lived with us for

124

three months, but then she had to go back to school. It was difficult finding someone reliable, preferably not a live-in, to take care of her during the day. We had used a few people after my sister left, unsatisfactorily. They were unsatisfactory because they lacked commitment. Things would come up that so-and-so wasn't available. Even as little as I needed a sitter, there would be days when I would have somebody cancel. I was using local sources when I worked during the day. Not knowing many people in the area, I ended up contacting people through ads in the local paper. These were mothers. I was looking for something better.

After I read the ad for the co-op, I called up and got a better idea what it was all about. A few days later I went to a monthly meeting and met a big percentage of the mothers. There were five or six other new people. The members were very friendly, and very organized. The co-op had been going on for a couple of years. It seemed like the perfect solution. Everybody lived in this area. They were all basically the same economic level. At that time no racial mix. As far as I know, none of them was a working mother. I was the first. I was kind of shocked and surprised at that first meeting to discover that they were not working mothers. The co-op to them was a means to getting out. They'd go shopping, take classes, go to the gym. But it was well enough organized that I could rely on the co-op to go to work.

My hours at work are an important factor in how I use the co-op. I work at an airline reservations office. We work a multitude of shifts and bid on these shifts monthly. It was never certain how many hours we would require of a sitter. It was flexible because I could trade hours with other people. I was working a lot of nights and could choose to be home with Monica during the day. I went to work at three in the afternoon and worked until midnight. So I only needed a sitter two-and-a-half or three hours until Rodger came home. And there were days when I didn't need a sitter at all, because I would have days off during the week. This is why we could consider the co-op.

There was no screening, at least nothing that I was aware of. Since then other new members have expressed surprise that we are so open, that we accept almost anyone who wants to join. I don't know of anyone who has been turned down. We don't go over the limit of thirty families, but there is no screening.

At that time the advantages seemed to be having free babysitting and, to some extent, other kids for Monica to play with. She was an infant. Since then I have realized that the other advantage has been getting to know other parents with young children. It's made such a difference in our lives. We have formed a lot of friendships within the co-op. I find that as valuable as the babysitting itself. To talk with other mothers, to compare other experiences, to find out that your kid is not weird and unusual. Comparing different doctors, different books. Even getting to know other couples socially.

The organization is simple. Each family pays two dollars a year for mailing expenses. A roster lists all the members, addresses, phone numbers, kids, ages, doctor's name and phone numbers, and some emergency phone number. This is kept very current. Authorization for medical treatment is always left with a sitter. No one has ever had to use it in the eleven years of the co-op, but it's important to have. At a monthly meeting, we fill the calendar. This co-op is basically for Monday to Friday, nine to five. It is not set up for evening sitting. Some of us are available for evening sitting, but the basic idea is daytime. So we fill the calendar for every weekday in that month. For every day of the month one member is designated as a primary sitter, and another as an alternate. When it is your day, you must be available to sit from nine to five. If you can sit only from nine to noon, it doesn't work, because there are people who need the entire day of babysitting. We call it *gadding* when you leave a child. Gadding hours and sitting hours should equal out. There is no money involved. At the monthly meeting everybody signs up for their days. It is all settled, and everybody gets a copy and knows who is sitting when.[1]

A degree of flexibility is built in. After a while you get to know the people who are sitting for your kids. If someone needs to go some place on the day she is to be the primary sitter, she asks you, "Is it all right if I take your kid to the dentist's office?" You take it as they give it, even though they are supposedly obligated to be home all day. This is not enforced, but it still works out because everybody expects these things to happen. We all try to be flexible.

Most of the arrangements for dropping kids, or gadding, as we say, are done by phone a couple of days ahead of the date, not at the monthly meeting. When your day to sit is coming up, people start calling a couple of days ahead of time.

The thirty families have about sixty kids. No large families. When I joined, there was only one family with more than two kids—they had three. Since then we have had three or four families with more, maximum four kids. But often a mother of four does not leave all four. One may be in school, or she leaves three while she goes to the doctor with the other. You are charged the same number of hours for two as one child. Three kids is one and a half times. The accounting bias favors two-children families.

---

[1]See the Appendix for the "Policy and Procedures" and medical authorization form of the Castro Valley Babysitting Cooperative.

126

They receive the same number of gadding hours as a family with only one child.

There is no numerical limit on the number of children at a sitter, but you are free to say when you have all the kids you can handle. Then the gadder has to call the alternate or someone else. Some women feel that they can't handle more than two kids in addition to their own, so that's it. There are days when I am the same way. There are days when I have fourteen to fifteen kids here. Nor is there a requirement that you use the primary or alternate sitter. Other considerations frequently come into it—geography, knowing the people. You may trade hours with a family you like more often than with the primary sitter. The biggest consideration is the age of the kids. Lots of times I call someone other than the primary sitter because the other has a child Monica's age.

Each month there is a secretary. She makes sure the calendar is filled and tallies everyone's hours. When you have sat, you call the secretary and tell her how many hours you sat and for whom. At the end of the month there is an accounting. The hours gadding and the hours sitting do not have to come out equally. There is a rule that nobody can go more than 25 hours in the hole. On the books, many people have surplus hours. The secretary earns thirty hours of sitting a month. That's just for doing the work, not for sitting. The secretary position rotates in the order of having joined the group. Each member serves approximately once every two years. Being secretary means answering the phone a lot and doing all the totaling up. Probably it comes to ten hours of work a month. The pay is thirty. Everybody thinks this is fair.

Almost everybody has a surplus? That can't be!

RODGER: You're thinking like an accountant. It doesn't balance. No one quite understands why there are so many surpluses. Two husbands who were accountants had fits trying to figure this out. They said no way, this isn't possible. Some of this is people who leave with extra hours unused. Somehow it works. Rather than change the system, even though it isn't understandable, we keep it because it works. It works marvelously. If lots of members tried to cash in, others wouldn't stand for it, whoever was sitting would not take all those kids. Mostly, people do not have the necessity, and that's why they don't use the hours.

JUSTINE: I earn enough by sitting during the week. I can leave my kids three days a week and still earn enough hours by sitting for as many as fourteen kids. Rodger sits evenings while I am working. Also, I became an officer because officers get free hours. The president gets fifteen hours a month. She is elected by secret ballot once a year at the annual meeting. The president keeps everything together, keeps track of the secretary, settles disputes. The biggest dispute in the co-op is people leaving their kids longer than they said. It's specifically in the rules that if you are going to be more than a half-hour longer than agreed, you will call and clear it with the sitter. The president reminds the offender, nothing more than that. Some people forget to call in their hours when they sit, but that's their problem. The president presides over the monthly meetings. She takes care of tallying problems if the secretary is not too good at figures. Sometimes there is only one person interested in the job; sometimes it is contested. I have been president twice.

I became more involved in the working of the co-op because it was an easy way to get hours. I wasn't afraid of taking on more responsibility, whereas a lot of these women did not want any more involvement than just the sitting. Also many did not have the self-confidence to do anything more. This particular co-op was good for me because it didn't have many working mothers. Before she went to public school, Monica was one of the few children who would stay all day. For a while we had a mother who was a substitute teacher and she would leave her son all day for a week. There are now five working mothers.

It is pretty much assumed that everyone in the co-op will do a competent job. The only basic rule is no corporal punishment, unless the mother has specifically requested that you spank the child. Whatever the gadder and the sitter agree upon is what goes. Generally, if you are gadding during mealtime, you bring the kid's food. This avoids problems of Mary's allergic to such-and-so, or Mary doesn't like this. It is in the rules that if the sitter has to feed the child she gets an extra half hour. When I leave Monica from nine to five, I bring a lunch and snack.

There are thirty active members, enough to cover weekdays plus a margin. In the summertime it is harder to fill the calendar because of vacations, but usually there is someone who needs the hours and is willing to sign up for two or three days. There are also two other statuses of membership, associate and inactive. Associate members sit nights and weekends only. These are working mothers. They gad during the day and sit during the night and weekends. They have a different status because they cannot sign up for an entire day. Usually these are people who have been active members for a number of years and then have gone to work. They have a vote. Inactive is someone who is getting out and just using up hours. If I knew that I were moving in three months, I would go inactive, and simply use up the hours I had accumulated.

Geography is basically limited to Castro Valley, but there are some exceptions. We have a couple of members who live in nearby communities. When a member moves outside Castro Valley, it is put to a vote, and majority decides. You have to take your kids there so you don't want it to be too far away.

How good is the babysitting that the co-op furnishes?

It depends on the mother. I would say that it is superior as babysitting goes—superior to teenagers in your home or relatively unknown people. You can count on getting a mature, experienced adult taking care of your kids. Basically when you are sitting for someone else's children, you tend to be more careful than with just your own kids. Since it is just one day a month, that day you are on your toes. If I have a big group, I let them run in the backyard, which is fenced. As the kids begin to talk, you get a pretty good idea of what kind of babysitting you are getting. As infants, you don't know as much.

There are mothers that I won't leave my kids with. Maybe ten, some of them only because their kids are a different age. Say just a small infant. I don't want to leave a four- and an eight-year-old with that family. If she has only an infant, she does not have experience with an older child. One member sat the kids in front of the television, so I did not send the kids there. There is no attempt to discuss this at monthly meetings because this is a matter of values. For some mothers, having their kids sitting in front of the television is all right. It is handled on the level of individual selection. If I work on the day when this mother is the primary sitter, I will call on someone else. That person is not obliged, but usually you can work out something.

RODGER: In seven-and-a-half years, there have been only a few times that we had to leave the kids at a home I wasn't happy with. There was one case of an alcoholic. The co-op made no formal attempt to exclude this mother. That was scary. I picked up Monica at 5:30 on the way home from work. Justine had left Monica at three, and everything seemed normal. The woman had three kids of her own. Since I didn't go to the meetings, I didn't know the people until I picked up the kids. I was used to seeing a wide variety of homes and people. But this place seemed very strange. The woman did not immediately recognize why I was there. I asked for Monica, and she didn't seem to know anything about it. I went in, and the living room was basically bare, no furniture. The lady was very nervous, running around. A man with her seemed to be trying to cover her inadequacies. He realized what was going on and tried to help her. At that point I decided no more of this. People do have problems of medication—maybe she was a diabetic. I didn't want to accuse her, I just wanted to get my kid out of there and go home. The other co-op members do not formally exclude a family like this. Once word gets out, people stop taking their kids to her house. Most of the new people have come with someone else—"This is my cousin, my neighbor, my friend." It is very rare to have an unknown join. Of the original group when we joined, there are five families left. Turnover is about five or six families a year. As kids get older, people drop out. We'll drop out eventually. There just won't be the need for the co-op in our lives.

JUSTINE: Education levels are not uniform. We have a couple of mothers who haven't finished high school, a couple who are teachers and nurses, a couple who have earned master's degrees. At one point I went back to school to study library science. Most of my classes were at night, and I arranged my work schedule around the classes. I earned the library degree and work one day a week at the junior college in Hayward. I haven't been able to find a full-time librarian job because I will not relocate, and there are hundreds of unemployed librarians in the Bay Area. At the time I was going to school I worked part-time. I have a very flexible job. That has been very important to us both.

RODGER: I think the co-op's been great for my children. They have met a lot

In the babysitting co-op each family's house has its own attractions for the children who visit as part of an exchange. At the Balls', older children run right to the backyard.

of people, adults and kids, that they would not have otherwise. They have gained quite a deep experience with different types of people. More than Monica would have gotten if we had just one sitter at home all day. Or if her contacts were just with the neighborhood kids. Our children are not afraid of strangers and never have been. I don't know of any truly bad experiences. Monica may complain, but that's a kid's perspective and very relative. I think it has kept Monica open to different people, to different homes, different lifestyles. Castro Valley does not have a great range, but it has a range nevertheless. She gets to see rich homes and poor homes. Ours is probably the poorest home. We haven't invested a lot of money in this house. One family has a pool and another is *very* wealthy. Monica loves it! She doesn't want to come back home! From our point of view this is fine because she likes to go to these places. Like any kid she comes home and says why can't we have a pool. We say we don't want one, and we can't afford one. She has understood this reasoning ever since she was small.

When the sitter comes from the outside, I think that her individual style becomes lost on the kid's turf. In her own home, she can be herself, freer. At home you feel much more confident and at ease in dealing with a bunch of kids. I think the kids pick up on that. They realize they're visiting. It's not like going to school. It's not a neutral territory, not an administrative locale, it's somebody else's home. This has an effect, a good effect.

JUSTINE: There are a number of babysitting co-ops in the area. At one time there were three in Castro Valley. Some of them are run differently. A friend of mine belongs to one for evenings and weekends so that parents can go out. In that co-op you just take people as they come up on a list.

In addition to the co-op, we sent Monica to a Montessori nursery school for two school years. While she did not pick up a lot of the Montessori concepts, she did pick up considerably more than the average kindergartener. She had had so much experience with other families, other kids, she was way beyond the other kids in kindergarten, those had never been away from their parents. So she skipped kindergarten. I was flabbergasted to see kids showing up at school holding onto their mother's apron strings. Monica would wave goodbye and run off to the playground! She is a year younger than her classmates and tests above the national median. But she is not wild about school.

Both kids have had a wide *range* of child care. Often in the co-op we could not afford the hours to leave Monica all day. So we left her in a day care center one of the mothers in the co-op ran in her home. She took care of Monica several days a week. When I was in library school, Monica was in Montessori half day. I had two different mothers who would pick her up at school and feed her lunch, and then I picked her up in time for her nap.

131

Was the delivering and picking up as formidable a matter as it sounds?

RODGER: We had some tricky schedules. I have a lot of respect for Justine's scheduling. She would be going to work at different hours and going to school, I was going to work my usual hours, we had sitters spaced all over the valley, and we had the day care center. Monica would be going to Montessori school, Geoffrey would need an all-day sitter, then Monica would be picked by another sitter. In my lunch bag, Justine would give me a note and a map. I never tried to keep track in my head who was where, it was just too much. So Justine would write it down for me. Now and then she would use a sitter who was new and whose address I did not know. One time I had read the instructions in the morning over breakfast and stuffed them in my lunch bag. Somehow I threw the instructions away with the lunch bag at work. I didn't think about it until I was driving home on the freeway. I would keep the instructions under the seat of the car and reach for it at my usual turn off to figure out how to pick up the kids. But it wasn't there. I panicked! There could be thirty places where my kid is, and I'm only familiar with ten of them to begin with. Where is she?

I could have gone home and called Justine at work, but this would take an extra half hour because I cannot call direct, she has to call back. I couldn't remember the name, all I could remember was the name of the street but not the number of the house. I got as far as the cul-de-sac and decided to chance it.

At the cul-de-sac there were all these houses, and one kid playing with a ball outside. I got out of the car and asked him if there were any strange children in the neighborhood. He must have thought I was a real nut. He scratched his head and looked at me funny. I asked again, "Is there anybody here visiting other kids?" "Oh," he said, "you must mean so-and-so." "Yes, where do they live?" "Right over there." I knocked on the door and asked, "Do you have my daughter here?" They said, "Who are you?" And I told them, and son-of-a-gun if that wasn't the place.

JUSTINE: I'm glad those days are gone. Geoffrey was at one place, Monica at another. It made it very complicated. That's one disadvantage to taking them to different houses as opposed to having the babysitter come to your house. Another disadvantage is when a child is sick, you cannot drop them off at someone else's house. In general, parents are good about not leaving off sick kids, at least not knowingly. Twice in the seven-and-a-half years since we joined, chicken pox swept through the group, but you don't know about this until it's too late. If the kids are just sniffling, we take them. One time we took Geoffrey when he was sniffling, and he got worse very quickly. The sitter was upset, understandably so. We didn't realize that he would get a high fever. Nor did she take the initiative to call one of us. If one of the kids is sick, then Rodger or I is "sick." We take turns. It may not look good on our employment records, but it has worked out all right.

RODGER: This type of co-op works well in this type of community. It would have to operate differently in a community where more mothers worked, where hours were more rigid, where the population was more heterogeneous. For example, central Oakland: there you would have to insist on more screening. This is a kind of "laid back" co-op. It works well because the people in it are flexible. Commitments are easy to make here, and easy to break.

A valuable reference book for anyone who wants to set up a babysitting cooperative is How to Organize a Babysitting Cooperative and Get Some FREE Time Away From the Kids, *by Carole T. Meyers. For mail orders send $4.75 (including tax, postage, and handling) to Carousel Press, P.O. Box 6061, Albany, California 94706.*

COOPERATIVE NURSERY SCHOOL

What the best and wisest parent wants for his own child that must the community want for all its children.

Thomas Dewey

The Sterns are a family described as child centered by their son's nursery school director Toni Liebman, who means it fully as a compliment. Carol's parents' affluence provides her and Arthur with a financial cushion that frees them to concentrate gracefully on living well *with* their children Benji, five, and David, two. Their house is located on a four-acre estate in Old Westbury, one of the most attractive suburban communities in Long Island, New York. Also living on the estate in two other houses are Carol's parents and a widow tenant, who is a friend of the family.

The Sterns' house is well built and lived in as opposed to "decorated." There is no materialistic show, and evidence of the children's lives is everywhere. When I talked with Carol about her involvement in Benji's nursery school, we sat at a large butcher-block table in the kitchen, overlooking a landscaped, swimming-pool terrace. We could see Carol's younger sister's fiance tending to the flower garden.

Carol is an unusual-looking, most attractive woman. Her fine brown hair is simply coiffed to shoulder length. She is not tall and has features both broad and delicate. She wore a turquoise tank top and denim skirt that accentuated her curvaceous figure and dewy tanned skin. I thought of pre-Columbian nobility.

When Benji came into the kitchen and asked to get the "robot" (his tape recorder) he had left at Grandma's the night before, Carol waved him off with, "Sure, fine," and noted to me, "She's right next door." At that moment her father strode in dressed in tennis whites asking if he could borrow her racket. Three generations of one American family living in one housing compound being unusual, we started there.

Carol Rosenfeld's Commentary

Neither of my parents is at home a lot. My father has his business, and my mother, her civic work and friends. But when they are, in the morning and at night, the children spend a lot of time running back and forth between the houses. It's nothing special my parents do. It is a total outpouring of love whenever they see David and Benji.

Arthur works in Brooklyn in a car dealership that is my family's own business. We knew each other slightly in high school and are the same age, thirty-one. We remet at the occasion of a friend's wedding and married two years later in 1972. I went to Boston University for my first two years of college, and then transferred to Hofstra. Somehow I managed to graduate, I did get through. Arthur completed two or three years of college, but he didn't graduate. He dropped out and began working for a magazine based in Manhattan. Arthur always was interested in cars. When my father offered him a job, he discovered he was a good salesperson. After David was born, he left the firm for over a year and bought and sold cars on his own. Then recently he went back. He liked spending more time at home with the children and working his own hours, but now he has the feeling the company is his, not just my father's.

We don't live rent free, but our landlord is my parents, so if we have a money problem we won't be thrown out on the street. Like other families whose children are small, we find we have less money and less flexible earning power than at other times. The difference is we don't have the underlying insecurity, the fear of being out in the street.

I think that I probably will take my schooling further. We are very keen on all questions of our children's educational future. I feel I'm doing things that weren't done for me. Educationally, I am more involved and more critical than my parents were, more interested in a different way. I care principally about quality. My parents were interested in my success in conforming to the system. I'm interested in the educational system's being successful in giving the child what he should have. I want to help Benji to deal with the good and bad aspects of education and not always take the teacher's part. My parents never questioned the institution. "Why aren't you getting a good mark?" or "Listen to the teacher," they'd say. I'm less inclined to criticize my child and more the school.

Arthur is more easygoing and less critical of the establishment. I tend to meet things with a critical eye. With regard to schooling too, I'm the one who feels more strongly the importance of school and who also has negative feelings about going through school. He thought high school was a ball—friends, freedom—and I was miserable. I had a lot of love but not the understanding or freedom. I've worked very hard to try to instill certain good feelings about themselves in my children, and I want these fostered in school, especially in their first nursery school experience.

In this built-up area of Long Island the choices of nursery schools are numerous. I asked Carol how she went about selecting one.

Before I went and looked at schools, I sat down and made a list of questions, points I thought were important. I took my list around to all the schools in the area that I'd heard about and interviewed the directors. I would take out my little list—a lot of them thought it was quite unusual!—and go through all the questions.

I asked for specifics such as size of class, student-teacher ratio, professional qualifications of the staff, who would be in the room with the children, details of the program, how the day was spent. Then I asked about nutrition consciousness—what kind of snacks did they give the

Maxine Danowitz

The Sterns are a family described as fun loving and child centered.

children?—and whether they divided the girls from the boys in any way—was it sexist?—because I wouldn't have gone for that at all. Did they have special activities in music, dance, cooking, gardening, environment, science? Then I asked the director for the philosophy of the school and what they hoped to achieve in the classroom. I said what I wanted and explained how I raise my children in a very tolerant way and try to let them be. Of course everybody needs socialization, and I try to teach them right from wrong and not to hurt others, but basically I want them to be stimulated in the direction that they want to go, not forced and channeled to do certain things. I stressed at that point I wanted Benji just to be in a very loving, tolerant, supportive atmosphere, not to do academics or preparation for it. And I got the reaction to what I wanted at many schools in the area. After that I was able to make my decision.

At the Roslyn-Trinity Co-op, which I selected, I was impressed by Toni Liebman, the director, as well as by the fact that her school was a

137

cooperative. But at that time I had no experience with cooperatives, so I didn't know what it would be like. What I knew that I liked about it was the parent participation once a month. I felt that would give me a chance to see firsthand what was going on, to observe the teachers and see the interaction, and to take an active part. I wasn't ready to entrust my three-year-old child entirely to somebody else's care, to relinquish all responsibility. I still wanted that opportunity to play a part. That was a big selling point. Plus I liked Toni, the philosophy, the facilities, and the two teachers I observed.

Benji was going to be three years three months in September. Originally when I had a baby I didn't expect to send him to nursery school at three years old. But as he grew up, I realized he did have a need for play experience with other children. Especially since we are quite isolated living here. I wanted to send him to a loving, supportive atmosphere where he could meet other children and be understood, tolerated, and loved. That is what I thought I would find at the co-op, and it turned out that I did.

Carol's involvement in the co-op changed her ideas about volunteering.

At the orientation meeting in May, sheets are passed around listing all the different committees. You have to join one. I was about to give birth to my second child, and I nursed my children, so I knew I would always want the child with me. So my first two choices were guided only by work I knew I could do at home. I signed up for telephone and typing. My third choice, since I like to be outdoors, was maintenance. The telephone committee is a popular choice. Everyone likes it because it doesn't require any time away from home. When they saw I had selected maintenance, they recruited me instantly. In August the president called to ask if I would like to be a chairperson of the maintenance committee.

I didn't have any mechanical ability when I jotted "maintenance" down on the list. It so happens I'm developing an interest in carpentry and would like to learn more about it. I put down maintenance because it was outdoors and I thought of raking the leaves.

So I felt first *why* do they want me to be chairperson? Then I felt flattered about it too, that they had singled me out. I asked what it meant to be the chair. It meant certain responsibilities to do the work, getting the other committee members out to do the work, and also that I would be on the board. I thought about it for a day, and as I thought my attitude about volunteering on some deep level changed. I examined my feelings, how I'd been in the past, and how I think most people are. They have an attitude where they want to do as little as they possibly can. It's the way they're brought up, the way our institutions are set up. It serves the establishment that we remain as passive as we can, and let the higher ups take care of business. I realized that I also had that inclination, to do as little as I could. Just no, *no* was my first response. But now my children were involved, so it was different, and I decided to say *yes*. From then on I was going to say yes, or my first reaction anyway would be, "Yes, but let's see if I really can do it"; instead of saying, "No, I don't want to do it. Leave me alone." So I decided to take on the chairmanship. I took a chance on it. That was the first time I had ever done that, and it felt really good. The same thing happened later when I became president. I had a "yes" feeling.

The maintenance committee and the fund raising committee are the two busiest, the most worked. The job of maintenance is to oversee the playground area, buy any new equipment, install it, and repair the old equipment; maintain equipment in the basement area, such as the tricycles that are constantly breaking down; and straighten up room 6, the everything room where the refrigerator is. Two consecutive Saturdays before school opens the maintenance committee cleans up the school. They devote one day to inside, one to outside. They get the school ready, scrubbing the blackboards, walls, desks, and closets; sprucing up and repairing all the equipment in the classrooms and on the playground. There are also two spring workdays, one before school begins after vacation and one at the end of the year, concentrating on getting the playground in shape.

Many of the tools we needed were at school. But many of the workers on the maintenance committee were fathers who had tools. For a particular job, I made sure the equipment was there. Some of the work required expertise that I did not have. I had to call on people more knowledgeable than I. Climbing equipment needed to be repaired and sanded down. Some of it was rotting so we sawed off and repositioned the bottoms. We lifted up the shed and put it on blocks one Saturday. Swings had to be repaired. One particularly big job was that all the wooden blocks needed sanding and varnishing. One of our parents took them home. Her husband is a contractor so he had a lot of equipment home in a big workshop. They sanded all the blocks down and varnished them. There were about twenty or more of them, and they were very large. That was a tremendous job.

Different things break. It's always something. Every year I'm sure the committee is fairly well run. There's just a large amount of upkeep, and much of the equipment has been there for quite a number of years.

We had ten on the committee, ten families; in some the wife, in some the husband, in some both participated. Half were very willing, and half seemed unwilling. I did manage to bring a majority of them out there at one

139

time or another. I always called first the people who hadn't been. I encountered a "yes" feeling from about half of them, and half had the "No, I can't do it."

There are different levels of cooperation. A very small percentage come because they realize it's a cooperative and we all have to pitch in. Others come, but you have to prod them a bit. A very few just refuse. Either they didn't understand what they were getting themselves involved in, or they have no inclination. It's attitude more than other demands on them because you find people are mostly in the same boat. I might call one woman, and she'd say, "Okay, I'll be there. I have a baby. Can I bring her?" Another woman will say, "I can't come. I have a small baby." It's all in what you feel you can accomplish. Some people who work come on weekends.

I have no personal history of volunteering. Before the co-op I really had not gotten involved. Now I'm more in a position where I will become more active. I find the things I do mostly grow out of my role as mother. I find my children bring out the best in me! I can see myself being very active within the school system in whatever mode of education we choose. My activity comes from that. With regard to things I think are important, I want to make sure they are done in a certain way. Before the co-op, no, I was isolated from the community.

How did Carol ascend from committee chairperson to co-op president?

I think chairing the committee was the stepping stone. I was a fairly responsible chairperson. I managed to get the work done. That was something in my favor. Going to business meetings also showed an interest in executive leadership. The way the co-op president is chosen is the current president picks a nominating committee of five who meet and choose a slate for the executive board for the following year. She might choose a person from the "fours" group, another from the "threes"; a person from Port Washington, another from Roslyn, and so forth. They try to represent all different types of people on the board. There may be input from both president and school director on the nominating committee, should their advice be sought. Who would know better who will do a good job than the director and president who work with the most people in the co-op? Any co-op member is free to make suggestions. The nominating committee mulls over the suggestions. The final decision is strictly theirs.

When I got the call, from a person whose son happened to be in Benji's class, I knew she was on the nominating committee. She said, "Hi, I'm on the nominating committee this year, and we're choosing the executive board." I thought to myself, "Oh God, they want me for recording secretary—I don't want to do that!" Then she said, "And we'd like you to be president." I was really floored. First of all, I didn't think anybody knew me that well. It was February and Benjamin had started school in September. Again, I couldn't help but be flattered. I said I would have to think about it. I called the president afterwards and tried to find out what the job entailed. I thought about it for a while, and found a lot of pros and cons. But then again, I decided to take the plunge. My main concern was I still had a baby home, David, who was nine months. I was nursing him and very much attached to him. I didn't have much mobility and thought that might create a problem. But that didn't seem reason enough to say no. I felt I could still work it out. So I accepted the job.

Elections come at the end of March, and the term goes from then through March of the following year. The slate comes up for a vote of the whole membership at a general meeting, but I don't think there has ever been one they didn't pass. The idea is at first you work in league with the outgoing officer, depending on how cooperative the person is. Unfortunately, when I became president, my predecessor was very ill in the hospital after being operated on for appendicitis. Also I was very new to the school. So I felt in the dark about everything. I only hoped I would learn as I went along. I took over in mid-March. It was like a whirlwind right away. It almost threw me for a loop. New member teas start up then, the orientation meetings and budget reviews. Somehow I muddled through.

Every three years the co-op reviews the bylaws and that was also happening. We changed a lot of semantics, for example, chairperson instead of chairman. It was sometimes difficult to get a quorum at meetings so we worked around that and instead said we needed a certain number of people. We changed the nominating procedures so people would have more time to become acquainted.

I think the biggest challenge was the initial accepting of the responsibility. I wasn't accustomed to assuming a leadership role. I had a certain amount of shyness to overcome in that area. Taking charge, even making the phone calls, was new. The way it usually worked was that Toni communicated something to me that needed to be done and I passed word on to the chairperson. She and I talked every day on the phone or in person. Either there was a fund raising event underway or a maintenance problem or just "Shall we close school? It's snowing." That was one facet of the job, checking in every day. Toni says it always takes a while to adjust to each other.

Running business meetings every month and speaking at the general monthly meeting was another big challenge. That was something I never felt comfortable with. Even to the last meeting, it always bothered me. I never felt at ease speaking in front of a crowd, running meetings. Some of them went better than others depending on how I felt at that particular time. I can't look back on it with a feeling of accomplishment because I don't think that's where my strong point was.

The third challenge to me was organization: getting myself organized to the point where I could run the school's parent machinery effectively. I tended to be much more organized after I became president than before. Being president you have to plunge in. You make that call *now*. You forget about procrastination. It helped me in my personal life as well. Very gradually I gained a definite sense of accomplishment that I could organize myself in such a way to be able to perform my job well and without stress. Even with housework, not one of my fortes, I'm doing better.

The job took a lot of time. I felt I was working like a regular job holder, and found myself looking forward to the weekend as a time to relax. Every day there were meetings, committees, problems.

I had the help of the executive board, made up of the two vice-presidents, one of membership and one of fund raising; the treasurer, who pays the bills; and the financial secretary, who receives tuition. These are the most active positions, and they have all been women. Other members of the executive board are the recording secretary, corresponding secretary, the class parent coordinators, and the program chairperson, who arranges for the three general meetings a year when we have speakers.

Is there a financial break given the president? No, but one thing that might be done is some kind of financial accommodation for the telephone. Even though I switched to unlimited service, my telephone bills went up quite a bit while I was president. That was something I found difficult, and I had to deal with that. It probably *can't* be remedied, though. If the president were reimbursed, other executive board members who do a lot of telephoning—the two vice-presidents and the financial secretary—should be too. The jobs are purely voluntary, and this is part of it.

The value of the nursery school experience for my child has been great. The school provides a wonderful learning situation. Then the fact that the parents are involved in the school adds a whole other dimension. This is something I used to try to communicate when I mobilized people, that the parents' input is as crucial as the teachers' and the director's. The parents have such a special point of view and so much love to give. It creates good feelings all around. The parents come in and work with the teachers. It becomes like a family. I think the children are the real beneficiaries of the kind of atmosphere where people come in and give of their time freely.

I remember feeling good about what I did for the school. After doing my part I always left with a good feeling. On the maintenance committee

A participating parent watches her son and his four-year-old classmates involved in water play—a nursery school staple!

there were some awful jobs we had to do. Even those I basically enjoyed. For example, in the basement are piles of paper that had been donated for art work. Teachers pull out the paper. Periodically Toni says, "We have to do something about the paper." It is the worst job to organize the gobs of paper, heavy, slow work. I'd call a few people in, and we would start moving the paper. The job was tedious but we were all working together for a common goal at our children's school, and there was a sense of community. I don't know how everyone else felt, but I always enjoyed it. It always seemed to me a happy atmosphere.

Sometimes at the co-op we had disagreements like a family too, but never profound ones. Christmas gifts were the subject at a volatile business meeting I recall. Traditionally the parents all chipped in and presented the teachers with cash or gift certificates. The teachers preferred this to getting a bunch of little gifts that they might not use. At this particular business meeting—the president before me told me it might be difficult—people became very worked up. They felt strongly on both sides, some wanted the group gift and some didn't. Finally we took a vote, and it was in favor of the group gift. A lot of tempers flared that night, but after discussion and debate we voted and the majority ruled.

Did I make friends at nursery school that are friends outside specifically co-op activities? I made one friend because my son and hers were friends in school. Our friendship was originally based on the children's friendliness. Through the co-op I also made many pleasant associations. With people I worked with on the executive board and with the new president also, I feel maybe closer than an acquaintance, a very pleasant association.

Arthur's participation in the co-op? I guess he was involved through me. He went to the first orientation meeting with me. Since I became chairperson of the maintenance committee and I had trouble getting people at various times, he was the first person I enlisted. So he did a lot of maintenance Benji's first year. He fixed several pieces of the yard equipment, he painted in the yard, he came to all the clean-up days. I used to beg him because I never thought anybody was going to show up. Then when I became president, he was very busy babysitting and taking care of the children for me. It just so happened that he quit his job about the time that I became president, and he started working from the house on his own. So he did happen to be home a lot and was available for me.

I was still breastfeeding the whole time I was president. With your second child it's different than with your first. If someone had asked me to volunteer actively in an organization when Benji was a baby, it would have seemed all wrong. When David came I had to do for my first too, so I found myself turning more outward.

For Carol, working with the director was a very exciting part of her job.

Toni was a revelation to me. She is such an active, interested person. Her interests go out in many directions. She's always thinking and doing. She was like a shot in the arm almost.

The school also has a summer program. The parents don't participate, but they set it up. They speak to the teachers, set salaries and tuition. Other children in the community can attend when there is room, but space is limited. It's all voted on in the last business meeting. The first year I was in the co-op, while I was chairing the maintenance committee, I sat at that business meeting, and Toni sat in back of me. They were asking for volunteers to run the summer program. Somebody raised her hand, a person who volunteered consistently. She was the treasurer on the executive board, a wonderful woman, one of those people who can't do enough. Then they said she needed an assistant. I sat there thinking I was very interested in the summer program and wanted to send Benji. But I had the same old familiar, "Gee, why get involved? I don't want to do it" thought process. I was almost sitting on my hand because I wanted to and didn't want to. All of a sudden I felt a little kick behind me. It was Toni, and I put my hand up! I kidded her about it later. I said, "Next business meeting I'm not sitting in front of you."

She is a dynamo and does a lot to motivate others. She is genuinely interested not only in the children but the parents. I can tell she likes to see the parents grow as much as the children. At first it was overwhelming being president and working with Toni: not knowing what I was doing and having her calling me with a million ideas and my writing furiously. But I came to admire and love her very much. She's an inspiration, I think, to all the women in the co-op.

The co-op was a well-established school years ago, but competition to get in has increased greatly while we have been there. When I first came for my interview in the late winter, I registered Benji for September with no problem. During the year I was president all of a sudden it took off, and it was filled up by November of that year for September of the next. Because of Toni, the school's not standing still. She's the impetus, because her mind keeps on going! She's the spearhead for ways to involve the school more in the community.

While I was president, Toni began to share with us her concern over the influence of television. At staff meetings the teachers remarked that they were finding a distinct change in the quality of children's play. With all the superhero influence, the children seemed less creative than before. They attributed a lot of it to the quality and amount of the children's television watching. There began a big consciousness-raising campaign. We had a general meeting at which Toni spoke. That led to the formation of the television committee. Toni brought a lot of articles to our attention. Her latest idea is to see if we can play an activist role in Action for Children's Television.[1]

I was always leary of television and the commercialism. Benji was never the kind of child who sits in front of the television for hours and hours. But sometimes in the morning he ended up watching program after program. It hypnotized him. When he was younger, I watched what he watched and discussed what we were seeing—the fact, for instance, that a

[1]Founded in 1968 in Newton, Massachusetts, and now based in Boston, Action for Children's Television (ACT) is a national citizens group that has had remarkable influence in its campaigns to upgrade children's programming. It works at both ends, pressuring the broadcasters to eliminate harmful advertising and increase quality shows, and encouraging families to regulate and limit their television watching. Concerned local groups such as parent-teacher associations join ACT's efforts.

commercial was selling a product. I did! I actually sat and watched them. I was an old television addict. I was brought up on television, my whole family was. So I could sit and watch the cartoons with him, though it wasn't easy! I thought it was important that I did. But the focus on the issue at the co-op spurred me on. I used that general meeting we had as a springboard to sit down and discuss with Benji that it was a health issue, that television would adversely affect his health. I discussed the need to limit it and think about what we watch. He is a sophisticated and less frequent viewer at this point.

An extension during my time as president was a program Toni set up between the co-op and Sunharbor Manor, a nursing home. Toni and co-op teachers and parents work side by side with staff members of the nursing home. The nursery school children visit weekly, and there are group songs and games to activity records. Then for arts and crafts and snack time, the children are paired with the residents to encourage the development of close individual relationships. This was my first taste of community work. I enjoyed immensely working with the very old and very young. This is how co-op activity leads parents into work. Two of us drove children over Thursday mornings. It put a fire in the other woman who now intends to go back to school in this area. She might never have become involved in community work otherwise. Next year the co-op will have a Sunharbor committee.

There was a controversy over junk foods and sugary snacks at the school before, during, and after my time as president. Parents were asked to refrain from bringing in sugary snacks on participation days to supplement the juice and crackers supplied by the co-op and instead encouraged to bring fruit, raw vegetables, cheese, or ethnic dishes. The co-op used that as a taking-off point in an effort to extend good nutrition to the homes. A committee was formed that communicated regularly with the parents. They put out fliers and had a regular space in the newsletter for recipes. There was quite an emphasis last year.

I asked Carol to characterize Benji and tell what she credits to his nursery school experience.

Benji is sensitive. He's imaginative and creative. He enjoys being alone, as well as playing with other children. He seems to occupy his time well. Often his friends' parents tell me that their children are always asking to see their playmates, and "What are we going to do?" Once or twice in his whole life Benji has told me he has nothing to do. He's independent in that way. He also seems to excel in all different activities. He's athletic, musical, likes to read and to draw. He is well rounded. I think what he got from

146

nursery school was learning to live with others, the give and take, relating, sharing the attention, physical space, and material things with other children.

His brother was just born when he started school. We all had a tough transition. I felt guilty about having the second baby. When my husband took Benji out, I felt relieved that Benji would finally get to go out and that I could then give all my love to the baby, and then I felt guilty about feeling relieved. For him of course it was a big adjustment. He was very attached to me. I always spent a lot of time with him, and he was very jealous. So he had more problems the first year of school than the second.

Also Benji went in the morning the first year, in the afternoon the second. He never liked to bound out of bed and rush right to school. He liked to be around the house in the morning and play. I sensed that was one of the difficulties. But I was afraid he would be too tired in the afternoon. Although they do have an afternoon program for the threes, it was a mixed group for older threes and fours without previous school experience. But in his case it might have worked better. By the next year I was sure the afternoon program would be better for him. The second year he enjoyed nursery school a lot more.

The day in the classroom? I participated when Benji was in the threes and in the fours. It was a challenging day. In the threes class he was so possessive it made me unsure of my situation and role. How could I help the teacher? Benji would be clinging and needing me almost as much as at home. I felt torn that I wasn't fulfilling my responsibility to the class. The fours are friendlier, which caused a new problem. Benji was very conscious of their friendly overtures. At the beginning of the year if a child said, "See what I built?" or "Tie my shoe," Benji was there to hold my hand, sit on my lap, stand around, and keep me to himself. If other children came to hear a story, I was conscious Benji didn't like it much. That was true right up until the spring.

Yet I *liked* being there even though I didn't always have a great time. It was never a bore. I enjoyed seeing Benji in the class. Although I know it wasn't a true picture of him because he was very different when I was there from when I wasn't. It is a special day for the child. That is what the staff tell the parents, that they are there to help out when they can and help the teachers as much as they can, but first and foremost it is a treat, a special day for your child because you come in. It's an emotional day for the child, too. It was never a completely natural kind of thing, but by the end of the year you feel less tension, you know your place and can have more fun. When I was president, new people called and said, "What am I supposed to do? Help the teacher?" I told them, "Primarily you are there for your child. It takes a while to condition yourself, and then you'll look forward to it."

147

I admired this year's teacher greatly for her patience and tolerance. In a conflict she had a certain way of addressing children. I found myself adopting the expressions at home. If kids were fighting in the playground, she would walk over and say, "No rough stuff, boys." Or "It's time now to do such-and-such," if they were doing something they shouldn't. I did emulate her in some ways.

I can't say the co-op is ideal because it's human beings with human shortcomings. But I can't think of anything that I would like to see that isn't being done. The parents' participation is something you really can't put your finger on. It's an intangible extra that enriches it.

Toni Liebman's Commentary

Toni Liebman is a brisk, small, bright-eyed woman of forty-six, with a cap of black hair, sturdy shoes, and a touch of makeup. A graduate of Wellesley College, she says nursery school must be in her blood because her mother was a nursery school teacher before she was born. My most lasting impression of her is orchestrating the calm and incredibly swift 11:45 A.M. dismissal. All the children know their car-pool numbers, from one to twelve. When a number is posted, four or five children break away from the others, gather in a group, and proceed to the bus or car. The way Toni looks on with sheer maternal pleasure you'd think it was a Brownie fly-up, or her own children's first time at nursery school.

The North Shore of Long Island is basically an affluent area, although in every community there is a mixture of both extremes. Up the road is a shopping center of the most chic of American and European boutiques—people call it "the Miracle Mile." Roslyn is a beautiful old historic town, some of which has been preserved, some of which is being changed in the name of progress. Here we are in a middle-class area, mostly upper-middle class, and many one-income families. We draw from Manhasset, Roslyn, Port Washington, also from north and south of here from areas that are not so affluent, such as Albertson and Glen Head. From here east gets more rural, and we draw from there too, Old Westbury, Brookville, and Oyster Bay.

There are a lot of other nursery schools in the area. There are commercial schools that I think of as primarily businesses, but I'm sure you could find good teachers and good classes. However, their primary motivation is profit. Then there are the large day schools that have children from nursery or kindergarten up through eighth grade. Finally we have temple and church schools, which are nonprofit as we are. Although we are located in a church, our autonomy is protected by our bylaws, and our own members form the board of directors. They are not necessarily church members. The minister is on the board of directors, but he would only come to a meeting if there were a substantial problem.

The school resulted from a marriage of two schools. The one my children attended was the Roslyn Nursery School, begun in 1951, which operated in the Methodist church for many years. It merged seven years ago with Trinity Day School, which was located in and run by this church. It was nonsectarian even though the church ran it, but it was not a co-op. We took this step at a time when we thought that the schools were going to have a problem. Birthrate was down, enrollment was down, and we thought that one fewer school in the community would be a good idea. But the population of young children in our area has recently seen an upward swing. We have been filled since November for next year. That creates other problems, but it is better than not having enough children.

Our enrollment for morning and afternoon sessions totals 125 children. In the morning we have a three-day, three-year-old group; two five-day, three-year-old groups; a five-day group of fours; and the kindergarten that stays till two o'clock four days a week and 11:30 on Wednesdays. In the afternoon, we have a three-day program for older threes and fours, and two five-day groups of four-year-olds. Each class has two full-time teachers. The ratio of staff to children is one to six or eight three-year-olds and one to eight or nine four-year-olds.

Somebody asked me, "To what do you attribute the fine reputation of the school?" I really think it's because we do what's best for the children even if it isn't always easiest for the parents. I was accused once of being too child-oriented, and I think that's fine. We *are* running a nursery school!

For example, at the beginning of the year when we have orientation, we insist that parents be around. The children have a chance to adjust to a small group, half the class, with both teachers, and the parents must stay in the building. Occasionally there are parents who do not want to hang around. We feel it's important for the child at the threshold of twelve years of schooling to make a really solid adjustment. It pays for the parent to stay the first week or two—both child *and* parent feel reassured! Some nurseries take a child and say, "Don't worry. He will stop crying as soon as you leave." He might, but at what price?

The idea is not just to stop crying but to have a good, comfortable feeling. So after the first couple of days, the whole group comes for two hours for a full week before beginning the regular schedule of two and three-quarters hours. Some of the three-year-olds' parents have to stay through the week. The three-day children have the hardest time because they miss the continuity, they're in and they're out every other day.

Jon takes time out from playground activities for a word with Toni Liebman.

Usually the parents are in a room across the hall. The child can go back and forth and say, "Hi," to get that feeling of security. By the end of the week most of the parents are gone. Chances are that if children have been left with babysitters they have learned that parents leave and parents come back. In the last several years we have had fewer and fewer children who have not been enrolled in some type of program *before* ours. Much to my dismay!

How does the school make a go financially?

It's surely not a moneymaker. The bulk of our expenses, over 90 percent, are involved in salaries, substitute salaries, social security, and unemployment taxes—in a word, staff. The next largest expense is the contribution to the church, which is about 6 percent of the yearly budget. The rest is peanuts. In the least essential areas we cut corners. We have our own parents do a lot of the maintenance.

Nursery school teachers' salaries are pretty bad. We exchange information with other co-ops on the Island. At some the salaries are even worse than ours. The school tries to give us bonuses when possible as it did this year.

We figure the salary per session. For example, some teachers work three mornings and three afternoons, or six sessions. Some work only five mornings, five sessions. A more experienced teacher earns a higher salary per session. Then you multiply. So if a person works at $950 a session, full time, that amounts to $9,500. That's a person with a master's and experience. She gets no extra financial benefits—zilch. We've looked into benefits, and the cost would be prohibitive. Fortunately most of our teachers are covered under their husbands' benefit plans.

There has been a lot of stability in the staff. This is my fourteenth year. There are five other people who have worked with me since then; a few more who have worked for seven years, or since we merged; and a new one here or there. The stability is nice, but it's also beneficial to have someone new every now and again. It changes the chemistry.

Every time we raise the tuition I worry that we're going to price ourselves out of the market that I would hate to lose—those families who just manage to pay tuition. To raise money, we have a fair in December with gifts to buy, food, and games; we publish a phone book of all co-op members for which we sell ads; we offer a children's art workshop in the spring; and we hold a raffle of art objects, dinners, theater tickets, a night in the city, you name it, with the drawing at the last-day picnic. Together these activities bring in a few thousand dollars. Most of the funds raised go for partial scholarships, where the family may pay $50 a year, or a third or a half of tuition. Often these families are referred to us through a social worker. We have parents who divorce in the middle of the year and can't pay the rest of the tuition. We have never expelled a child for nonpayment, if there was a valid reason. We had a woman who came into the office the other day who lives on $4,000 a year, can you believe it? Her husband walked out the day the baby was born. She refuses to go on public assistance, so she is working part time. We'll give her child a full scholarship.

The scholarship committee is comprised of myself, the president, the financial secretary, and membership chairman. We do not discuss names just situations. We don't require W2 forms. When we finally decide on who receives a scholarship, only the financial secretary and I know the family's identity.

The cooperative idea gives the school a distinctive coloration. It is not enough that parents like the idea in theory, explained Toni, they must give of themselves to carry it out.

Before any family is admitted I sit with them and tell them why a co-op is different from other schools. It's important that they understand what's expected of them and what our educational philosophy is, because the school is not for everybody. There are times when I'd like to have certain families self-select out—those that I sense come only because they hear it is a good school, not because they honestly want to be involved. I explain to prospective parents when they come here, that they are going to have to participate once a month, either the mother or the father or occasionally a grandparent or another relative. That is part of the responsibility. This is not a school where you send a child and that's it. You have to participate, drive on trips, and serve on a committee. Some are very active, some less active. Everybody is given the opportunity to choose a committee and is assigned to work on one. The core of workers includes the executive board of eleven officers plus committee heads, all of which comprise the governing board. The board meets once a month in a member's house, and we usually get a turnout of twenty or twenty-five, out of about thirty-five.

An essential parent committee is maintenance. Although the school building is taken care of by the church, the parents maintain the swings and the large climbing equipment in the yard, and the equipment in the basement. I do a lot of it myself too. It's so much easier, and I happen to be handy with tools. I am the only child of a very handy father and I learned to do a little of everything from him. The problem is that I often don't have time, but if something is loose downstairs, if a rung on a climber has to be replaced or a tricycle part tightened or oiled, I keep a cache of tools and nuts and bolts to do it. Other jobs may require several parents working together.

In addition to maintenance, parents serve on various other committees important to the life of the school. The purchasing committee does our shopping: juice, crackers, cleaning supplies, and odds and ends like animal food and shavings for their cages. The hospitality committee works at every school meeting or function. The health committee does amblyopia testing and arranges speech and hearing screening. The library committee takes care of cataloging and mending books for the children's library, as well as the books and materials for the parents' and staff library. Our newsletter committee publishes three times yearly. The nutrition committee has researched and found out which snack foods we should or shouldn't buy. I can no longer simply telephone a wholesaler like Nabisco and ask for cookies because we have become cautious consumers. No more doughnut holes, no additives or preservatives, no more junk food. We encourage parents to bring in food they make with their children.

Regarding parent participation, the important fact to remember is that there has to be a demarcation between the staff's function and the parents' function. Some people join the co-op and think, "Oh good, I can run the school. I can tell my child's teacher what to do." That's not so. When co-ops got going in the early 1920s,[2] the idea was, for economy's sake, to have the parents assume the teaching role. What has developed, and certainly is the case in our school, is a very professional organization but with the parents still involved.

There are co-ops on the Island that have done away with parent participation. I think that's a mistake. To me, parent participation is one of the joys of the program. We have as much to offer the parents as the children. Parent education is very important, now more than ever. We know what good early childhood education is supposed to be, and it's being bastardized. There are books like one entitled *Kindergarten Is Too Late*[3] that frighten parents into thinking if their children don't master many skills in the first five years, it's all over. There are some educators who would cram children with facts and information. The kids are likely to come out like computers, instead of sensitive, caring, well-rounded human beings.

So our job in terms of parent education is bigger than ever. It's not only right, it's imperative that children learn through play. We see such an anxiety level among parents today. We try to get them to relax a little and enjoy their children and not worry so much about what they're learning all the time. They're learning lots, but it doesn't have to be squares, triangles, hexagonals, 2×2 is 4, and ABCDEFG. Parents are surprised when we have discussions about television and I suggest that *Sesame Street* is not education's be all and end all. When children verbalize all the stuff they have memorized by rote, we're not impressed.

A mother asked me to help her decide between the public kindergarten and one of the private commercial schools that promises to teach your child to read at an early age. It turns out that this bright little boy has taught himself to read. But as I talked with the mother, I found out that her son is not socially or physically very mature. The father is a physician and very academically oriented. They keep reinforcing this area and neglecting the others. Young children want their parents' approval, and are smart enough to know how to get it!

[2]The first cooperative nursery school was opened in 1916 by twelve faculty wives at the University of Chicago. Six more came in the 1920s: in Cambridge, Massachusetts; at Smith College; in Schenectedy, New York; at the University of California at Los Angeles; and two in Berkeley, California. See Katharine Whiteside Taylor, *Parents and Children Learn Together*, 3d ed. (New York: Teachers College Press, 1981), p. 322.

[3]Masaru Ibuka (New York: Simon & Schuster, 1980).

So *many* of the children coming in now have had a formal group experience before. Again, I patently disapprove. The parents think this is wonderful, that they're preparing them for nursery school. And we are finding to the contrary that more and more the children are *less secure*, rather than better prepared. In some three-year-old groups if we had sixteen laps it wouldn't be enough! Children need a great deal of nurturing, and many are not receiving it.

In what might be called "self-defense," we started the Two's Company program. As it happens this year, the children who started in the second group can't even enter the nursery school in the fall, because the co-op is filled, so it is not meant just as a feeder. Parents and children two-and-a-half or older attend once a week for a two-hour session. The value of the twos' program is a bit of group experience for the children without a forced separation from their parents. I love the parent discussion part of it for those who *can* separate for the second hour, beginning six weeks into the first session. Parents have always needed this, but they need it *more* now—partly because of their anxiety and frenzy about raising their children, partly because there are so many experts telling them what to do, and partly because families, at least in this particular affluent suburban area, are very success-oriented. So much pressure descends on the parents, and they don't have the extended family around them to give them the emotional and physical backup. And since there are many smaller, even one-child families, the focus is often intensively on that child.

Especially nowadays, people like the sense of belonging to something. The friends that my husband and I made and have kept for eighteen or twenty years now—my daughter is twenty-two and she came to the Roslyn nursery when she was three—are people whom we met in the co-op. You get to know people a lot better if you work with them than if you meet at a party where, unless you are an unusual person, you just scratch the surface. In the co-op you work elbow to elbow with people and learn whom you can or cannot depend on; you share a common interest and concern because you have little children. I see it happen year after year. People develop very meaningful friendships. So aside from the children benefiting, the parents benefit as well.

Also when I look at the list that comes out each year of the active PTA members and members of the Roslyn school and library boards, they are always loaded with former parents from the co-op. Now that we are drawing heavily from Port Washington as well as from other neighboring communities, I see it happening elsewhere too. The co-op is like a grooming ground for people who remain involved.

Not everybody is thrilled by monthly participation, but it *is* the lifeblood of the co-op. Sometimes we have a mother who is going back to work who says, "Why must I come?" I answer it wouldn't be fair for a child if his or her parent were a nonparticipator. If we allowed that parent not to participate, and that child saw every other parent participating except his or hers, it would be very *sad* for that child. The day the parent comes is special. It's the day the child can be first to the basement or to the yard, gets to set the tables and fix the snacks, and feels very important. Why it's a day that child shouts, "Here's my Mommy [Daddy, Granny], and here am I!"

FAMILY DAY CARE

Here is the enlightened skillful teacher strolling in the street, agog with interest in whom he meets, engaging in conversation. An interesting person at the least, so that people from the houses, the native inhabitants, are disposed to come out and meet him, exchange greetings and ideas with him. Sometimes with him and often without him, they feel free to think and do things . . . outside in the world. A street named Variation.

Sylvia Ashton-Warner, *Spearpoint*

Irene Kricorian, family day care provider, lives in a two-story frame house in Watertown, Massachusetts, just off the main trolley run to Cambridge. Watertown is an old and "in-lying" suburb of Boston. It has the largest concentration of Armenian population of any city or town in the United States. Around the corner from the Kricorian's lie Armenian groceries, butcher shops, bakeries, radio shops, tailors, and carpet dealers, where the second language of commerce and the writing on many products are Armenian. But Watertown also has a new element of academic and professional families, a population that has fanned out from Boston and Cambridge as rents and real estate there skyrocketed during the last decade.

Irene's husband's family has lived in Watertown for three generations. Eddie and Irene raised both their daughters, now seventeen and nineteen, here, and a neighborhood Armenian church has been a religious and social center for much of their lives. Irene, however, is Armenian by marriage, not blood. Her rosy cheeks, widespread brown eyes, and freckled face bring to mind a French country lass, and she is, she explains, a Quebecoise, whose parents came to the United States from French Canada. One of seventeen children, she was brought up in a state-operated orphanage in Dover, New Hampshire. "Because of my training, I like method," she said. "I order and I plan, but I believe in showing a lot of love and fostering real independence, which wasn't the orphanage's way."

The Kricorians live comfortably and within their means, and in money matters feel that they are doing well. Eddie is the head of the meat department of the Broadway supermarket that is just off the Harvard campus and heavily patronized by the university community. Since their daughters were tots, Irene has been a family day care provider—for many years she thought of it as babysitting. Their elder daughter now attends Dartmouth College on partial scholarship, the younger is still at home. Living in the house as well are Eddie's mother and younger brother, a lead guitarist for a rock band.

Most children Irene cares for come from the near vicinity, though they often move out of Watertown to the further suburbs. I met two families who use Irene's place very differently. For Richard and Sue Rasala of Newton Corner, Irene's has been a main entrée of the preschool lives of their daughters Kathy, six, and April, four, and even partly determined where they moved when they bought a larger house just before April was born. Sue, a kindergarten teacher in a Newton school, sews, makes jewelry and stained glass, and likes to see her creative work and her children's displayed in their home. Richard, who looks the cerebral abstract thinker that he is, teaches computer mathematics at a university, does some consulting, and is writing a textbook using his home terminal.

The Holdens have sent their son Andrew to Irene's on a more part-time basis, first as a dessert course and now so that Jane Holden can return to work twenty hours a week. Jane is a horticulturist employed by the State of Massachusetts. She works in an experimental agricultural station on breeding disease-resistant vegetables. Dick Holden is a camera man whose specialty is flower gardens. He works on a free lance basis, often for public television, and *Crockett's Victory Garden* was, he says, the credit that put him "on the map." Tow-headed Andrew is three. The Holdens have bought and beautifully restored a late-nineteenth century house around the block from the Kricorians.

Before talking with the Rasalas and the Holdens, I visited Irene at her home. As I entered the front door, the rhyme of "Polly Wants a Cracker" issued up from the floorboards, led by an authoritative woman's voice and pronounced in a Boston accent. The tiny elderly woman who met me at the door identified herself as Auntie. She had her iron gray hair in a bun and wore scuffs with heavy stockings. Like a fairy tale helper, she bobbed me on to those whom I was "destined" to see: Mrs. Kricorian and her charges.

The basement center of activities was furnished like the best nursery school, but on a smaller scale: big modular couch, two record players, wall-to-wall red carpeting, play kitchen equipment, table and chairs to seat everybody, a half-size refrigerator, an upholstered rocker. On the wall were pussy willow branches and a big mural with children's hands in hues of blue and purple. Fluorescent light came from ceiling panels, natural light through a rim of high windows. One big cabinet, piled with games, art supplies, and toy sets, lay open; several others were closed. Irene was dressed in suburban preppy clothes with housewife's slippers. She had on a navy blue turtleneck, dark blue crew-necked sweater with patterned yoke, and straight wool skirt. On carpet squares with her in the circle sat her "kids." I counted five, both boys and girls, and read from a poster that their ages ranged from two to five.

They played "Ring Around the Rosy" with a different twist. Lily didn't want her turn at the game so Irene gave her a big hug and Paul patted her. "One potato, two potatos," decided turns for the game after that, a hiding game with plastic fishes.

Fishy fishy in the brook,
Papa catch him on a hook;
Mommy cook him in a pan;
Georgie eat him like a man.

Everybody got two turns guessing. When a child guessed right, Auntie went into a trill of laughter or a wreath of smiles, and hugged. She hid the fish too. Auntie guessed each time: How? "Because April was very QUIET!" she revealed.

They played a repetition word game about "an egg, an egg, a——egg." "I think we're into sillies," Irene said when somebody led with a "television egg," and she steered them to some "real" eggs for a while. "What kind of egg stays the same in the shell?" "A hardboiled egg." Each child joined in the clapping, the older ones in the chanting. "An egg, an egg, a rotten egg . . . a real . . . a chocolate . . . a scrambled egg." "An Easter egg, a dinosaur egg," added Irene, raising her arms. Then came the sillies—a buffalo egg (some thought it was and some it wasn't).

For snack the children watched Irene craft wagons of carrot penny wheels on celery chassis, with toothpick axles. Each child put on either peanut butter or cream cheese, then nuts or raisins, using a plastic knife or a finger. One child made an ant on a log instead of the car. The younger children turned theirs around wondrously. Paul wanted another after breaking his willfully. "You know you are the only troublemaker in the whole group!" scolded Auntie gently. Irene got Paul to admit that the celery car was not the problem when she leaned him against her. "Paul, don't say that—I'd be really sad." Each child tried to give Paul something to stop his crying, but, "No giving me stuff!" Then Irene directed the children quietly to collect Lily's hat, mittens, and snowsuit, and get their own coats: they were going outdoors.

Each shared something with Irene before going out, touching base with her as an individual and grappling with Paul's bad mood. The children referred to the book *Alexander and the Terrible, Horrible, No Good, Very Bad Day,* by Judith Viorst.[1] In the story, Alexander is having a very bad day; nothing seems to go right. His mother forgets to put dessert in his school lunch, the cat wants to sleep with someone else, and so forth. Alexander thinks that things might be better in Australia and threatens to go there whenever things get bad. "Paul wants to go to Australia," and "Alexander didn't find it any better," two say. "When one of the kids is having one of 'those days,' we refer to it as 'an Australia day' or 'an Alexander day;'" explained Irene. She frowned at Paul's exit line, so dispairing and different in key from the words in flight of the other children—"I wish I were dead."

During the play time when Auntie watched the children outside, and they started to dig in the thawing March soil, Paul came back in, looking a little red-eyed and feeling tender. With Irene he talked about a children's book with a car crash of a red-and-silver motorcycle. They went on about

---

[1] New York: Atheneum, 1974.

boo-hoos on the forehead, scratches from rosebushes, falls from bikes, then how to ride a bike *safely*. Paul was most interested in being hurt and getting safe. As he chatted with Irene, his intelligent face cleared of its troubled look and became bright and trusting.

Paul helped Irene prepare the salad for lunch. He told me all the vegetables he could cut, then settled in, self-forgettingly, to slice his cucumber. One senses a child like Paul has a "corrective" emotional experience with Irene, participating in an extended family life that rarely exists at home.

Irene Kricorian's Commentary

I firmly believe that family day care is the best alternative to mother care. I feel that it is learning in a home environment, plus when a person is truly committed to *family* day care, there are other benefits as well.

We use the home, and we also use Auntie, my mother-in-law upstairs, and "Uncle Leo," Eddie's brother. Children have all these people who care about them, and to care about. Families nowadays are so isolated. One little family without the grandparents, without aunts and uncles nearby. Kids miss out on the generational type of living that explains how a child becomes someone big.

One day Grandma "blacked out," and the ambulance had to come and take her to the hospital. The children were so concerned. As it happened, she was released the same day. When she came home, the children all gathered around her to say they were happy she was okay. They brought her little trinkets—flowers, pine cones, and buttons—and promised her they would be very quiet in the yard so that she could rest. Each day after that for several weeks they asked for her and did little errands for her. How could they have had this kind of sharing-caring experience in a day care center?

When my husband was in the hospital, the children were as concerned as they would be for a member of their own family. They called him at the hospital, made him get-well cards, and sent them to him. Their parents would drive me to the hospital in the evening, and the children felt that they were helping Eddie and me. It gave them a real sense of helpfulness and caring. I think that this is one part of life that many kids miss out on—this nurturing of one another.

When Rebecca's grandfather died, we all baked an apple pie for her family to share after the funeral. Then the parents donated some money to purchase a book for the children's department at the library. The librarian explained that this was a special book from Rebecca's friends to the library in memory of her grandfather. She was so proud, and the day care children had another great experience of sharing and caring.

"Auntie" comes twice a week. Auntie is older, and her whole approach with children is different from mine. Auntie's first language is Armenian. In Lebanon years ago, Auntie was a governess. Then she came to America and did other work. When her husband died, Auntie was all alone: she has no children or family. These children have adopted her. It gives her a whole other reason for living. And the children invite her for birthday parties. It is good for everybody—for her, for the children, and also for me. Auntie has been helping me now for two-and-a-half years.

She is my mother-in-law's friend. After her husband died, I called her one day and asked, "Would you like to help me a couple of days per week?" "Well I don't know if I can do it. I haven't done it for years." I said, "You won't be alone. I will be here. It will help me, and it will be good for the kids and for you."

I pay Auntie the minimum wage and generally have her two mornings a week. Those are the times when I plan really messy activities like cooking. We usually cook on Friday mornings. That is a time when even with only five, you truly need another adult. With that person it goes smoother. Without help it is havoc, the kids aren't learning, and it is unpleasant for everybody.

Irene belongs to the Massachusetts Association of Family Day Care Providers (MAFDCP), a non-profit organization of independent providers whose goals are (1) to offer education and training for family day care providers; (2) to ease the isolation of providers; (3) to increase visibility and publicity for family day care; (4) to provide a liaison between the state Office for Children and family day care providers. All work done for the association is strictly on a volunteer basis. She loves the association and the work.

It's rare for a family day care provider to have an adjunct person, but it happens more and more now. It eases the isolation, which is the basic problem in family day care. Many women keep themselves so boxed in they get frustrated and bored. It's a terrible thing, that isolation. Because I am education chairperson for the Massachusetts Family Day Care Providers Association, the issue is my concern. I emphasize strongly that no woman needs to keep the children locked into her home. I encourage providers to go to the libraries, which have story hours and toddler drop-ins; to use the neighborhood parks. Don't always go to the same one. Every town has three or four parks; you can move about. On a pretty day take a little *longer* walk. Visiting the fire station is always exciting. The kids can learn from anything that you do.

A lot of providers feel that they can't move about with six children, that it is too many to handle. That was the reason I hired an assistant, to give me more mobility with the older children. When Lily was younger, Auntie would come and take care of Lily and another little child under a year old who was part time, because I didn't feel like taking the little ones along with the older ones. It would have kept me from spending the time that I ought with the children whose understanding was greater. People can do that, they can get an assistant. On my license I have two, Auntie and my husband. Almost any provider can have an approved assistant—their husbands almost automatically, then a mother-in-law or a neighbor who can be called in for field trips. It allows that much more freedom.

You'll find that many day care providers have husbands who work shifts different from the nine-to-five. My husband, Eddie, is off on Tuesdays or Wednesdays. When he is home, the whole complexion of the day changes. We go on field trips, and he is very much a part of it. The children are attached to me, but they like a male influence. With Eddie they do different things than with me. Eddie acts altogether differently with them than I do. He gets them more excited. He allows them to work themselves into a peak. He runs across the fields with them and does very active things. He is another person they are able to relate to and enjoy. Because Eddie is technically on my license as an approved assistant, if he wants to take the kids to the car wash, and if I have a baby here and can't go, then he can take them, *legally*. Eddie has always been very much involved.

I take the children to museums and zoos and city sights, but always with my husband. Even if we go with only the four older ones, I want two adults there. Also, Eddie usually drives us in, unless the bus and subway are part of the treat. Transportation is always a problem. Until recently on our group liability insurance the children were not covered while they were in our car. Now they are covered for medical advances; this step represents a great gain for the Massachusetts Association. A lot of providers will not take their day care children anywhere. There are other day care providers who don't have *any* insurance and still take the kids out all the time. A lot of providers are not aware; others are aware and don't care. Day care exists at all levels.

We use both the first floor and the basement of our home for child care. Upstairs we cook and eat lunch, and the children take their naps in a bedroom off the kitchen. According to state law, when they sleep, they have to be where I can see them. There are so many rules and regulations that many people don't know or ignore. But you will find that a good family day care person will enforce them herself. The Office for Children cannot

Storytime is special when Eddie is home to read to the children. The older children cluster around him on the floor, while Auntie and Irene hold the younger ones.

possibly get around to check. I have not seen a person from the OFC but twice in fifteen years. We have now in the state over 4,000 licensed family day care homes and about three times as many unlicensed. The Office for Children works mainly to register the unregistered people and renew licenses of registered providers. They don't investigate unless a parent calls in with a grievance.

Parents trying to judge a particular day care situation should be sure it is registered and has a good nutritional program. They should also ask about the provider's liability insurance. For example, less than a fifth of the Massachusetts registered providers, but all the MAFDCP members, are covered.

As a member of the association, our insurance comes through a group plan. It covers if a child is injured and if a parent accuses the provider of neglect or abuse, for example. I have not had a chance to use it even though my parents could have given me occasion once when April's older sister Kathy was two. She was leaving, it was after hours, and I was in a hurry to go to a meeting. The father walked in, and I told him, "I'm in a rush, I don't have time to talk." I ducked into the bathroom to take a shower, and he left.

All of a sudden I heard a horrendous scream. I came out of the shower and put on a bathrobe and ran outdoors. And there was Kathy! It was her wagon that tips very quickly—not my wagon—and he was running with it, and it tipped. He had it waiting outside. He put her in, and was going to pull her over to the car. Kathy lay across the concrete walk, and her two front teeth were ground up to the roots. She was a bloody mess.

The Rasalas could have asked me to cover the accident under my insurance, and I did offer. But he analyzed and said, "It was after hours and my fault. It merely happened on your property." So they didn't do it. That was the only time I have had possible cause to use the insurance. Kathy's permanent teeth still haven't come in, and she's six! But they'll be coming in soon. It was an ordeal. I have not used my liability insurance, but other providers have.

Irene Kricorian is licensed to take children any age, even a newborn, and she insists that a range of ages, family-like, is the best way.

I have had youngsters as young as a week old. One of my children, Loren, came when he was seven weeks old, and he is almost five and is still with me. He comes at one o'clock now. This is like his home, because he has come over since he was seven weeks. He has so integrated into our family that we thought he might need a little time to adjust before going off to school. He attends nursery school from nine to 12:30 and then comes here afterwards.

It was difficult for Loren not to be here. He would be upset and cry and really act up with me: Why did I take the kids on a field trip when he wasn't here? Why didn't I wait? That was like what my daughter Susan used to say, not wanting to miss out: "Don't you go anywhere with the kids until I get home!" Their reactions were almost identical. So I changed two of the field trips to the afternoon, in order to include Loren who was taking it so hard. I didn't want him not to like nursery school because he was going to miss out on what the other children at Irene's were doing.

I think that having children of different ages in the group makes for a very good experience in family day care. Some of the positive aspects are learning to be considerate of others, having models, and feeling competent as a bigger kid. With a mixed group, the older children are protective of the younger ones, remind them of the rules, and help them with simple projects. Here at my home, they also help one another understand how to deal with my mother-in-law, who has a heart condition. They are so sweet to her! She benefits from their presence as much as they do from hers. The older ones have to "watch out" for the babies, not to knock them down while running and to hug them gently.

The children as young as two and a half help by holding the bottle for the babies, getting diapers, and entertaining the little ones. Some of the children come from homes where they are the only child or they have a much older sibling. Family day care gives them an opportunity to be part of a larger, extended family. They can learn from the older children. They can teach the younger ones—and they so enjoy the role of teacher!

I like the difference in ages because I don't like the idea of a group of "twins." All doing the same things at the same age would make caregiving more difficult. At each age something different is happening, and I can't think of any age I don't enjoy. Even the "terrible twos." I certainly don't find them terrible when they're in my little group. With most children at this stage, parents are in a spot. They don't know what the child can do, and they are afraid to let them try too much. They *contain* the child and "overcontrol" them. Which is exactly what the child is fighting. Then you see the pushing and pulling. If you are not on the children's necks all the time, they don't get pent up. Here they are in a safe place where they really can't do much harm. They're not boxed in socially either.

Although I'm licensed for six children, I like to keep it at five. I like that one opening, that one space available should an emergency arise or should an older brother or sister of any of these children need care for the day. If I were desperate for the income, I could easily fill that space, but I am most comfortable limiting the number to five. When I *have* that one extra charge, it stretches me a bit too far. Now I have six, but one, Andrew, comes in the morning, and Loren is here only afternoons so it balances out to five.

I had only three children that I thought would do better in another situation. One needed a group even smaller than family day care, a one-to-one, and I just could not give it to him. I told the parents I would try for two weeks and then saw I could not keep up that level of interaction with him and give care to the others. The other two that I took on trial were two little girls, eighteen months and two-and-a-half years, who were constant whiners. I couldn't take it! It was not worth it to me to listen to that, and there was no way I was going to change them. Children learn very young what works and doesn't work. Apparently the whining with the mother worked. My head at the end of the day! I would rather have a baby outright crying than a child whining at me all day. I told the parent I couldn't continue with them, and she went berserk. She cried and fussed and boo-hoo-hooed, and what was she going to do. I thought to myself, "I know how these kids get it." I could see easily that the way the mother dealt with things was how the children were going to deal.

Those are three cases in fifteen years. I am *careful* in interviews. If I don't have the feeling it will be a good relationship with the parents, I say I don't have an opening right now, or that I have the opening but would like to keep it that way for a while. At the beginning I felt that I couldn't say no to anyone. That was really crazy on my part. Now I know this is a two-way street. You don't have to take every child that appears at your door. A lot of other providers have a difficult time with saying no.

This discussion brought Irene back to the subject of her professional organization. Activity in the organization clearly means a great deal to her. One senses it is the reason her interest in her job has not dipped. The association is a source of her continuing education, a platform for carrying out the changes in the field she wants, a cause of pride, a testing ground for the self, and an outlet for doing good. It is not important as a friendship set; Irene is too busy and has at this point no need to share frustrations with other providers.

The association helps members by giving monthly workshops. They are really catching on now. Three years ago there would be two or three of us at a workshop; the year after that, twenty. Now there will be ninety of us. The association is beginning to be important. We don't insist everybody conform to standards, the group is more for learning, for support, and for communication with the state authorities.

For example, we don't have a contract that we hand out to everybody. That is not the philosophy. Your contract should be whatever you are comfortable with. Some providers have horribly elaborate contracts. Others have no contracts, and they constantly run into difficulties. I'm in the middle. I do have a contract, but it is not rigid. It tells the parents what I need and want, I have not had any problems with my parents paying for holidays and vacations.

At the beginning of the year at the first education meeting we ask everyone to write down things they are interested in and needed help with. Discipline, taxes, and business are always on the list, contracts, and arts and crafts. We use that as a basis for organizing the workshops over the year. We have done other workshops on first aid and on being assertive— so many providers do not know how to make a statement of their needs to the parents.

We don't know how many day care providers continue beyond their children's preschool years. There is a huge turnover in family day care. I am unhappy with that aspect of it. I feel when you are constantly having new, inexperienced people problems increase. There is a tremendous amount to learn to be good.

I wish it were mandatory that a provider had to have at least six months' training. Women sometimes call and ask if they can come and train with me. They come every day and observe for about two weeks. After two weeks I tell them, "I'm going to go upstairs and you handle the children. If there's a problem I'm here." I would like to see women in every area of the state who would allow other women to come in and train for a month. We could give them ideas, tell them about the books we use, and let them learn that it's easy to put new ideas to work. Training would cut down on the turnover. Too many women work for a month and decide they can't take it. Training would eventually lead to better day care.

Family day care is unique. It is not like a nursery school where the children arrive at 8:45 A.M. and leave at 11:45 A.M. Neither is it like a regular at-home situation with just mommy. A family day care provider tries to blend both worlds. In the small group, with varied ages, learning happens in a very casual and relaxed way.

Of course it would be a very long day for the children to be left to their own amusement. I have tons of toys downstairs—Legos and bristle blocks, beads, paints, and clay. You name it, we've got it! But right now, after a New England winter, the kids are sick of every bit of that. It's up to me to introduce new games and things to do. And they want to be involved with *me*. They don't want me to be off somewhere else. A provider can NEVER forget that she is responsible for their safety and their well-being while they are in her care.

One feature of family day care that many parents find very helpful is that most providers have flexible hours. My first day care child arrives at 6:45 A.M. and the last child leaves at 5:30 P.M. There are days that my hours are even longer because a parent gets caught in traffic or tied up on the telephone at closing time, and so forth. I must say that most of the parents I work with try to keep to the hours agreed to in the contract. Here, too, I must add that I have been unusually fortunate; some providers have parents who are not as considerate.

Irene has been a provider so long that she takes for granted how her housekeeping and cooking routines mesh with occupying the children. She is more excited by the new projects that come through workshops she now attends or the preschool curriculum books she has begun to read. But to the children the key thing is being in Irene's home. She shed light on both the homely activities and the "enrichment" ones.

I can do my laundry when the children are here. They help me to put the whites here, the colors there, and towels there. Then they put it in the dryer. From the dryer I bring it into the playroom, and sit on the couch and fold. Before you know it one or two of them will wander over. And they'll help me to fold the towels and socks and other things into rather untidy piles.

We go outside, and they help me with the yard. We do a lot, especially the raking. My husband has a garden out there. They help with the planting and weeding and go out after the vegetables. Strawberries, forget it! I can never get a meal of them for my family, the kids eat them so rapidly. Every now and then I say, "Okay kids, let them stay for two or three days because Eddie needs them. Eddie wants some for supper." Then they'll try. It's hard with the berries so tempting.

When they cook, it is usually what they intend to eat for lunch. If it is anything like a cookie, they get to take one home for mommy, daddy, and a sister or brother—anybody's that's in the house. What we make we eat that day; we don't make a lot of anything. Last week we did a soup with the meat and bones. We make Armenian breadsticks and pastry. It's always different. That's what I have found the most helpful about the workshops, that you get simple, easy ideas that the children absorb as if they were sponges. Like with the little games. Changing just the little sequence of "Ring Around the Rosy"—forming the chain and then the circle and then the chain again—changes the whole complexion of the game for me and also for them. It's elementary, but unless you are made aware of it you stick to what you know. I can't make up a lot of things, but if I see it then I can use it. The new activities encourage the children to be exploring and to be thinking and changing, instead of in a rut. They can become so bored that they drive one another crazy.

Some providers are only in day care for a couple of years, until their child is old enough to go into nursery school or kindergarten. For a person like myself, this is my profession. I need to be constantly learning and changing and having new ideas. The little wagons of the celery with the carrot rounds is so simple, and the kids like it. Ideas like that come from each workshop.

We go to the library every Tuesday morning for story hour. It's about a half mile and a nice walk. I usually borrow eight or ten books per week, and the children have their favorites that seem to be here more than at the library. After the library we go to the park. Then we play and come home.

Although sometimes Eddie does drive everybody to the Museum of Science or the Children's Museum or the zoo, the idea is basically to use what is happening around us. Last week we went to see a puppet show at the mall (in the afternoon to include Loren).

This sounds like a long day together, but they take a rest every afternoon. That's a state law too. I explain that to the parents, because many of them will tell me that the child hasn't taken a nap for them in a year or so. I take out my trusty rules and regulations and say that according to the Office for Children, every child needs a resting time, a minimum of 45 minutes. According to "Irene's law," it's one hour. So if at the end of the hour they are awake, the children may get up. They come into the kitchen here where I have crayons, coloring books, puzzles, and other things they can do quietly at the table. When I am alone, I need to keep everybody on the same level until the baby is up, to comply with the state law. So the nappers stay in the kitchen.

During the naps, after lunch, I asked Irene about Paul, the five-year-old who seemed so angry. Her answer is interesting because it shows the detachment yet understanding of a caregiver who has a long perspective on this child and on many children.

I've noticed for the last few days Paul has been uptight, touchy, always on the verge of tears. He is extremely sensitive but not usually like this. If anybody gets hurt, it is Paul who will be concerned and try to make them feel better. He came yesterday and was brooding about his dad. First he asked me could he have a large envelope. I said, "Sure." Then he went around collecting things like a pencil—"Can I have this? It's for my dad." I said, "Oh sure, I have extra pencils, you can have it." Then he found some walnuts and asked for some of those for his dad. In the newspaper was a colored picture of the Boston Celtics. He said, "Can I have this?" I said, "Yeah," and gave him that too. Everything was going into the large envelope. Paul wanted me to write, "I love you daddy." I wrote it on a scrap of paper, and he dropped that in also. Then he wanted to tape the packet all together. I said all right. He used yards of tape. He wanted to make sure it stayed together.

Last night at a workshop I told our early childhood adviser I couldn't understand Paul's wanting to collect all this and the great concern for his father. Our trainer told me that either Paul has had a terrible time with his father and was trying to make up to him; or if the family is separating and there is tension between the mother and father, that the child tries to keep the father tied to him by giving the father things.

Paul has been with me two and a half years, a long time, and yet not as long as some of the others. I think a lot of what happened this morning— Paul's sudden tears about every little thing—is tied in to what is happening at home, unbeknownst to me. I don't know the situation at home right now, so I will ask the mother. In order to help Paul, I need to understand. I can't just assume something. When I ask him about it, he only says, "I don't want to talk." When I know the problem, I can open communication with him.

How did it all begin? I asked Irene to sketch the background of her family day care business.

I was one of seventeen children. I was raised in an orphanage that was not very creative. It existed to care for children in order to keep them off the streets. A sister a year older and one a year younger were in there too. My mother died when I was three, and we were the last three in our family.

I went on to high school and secretarial training, which, without any guidance, I thought would be an okay field for me. If I had had good counseling, maybe I would have chosen a different way. I was married at twenty-three. Nancy was born when I was twenty-five.

Until Nancy was born, I worked in an office as a secretary: thirteen men and two typists and a clerk. It was *not* what I enjoy doing. I didn't have the patience to work with adults that I have with children. I always have the feeling that adults should know better, like knowing how to get their materials in on time, doing their own spelling and writing and rewriting. A report was thrown on my desk, and the men *assumed* I would correct the punctuation and spelling. What I resented was doing their work and mine too. I was too concerned that it be right, and I guess because I didn't enjoy the work, I didn't understand why the bosses couldn't do theirs properly. If the work wasn't done on time and properly, I took it as a reflection on myself.

With children you know they are learning and your job is to teach them this and that. I feel better because I can see the results. I feel rewarded right away. Whereas in an office I didn't feel rewarded, I don't care how many times they patted me on the back.

Susan, our second child, came along three years after Nancy. About this time we had a neighbor with four children, who was getting divorced. She needed someone to watch her youngest child who had cystic fibrosis and needed a lot of care. That one was Susan's age, and there was also a child Nancy's age. When my neighbor returned to work full time, I took care of all four children. The older ones came after school. That is how I began.

From that, other neigborhood people learned that I was doing child care. At that time the Office for Children did not exist, there was no licensing. Other people told other people who told other people, and I constantly had children coming and going without advertising. For a long time I kept the number at four plus my two children.

In the first years my children were excited about having constant playmates and enjoyed that greatly. But there came a time at eleven or twelve when they resented the intrusion of the day care children. Now that's true, it is intrusive. When we decided to redo the basement, initially that was going to be Nancy's and Susan's area, for privacy. But they wanted to be upstairs because they liked to cook after school, to have their friends in, and talk on the phone. We tried having the basement as the girls' room, but it wasn't getting much use. It was empty all morning and only used a few hours in the afternoon. So I took over downstairs for the day care kids and gave my daughters the upstairs. It eased a lot of tensions once we got the playroom.

It's no problem doing day care when your children are little, but as they get older they want a little privacy. Now my girls are beginning to come round and rather enjoy having the little kids here again. Nancy is at Dartmouth College, and Susan is in high school still. I don't ask them to help with the day care, but they will offer. If Lily isn't awake yet, Susie will say, "Can I take the older ones downstairs for a little while, Mom?" She does all kinds of things, and they love having her there. If I insisted, that would not work out well. It would provoke a conflict. Not demanding and having the help offered is an entirely different situation, a much better one. Susan especially likes Paul and greets him each day after school with a kiss. Her boyfriend acts jealous and chases Paul away, and it is a big game for all of them. Paul tells everyone that Susan is C-R-A-Z-Y about him, and he is going to have to get rid of Mark.

For a period of time my husband resented the fact that I was a babysitter. He urged me to go back to work, "Why don't you go back to work in an office? It would be easier, you wouldn't be so tired." I used to feel upset about that. His disapproval made a bad situation. What changed it all—and part of me was angry about it—was when I began to become involved with the association and to take evening courses, and refuse to allow him or anyone else to call me a babysitter. I would say, "I'm a family day care provider. I do much more than babysit. I don't want you calling me a babysitter."

Once Eddie had a title, a label, for my work he became proud of what I do. But it took time to shift gears. I would say, "I'm doing the same job that I did ten years ago, and ten years ago you were embarrassed, you didn't want to admit this was what I was doing. I was just a babysitter." From saying, "How can you? You were trained to be a secretary, you should be out *there*, you are wasting your talents," Eddie went to boasting about me. For the last five years now he has been so proud—because I'm a member of the association, the education chairperson, a vice-president, taking courses toward a degree in early childhood education. He feels now he can say, "My wife is in family day care!" I'm a trophy, and the label did it.

When I began to look at the day care in a businesslike and professional way, my daughters shared my confidence that what I do is important, that it is a necessary service. I feel that I do a very good job. I'm not being immodest because everyone tells me I put myself down too much. I give a good service, what I do I try to do well. I think I give the parents every bit of what they are paying for. Most of them feel they have gotten a good deal and that it has been the right choice.

Irene's income from day care goes towards her daughters' college educations; her husband's earnings are adequate to meet all other family expenses. Some of the parents who use her service are single parents and primary breadwinners, most are two-income professional families. Irene puts at a premium the feeling of giving them a good "bargain." For day care in a prosperous area in the northeastern United States, her rates are intentionally low.

Fees are a big issue with my husband and me. He thinks I'm under-priced. All my day care families tell me I'm underpriced, but they really appreciate it! The reason I don't charge more is that I have excellent parents. They are extremely thoughtful of me and of my family. I also have vacation and holiday pay. It all equals out. I can't always have the money side to my benefit. The parents have to have a little extra benefit too.

I charge $55 a week. The Massachusetts Association did a survey of fees around the state. The people in towns like Lawrence and Brockton are lucky if they can get $35 a week. Provide care in a town like Newton, Wellesley, or Brookline, and you can charge over $100 per week. In other towns like West Roxbury the rate is $85. So I see the state norm or average as $65.

You can go to the Star Market and get things cheaper because they buy in volume. So some of the day care centers operate cheaper than I do, and charge less because they deal in volume too. But is that what you want for your child? For him or her to be part of a herd? That's the only way I can look at it. Kids get so wound up and become very aggressive, like the mice in the scientific experiment who when they get too crowded start biting one another. Other mice in the same amount of space but in fewer numbers were calm; that one factor, the overcrowding, did it. What I find in my little group is the children *do* care about one another. They are a lot more protective because they don't have to fight for their right all the time.

Also, in family day care a child forms a bond with one caregiver. If the bond is not going to be with parents only and has to spin off to someone else, then let it be one other person, not five teachers or first this provider then that one. As a person raised in an orphanage and in and out of foster care, I know the anxieties, fears, and insecurities that come from adjusting to some new person's idea of what is right and wrong, good and bad. It's too hard for children. When parents select my home because we agree on the kind of care that is important, then we can work hand in hand. We are interested in the same child. I don't think children ought to be bounced around from nurse to infant center to all-day nursery school.

My situation, I realize, is unique in several ways. First, most of these children have truly grown up together from infancy or toddlerhood to getting ready to go off to kindergarten. The librarian comments that they have a real "family" feeling for one another. She sees it in the way they interact and support one another during the storytime and crafts programs at the library. It makes me feel good that they have learned that much at least. In addition, the bond has pushed out roots in the families' lives. The children visit one another on weekends and we *all* go to the birthday parties—Auntie, myself, Eddie, and the day care children. They have developed a close bond, not of dependency but of affection and support.

My income is basically for my kids' college education. We could not live on what I'm earning, even if I went up on my prices. This is what I like about the whole career. As a provider you can affect your income, by adding a third or a fourth, fifth, or sixth child. Eventually, after my children are out of college, I hope to have only a half-day program and go into training, opening my home as a training center for other providers to come in and take off.

Jane Holden's Commentary

Family day care operates flexibly to meet different families graduated needs, as typified by the two families I talked with. Jane Holden explained how her use of Irene's services evolved.

I work for the University of Massachusetts doing horticultural research over at the experiment station. I work twenty hours a week. But Andrew started going to Irene's before I had a job; he wasn't quite a year old yet. I wanted some free time. I had spent practically a solid year in the house taking care of him, and it was nice to have the freedom of two afternoons a week.

I had given up a job to have Andrew. When he started going to Irene's, I realized that it was nice to get some of my old time back. Then I realized that he could go more often, that he was doing well there, and that he looked forward to going over. That's when I got the job.

I work because I want to, for myself. I am not a mother who "has to" work. My mother-in-law cannot fathom why I work at all. It's totally strange to her why a mother wouldn't want to just sit home or shop and have fun with her girlfriends during the day until her child gets home from school. It's a luxury to be able to work only part time today. Sometimes it's hard to remember that.

In the paper you see people advertising for a grandmotherly type woman to "take care of my child and help with some light housekeeping" or just "take care of my two children while I work." That is what professional people advertise for. And I think family day care is so much preferable to it. After a child is a year old, to stay in the same house with the same toys and have a sitter doesn't do a thing for him. It's the same situation as if the mother were there but not as good. If you bring him to a place where there are new toys, a new perspective, and new children, or just playmates, it's fabulous. This is so much better for Andrew. He never was happy having a woman come here.

When I was trying to get some free time before I went back to work, I kept trying to find a sitter who would come and babysit. It was never successful. Older women do not play with children. They bring their knitting and expect to watch your child play. Well, Andrew is a very active boy. He wanted very much to be with other children. Irene's is great that way.

Some young teenagers would be, too. They love to sit and play. But teenagers are not available in the day. So people hire the older women who are not interested in getting on the floor and building with blocks. They are also very critical of the manners of your children. I'm sure that our family is much more child-centered than many of these women accepted with their own families. Andrew has a very relaxed milieu. We don't press down on him to be quiet when adults are around; we probably should. We did not find an older woman who made him happy. If he had another playmate it would have been fine, or a twin, but the older sitters we found did not do.

For a long time Andrew was the youngest at Irene's. Next year he will be the oldest, because the older children who are with her now will go to kindergarten. He goes three mornings a week from 7:45 to 12:45. His father takes care of him two afternoons. That allows me to work twenty hours, or two-and-a-half days. I would have used Irene more, but at the time she couldn't take Andrew for a nap, she had too many children. So we did this. Now we are happy with it anyway.

Part time day care seems ideal to me. I sometimes feel sorry for children who are in day care forty hours. It seems such a long day to be away from home. Irene's is the best possible world for that, but it's still a long day to be away from home for small children.

The other very important aspect is that it has given Andrew, who has no other relatives in Massachusetts, an extended family. It's on our street. Even the days he is not there, in the summer, if Irene is taking a walk, the kids come up our driveway and play in Andrew's sandbox for a while, which pleases him no end. We end up with *them* in our yard. For his birthday they came for a birthday party here. The two days he's not there he still sees the other children sometimes. On my day off, Tuesday, we may go for a field trip with them, for example, to the zoo. Plus he sees them coming and going—Irene and her husband Eddie on their evening walks. If you don't have relatives around, and we don't, it's one more base, a family feel. If I fell very sick, Andrew could stay overnight at Irene's. She feels close to all the kids and would pinch hit.

Andrew is an outgoing, talkative, active child who becomes, I gather from Irene and from my own observations, much more of an observer there because there are four children older than he is who act out and do interesting things. He is withdrawn and more interested in them, and tries it all out when he comes home—the big words or the aggressive play. "Paul did this today," he says. He takes a lot in. Here he can be a holy terror, because he has watched the kids all day long.

We've made friends with the other children's parents, so Lily will come on a Saturday or Andrew will go there. With young children alone, suddenly he takes the role of Paul and bonks Lily and tells her, "I'm sorry, you can't play with that, you must play with this." If they play house, he insists, "You have to be the baby!" He is bossy with the little kids alone, whereas at Irene's he is the child who watches more.

At three-and-a-half or four, many children go to a nursery school. We are debating this but think we are going to continue with Irene for another year and then send him to kindergarten. Next year the children in her group will be younger probably. My only criticism of family day care is—and many people would see it as an advantage—that I'd be happier if all the children were Andrew's age. Obviously the provider is *not* going to get five kids all the same age, and Irene is happier with the graduated ages. But I think a person might be able to gear activities better to one age level, ability, and interest. Andrew learns from seeing older kids, but he also learns bad habits. We are not always happy with what he learns, but that would be true playing in a neighborhood—you can't criticize family day care for it. Being the oldest will be another good experience for him.

We appreciate that the experience is more diverse than we might have been able to expose Andrew, an only child, to on our own. The family lifestyles represented at Irene's include traditional two-parent families, a divorced mother raising her children in their grandmother's house, and a separated couple sharing their child care on alternate nights. Some of the mothers work long hours at full-time jobs and can spend very little time at Irene's, while other mothers working part time spend time watching and even participating in the activities at Irene's. One child is very aware of her Jewish heritage and is quite proud of the Hebrew words that she has mastered. I feel that Andrew's view of life is larger and more realisitic because of this diversity brought together in a family day care situation.

In the summer when we take walks, we go and swing with Irene's children for a while. It's hard to persuade Andrew to leave! I don't feel Irene needs an *extra child* at that point! Having our day care around the corner is an enhancement. Irene says Andrew has actually told her, "My mommy won't *let* me take a nap here. I asked her to stay in the afternoon but she says no." At this age they often say what they think that you want to hear. To me if I say, "This is the day I pick you up at noon," he says, "Yippee." He gives the appropriate or expected response to some degree. That I say he can't take his nap at Irene's is a fabrication on his part. However, it also shows how at home he feels there.

Irene has the virtue of being less hyper about the children than I could be. It keeps her sane. She is a lot less on top of everything they are doing. That is good for the children. I am much more aware of Andrew's approaching the woodwork to dent it, or a table to topple something. There are times when Irene is pretty casual about the kids. She'll get involved with talking with her daughter, and the kids are left on their own. It's good, not bad. I don't have that makeup. I could never let Andrew and a friend play alone and not know what they were doing. Lots of times I can't stand being over there with the kids. It makes me anxious. I want to intervene. Irene more or less lets the children work their disputes out. She is very oriented to games and activities with them, but as far as the toys are concerned, she lets them play and work out their own grievances. Andrew does *well* in a situation where somebody is not listening to him every minute. Brazelton has said the kids are all fine until the mothers come into the room, then they have problems.[2]

If I ask Andrew, "What did you do today?" he might say, "I went to a park," but the interesting stories come out later. "So-and-so hit so-and-so and this is what happened," or "Irene tells us that dinosaur eggs don't fit in the refrigerator." Little by little in the course of the afternoon he tells me what is fun to hear.

Since Andrew is acclimated to Irene's, and Jane to the separations, leaving him in another neighbor's care overnight has caused anguish to neither. The arrangement with Irene gave Jane the idea of extending her support system by paying this neighbor to care for Andrew from time to time, while she stays home with her own young children.

[2]T. Berry Brazelton, *Toddlers and Parents: A Declaration of Independence* (New York: Dell Publishing, 1974), pp. 59–60, 80–82, 115–116.

What I did, when Irene couldn't take Andrew for the nap, and with Dick's work schedule so erratic, was to make some contacts in a nearby street, meet some mothers I had never met before, and find a mother with a child the same age as Andrew and ask her if for $2 an hour, Andrew could take his nap and play for the afternoon over there on an irregular basis on days when Dick was working. That has worked out beautifully. Irene could have legally taken another child, but she knew if she had too many kids no one would nap, and she would have a horrible afternoon of six cranky kids. The half days suited me before I started my job, but afterwards I had to be away two afternoons a week. If Dick was working too, I was at a loss.

I would do it again! I would always look if I lived in a neighborhood for someone with a child the same age, who hadn't thought of working, didn't particularly need the money, but realized it's an easy way to earn $10 now and again and to have a playmate for her child. That has worked out for me as well as Irene's has. As the neighbor's and my children grow, I think Andrew will end up playing with this boy simply as a friend.

Irene's younger daughter, Susan, sits for us too. She has at times babysat two nights a week. Andrew loves it. Susan is getting older now, and we can't count on her being our only babysitter. Nancy before she went to Dartmouth babysat too. Andrew feels that he knows that family! Susan, having a mother who does family day care, feels comfortable around little children. Andrew brags to the others in the group, "Susan came to my house last night." That is a point of pride with him. Staying at our neighbor's he sees as a privilege too. Andrew stayed with her when I went to the International Flower Show in Montreal, which Dick was filming. Ever since, Andrew has asked, "When am I going to stay overnight with Katy and Daniel?"

Jane Holden believes she has achieved the right balance between being with her preschooler and pursuing her career. Although as a part-timer she can't rise on the research ladder, she is not seriously tempted to double her hours to the conventional thirty-five or forty.

This schedule gives him and me two mornings when we can do something together. We go to Harvard Square and shop, and we sit in a coffee shop, or I may take him to watch his father shooting. When he was younger, he took swimming lessons with me one of those days. I would miss the two mornings. I don't think I'm ready to give Andrew up every morning of the week. If he were older, it wouldn't be so bad, we'd have afternoons. But he still takes a long afternoon nap. He would be happy at Irene's every day I suppose, and this way's a luxury, but I would miss it.

Especially in the wintertime, once the morning is gone so is the day for young children. And isn't childhood gone quickly too?

The Rasalas' Commentary

When I visited the Rasalas on a Saturday afternoon to talk about their use of Irene's family day care service, Sue was baking bread, Richard was immersed in a carpentry project, and the girls were about to be picked up for swimming at the "Y." We sat in the Rasalas' handsome wood block and white formica kitchen—the first room, they explained, that they have been able to redecorate in toto since moving in three years ago. When Kathy and April were younger, they agreed, projects on the order of redecorating were unthinkable, and they reminisced about how life was "back then."

SUE: When Kathy was born I had a huge, twelve-month leave from my teaching job. Then when Kathy was one, I could not get another huge leave, which I had thought I could, but I had an opportunity to go back to work half time. It was for half days, five days a week. Some whole days would actually be a better arrangement, but we decided I would go back to work and would take this position.

We talked about child care. Richard's schedule is quite flexible because, beyond his teaching hours, his office hours and independent work time can be manipulated around. If he moves an appointment from one day to another, it's not critical. Still we needed help. At this time we had no family in the area although I don't think I would have considered that. Young people interact differently with children than old people. Both are a nice experience, but . . .

RICHARD: It's hard for old people to maintain the calm for long periods of time. Also the pace is harrying.

SUE: I was thinking of a babysitter and read ads in the papers and realized they were expensive. Also, I'd heard stories of babysitters tending to be older women spending the day watching the soap operas. After being home with my child for a year, I knew that some of it was very boring. There were times when I craved adult companionship and could understand why somebody would sit in front of the television all day. But that wasn't what I wanted for my child.

I also had friends that had children in day care centers or had babysitting so that whole world was not unknown to me. Family day care was. I heard about it first at a meeting on child care sponsored by the public

178

library of Watertown, where we were living at the time. The person who spoke about family day care was very likable. From what she said I realized that was what I wanted. The multi-service center of Watertown puts together a well-organized booklet listing all the names of people offering various services. That's where we got Irene's name. On a town map I looked for people near our house and along a route where Richard and I would be going to work. I called up and made appointments to see them.

Several features appealed to me about family day care. First, that there would be several children together and several families involved with this provider. So that although my child wasn't talking and there was no way that I was going to really know what happened in the day, other children *were* talking. Other parents would be concerned with what was going on, not just us.

Second, as a teacher of primary children, I am very much in favor of children of different ages spending time together while preschoolers. Many day care centers, if they are big enough, classify the children by age, so the early threes only see early threes, late threes only late threes. They don't learn anything from a child who is older, who has had more experience. Nor can the older children learn anything from younger ones. I liked the family day care mix.

Last, I am more comfortable about a child being in a home at that age. I do things like cooking in the classroom and know how difficult it can be to import part of the home into the classroom, to try to create in an institution what is a very natural activity at home. The family day care environment *was* home. They were seeing a home kitchen and bathroom and the mailman. For little children the home has more variety and opportunity for the kind of things that I thought my child should be doing. I was more comfortable with that for her than with the halls of a school.

I interviewed people. I went to one person I liked fine, and the caliber of her program was very good, but I didn't care for the space. I wasn't comfortable with where her house was or inside it. The house was small, and she had a space heater on the first floor. Since then other families we know send their children to her, and one mother is grieving that this is the last child she has to send. Some of my objection was class conscious. The space was lower class, I felt, even though I knew that the care would be fine. Through telephone interviews I realized that lots of people don't like kids who aren't toilet trained. They would rather have them older.

After an appointment with one other person, who impressed me as not having much energy, I had an appointment with Irene. Irene's setting impressed me very much. What I saw when I was there was a child who was going to kindergarten, five, and a younger boy, three. The five-year-old kept playing around with a bucket of water. Irene told him not to, that it

April Rasala and Andrew Holden help Irene make a salad for lunch.

was something someone else was using. She persisted in it and spoke to him again and took it away to put it inside. I was impressed by that method of disciplining a child. I was struck by her calm, and I didn't quite understand it. It took me a while to realize that is just how she is, that Irene operates that way all the time with the children.

She used words well, so that they had meaning. After our long association, something that I would say is really important in preschool care is how the caregiver speaks to the child because language development is occurring at this time. That's something Irene does excellently. No matter what else she does, she speaks well to the children. Whether she is disciplining them, whether they are playing a game, she speaks in the same tone of voice that she does to anybody, which is nice.

Most people start off thinking of hiring the perfect babysitter. Then they realize that, number one, they don't exist, and number two, they are very expensive. A small group in the home with a good provider is a less publicized solution. The same as with any other type of day care, you have to investigate carefully. I suggested family day care to a neighbor, and after interviewing the first person, she called me up, just distraught: "The television was on all the time. The place was dirty." I answered, "Keep looking. You will know when you find the place you are comfortable with. I can't tell you how you will know. But after going through it myself, I'm sure you will." There *are* good people out there doing family day care, but you have to screen them. And you can screen them more easily than a baby-sitter.

One of our friends ran into a question she hadn't thought of before-hand: she is bothered by smoking, and it turned out that the provider smokes. Had she thought it was important to her before she got her child involved, she would not have sent her there. It turns out to be a totally positive experience for the child. The woman is a very happy person, and the daughter thrives there. But I tell people now, "If something like smoking or messiness bothers you, figure out how you are bothered ahead of time."

Something that would bother me is how much television some provid-ers allow children to watch. The particular place that my friend's child goes to, the television is on all the time. The children do not sit and watch it, but it is on. My friend has the television on a fair amount of time in her house so I suppose they match. This would have driven me straight up the wall. You have to think about your own ideas and lifestyle, not only child-rearing beliefs but idiosyncracies. Going through the interviewing process helps you define this for yourself.

It's fortunate that Richard and Sue are highly organized individuals; of the families I interviewed they stand out as having the most elaborate day care schedule.

RICHARD: For the last two years before kindergarten, Kathy also went to a nursery school, along with Irene's. That was a mixed experience. Kathy went to the nursery three mornings a week and Irene's two other days. It turned out to be absolutely strenuous. There were times I had to pick Kathy up at a certain point, get her to Irene's, and drive to school with no minutes to spare. When I had something critical going on, it was really crazy! The main reason we were doing it was to give Kathy the chance to be with a larger group of children part of the time.

Not only the driving but the participation took a toll on us. The nursery was completely parent-funded. Given the fact that they wanted to limit the children to twelve, it was hard to generate enough money to pay the two teachers and the rent. So parents were responsible for fixing things up and for raising money.

SUE: This is probably the end of our girls' experience with Irene—April is just four. We decided not to send April to nursery school this year. Next year I think she will go because there is a nursery school in the area that she can attend five days a week and that has the option of staying until 2:30, if you let them know the day before.

Now I work mornings and leave home at eight. The kindergarten is over at a quarter to twelve, and technically I'm done then. I always stay at least an hour after the kids leave, and if at least one afternoon a week I'm there for a couple of hours, I can get things together for the rest of the week. It makes the week go better. Richard finishes their breakfasts and packs Kathy off to school—or sometimes walks with her. Then he takes April to Irene's, and either proceeds to the university or returns home and works and later teaches in the afternoon. He arrives home at about six. If either girl is sick, he stays home in the morning, and I leave school at noon and come right back for the second shift.

Two years ago we asked Richard's parents to move right across the street from us—they had been further away. They help willingly, but we wouldn't have them do the stint of day care. They have their lives and are much better for the kids to sit just on occasion.

The issue now is that April wants friends in the neighborhood, because Kathy has friends in the neighborhood. Kathy can call somebody up or go over to somebody's house at four in the afternoon, and I'm not willing to drive April twenty minutes to somebody's house. April has a wonderful relationship with the kids at Irene's. Last week was her birthday and that was whom she invited: the children from Irene's, Irene, and Auntie. And sometimes we do exchange visits on the weekends. But as working parents we are very busy. All of us are ready for her to have neighbors she can play with as Kathy does.

RICHARD: We still don't want full-time day care. One reason why Sue works part time is to spend time with the children. My schedule too allows me to be with my children more than many fathers can. I do a lot of my work in the early mornings and late evening. Our teaching hours flipflop: she teaches only mornings, I only afternoons. This way, when I go to the university, it's okay for me to be held up or to go to extra meetings, even if they last beyond five. But we don't want the children away from us both until five or six o'clock, so we have arranged to put them in a day care situation in which they can stay only as long as needed.

SUE: Also, if you have opted for part-time work as I have, you receive part-time salary. We could arrange to pay full-time care and not use it full-time, pick them up at 2:30 instead of five o'clock. It would be a bit of a hardship, though. These organizations do not float in money and have to fill that slot. Irene is the same, but she takes a few part time kids by having them share a slot, as Loren and April do. Loren goes to a morning nursery and comes at noon. April leaves at one three days a week.

RICHARD: Irene has accommodated all the changes. Our arrangement with her now is that, whether or not we use them, we pay for a minimum of twenty hours. In fact we tend to use between twenty-three and twenty-eight hours per week. Wednesday April stays almost all day. That happens to be the one day this semester when I'm not teaching, and if I can have that day clear to do some work, then it's excellent.

Irene has been splendid about not raising prices. Her fees are $1.25 an hour, so it averages for us now $35 to $45. When we had two children in day care, two-thirds to three-quarters of the take-home pay Sue earned was covering day care. She was clearing only about one-quarter of her pay. But she was a teacher, enrollments were declining, and if she did not maintain her position in the schools, she would have had a difficult time finding a position again.

Maybe two days out of two different years of the nearly six we have gone to her has Irene been ill and unable to provide care. If she had been a person sick a lot, we would have had to look to the day care centers as offering more security.

We let Irene know if something unusual is going to happen. If she can't handle it, we start working out other plans. Usually there is a way out. Having my parents across the street makes life easier. They don't do picking up because they don't like to drive, but Kathy can walk from school there. You can feel very alone if you don't have parents and if all your friends are working. If something happens, we have my parents to fall back on, to depend on. As well as we have our schedules worked out, keeping the pieces together takes constant attention and can be absolutely strenuous.

SUE: In the case of almost all our married friends, both people in the couple work, usually one of them part time. In that sense we have a lot of support. Everyone we know shares our situation and can tell the same stories, about "How I spent an hour so that this fifteen-minute gap would be covered." It's far from unique. Transporting is a drag. If the good fairy would eliminate one chore, that would be it! There was a point one year when I did both the delivery, taking the kids to Irene's in the morning, and picking them up in the afternoon. The rare day when Richard could pick them up, I felt such relief. Our current schedule's much better because he takes them every day.

The day-after-day delivery and pickup is what is wearing. If it can be split, it's tolerable. If one person is doing both the chaufferings, the other person cannot appreciate how tiresome it is. It would have been wonderful had the day care site been close. But Irene wasn't particularly close to us when we lived in Watertown, either. I just felt it was a very good place. When we moved from Watertown to Newton Corner, a factor in our choice was a location close enough to still go to Irene's. We're not the only parents who've thought that way. When Loren's family moved, they chose a house that would still be in the area too.

What makes family day care at Irene's so very desirable?

SUE: Family day care offers this over a day care center: you are dealing with only one person. You make all the arrangements with one caregiver. It's more personal. By the same token I think it's a harder task for the provider to know where her lines are, what she is willing to bend on and what she isn't. Institutions by and large have to be more rigid in their policies. For example, the children sometimes have gone to Irene's not feeling as well as they would have had to in order to go to a day care center. Because they can lie down a lot, they go.

I took a college class one summer, and a number of teachers there were from day care centers. At one point in talking about family day care, some disparaging statements were made. I spoke up and defended it, said it was to me the *choice* solution. It turned out that several of the people were aware of situations with twelve or fifteen kids illegally kept by one woman. Such situations give a bad name to this highly satisfactory type of care.

Many providers do it while their own children are young. That seems to me trickier. At Irene's the toys that the children are playing with are her toys. Whenever there is a problem, I've heard her say, "If we are not going to be able to share that, we'll put it up for a while." So either it is a toy the child has brought and he is in control, or she is in control. There isn't a child there having to share territory and mother. That is nicer for our children though I understand a lot of women do this.

Actually I think that working part time as I'm doing, and the kids having the opportunity to go to Irene's is the best of both worlds. Having gone through the whole experience, the only way I'd redesign it would be to work three full days a week and have two days when I didn't have to get up and get out. But I never had that option.

Kathy and Irene always got along very well. She had a nice cohesive group, and April's is even nicer. Sometimes in family day care the older kids drop out, the fours and fives. Irene tries to have different ages and the right sexes to fit. At one point Loren was the only boy. She wanted, and got, more boys.

Our girls see Irene's as an extended family. We wanted them to have child care outside the home, so that when the family comes back home, the family is together. Neither child has ever used Irene "against" us. They may say that Irene lets them paint on their hands and you don't. So I say to the children. "Yes, you can do that at Irene's. Here you can't." Different people set different limits. What we have to do is be specific so they know. Sometimes April calls me Irene, and then she laughs. She calls Eddie's mother "Grandma," but she knows it's Grandma Kricorian. Eddie's bachelor brother is "Uncle Leo." When he had a radio station job at night, he used to be around a lot. Some of the relatives thought that was strange, but I didn't.

RICHARD: There aren't enough titles in English, so the children have to use the ones that are there.

SUE: Irene and Eddie are comfortable with the kids calling them Irene and Eddie. It's so good that Irene's husband goes places with the kids, too. And maybe it is not so rare for a family day care situation. My friend's day care provider's husband is a police officer who often works nights and in fact is around a lot in the daytime. Like Eddie he plays an important role. Anyway, we see it's not unusual for the kids to get to know the husbands.

RICHARD: The field trips have evolved in the last five years. Now almost every week there is some kind of outing on Wednesday. She thinks of what kinds of interesting events she can plan for a couple of hours with the children. She always goes to the library Tuesdays, and the children have a fairly long walk, nice exercise. This may be part of the fact that she has been going to school, which has stimulated her thinking about the possibilities of day care. She takes them to the supermarket, the fire station. She looks at the community as a resource for the day care.

SUE: There is an Armenian-ness, too. April loves yogurt, and we don't have it much at home. Last summer she was telling us to buy it and what to serve it with. We cook using some Armenian recipes because Kathy said Irene makes wonderful *choreg*, a sweet bread. April eats a large variety of foods because of the lunches at Irene's.

RICHARD: And we sample Armenian food independently. In that sense, Watertown is a very good area. It has a lot of opportunity for cultural variety.

Sue: Irene is also very involved in her church. The church is a very strong force in her life. When Kathy was going to Irene, initially, she had the children say grace before lunch, "God is great, God is good, thank You for our food." Kathy did it at home, too. I thought about that and decided it was fine, that when I'd gone to Girl Scout camp we had always sung grace with the meal. It was part of the camp life. It wasn't being taken to church. So we appreciated that the children at Irene's sit down and each lunch as people eat, rather than as animals eat, which can happen. I think our own meals here could use some civility! We appreciated the fact that Irene cared how the children ate. As long as no one dished out religious lectures, I wasn't going to object. Now Irene has dropped it. Whether because she is more involved in the professionalism or not, I don't know.

We've seen Irene develop and change, although Irene had already been a family day care provider for nine years when Kathy started. Now we have been with her for six years. I think she really would have had to go in some direction to keep involved. That is a long time for an at-home career.

Richard: Also, we have seen her children grow up through six years of their lives and that changes the picture too. Originally when she did day care, the day care children were approximately the same age as Nancy and Susie. As she has gone along, she has had to readjust the relationship with her children because they are growing while the day care children are remaining approximately the same. At times she has said to me, "Eddie and Susie have told me that if I don't stop doing this work and give them some time, they are going to divorce me." I think she has felt a tremendous sense of her own abilities by getting involved in her professional organization, but she has also felt the kind of pressures that come into being that involved. She is remarkable in that she intuitively senses the limits. She doesn't let herself get pushed to the point that it would take time to recover.

Once when there was going to be a hearing relating to family day care at the State House, Irene planned to go down, and someone else would take care of the children. I came at nine o'clock, and she wasn't dressed to go. I said, "Gee, I thought you were going to the state house!" She said, "Well, I haven't gotten things together this morning." There was still a tiny hint that she might go, but in fact she didn't. Somehow I think she sensed this would be one too many obligations in that particular week. She had the ability to back off and not let herself get into a frazzle over it because "I've made this commitment." Six months ago when the president of the state association of providers had to resign, Irene could have stepped in. Irene said, "No way, I'm not going to become president. I've seen what the job entails. I do what I can as a chairperson. The extra responsibility would be too much for me to handle." I marvel at that because I sometimes bite off more than I can chew.

SUE: Some family day care providers work up lesson plans, and I feel that is unnecessary. The language, the play time are most important, and Irene provides a lot of good settings for them. In the basement when I've gone down there have been sheets taped up to the ceiling and the kids have hideouts and rooms. The couch is moved around so there are different spaces. In good weather the children spend a lot of time playing in the sandbox. Irene is out there too. After the garden is over in the fall, they all dig in the earth and hunt for worms. When I went to pick April up yesterday, she was playing around with big sticks they had gathered and was building a pretend fire. Since Irene has become involved in the association and active in its education wing, she has more definite ideas of what she wants to do with the children. But her innate qualities with the kids are still there, and there continues to be a lot of playing time. She will say, "That's it," if something is not what people are in the mood for. At one point I thought, "Oh no, I'm not sure I want her to go in this direction," when she began to look at curriculum. But she didn't go beyond what her common sense said made sense with the children. And I do see people like Irene who are doing family day care professionally needing professional challenges too.

RICHARD: I've taken April in the morning for a long time now. There are times when Irene needs to talk to a grown-up, and she and I will talk for twenty minutes before I go off. Or there are times when I just want to talk about school's having been a chaotic mess for the last two weeks, and she'll listen. We don't see the Kricorians otherwise, which is probably good. You could have too much contact. But Irene feels free to talk to me about things that are troubling her about the situation or even the family.

I grew up in a family where my parents could get angry very easily and could ride us pretty hard. I have had a tendency to act the same with my kids. The old saying is, "You do what you learn." Sue has been very helpful; so has Irene been helpful as a model of handling children without becoming angry. Having more creative ways to solve a problem, or even the simple matter of stopping and listening and figuring out what the issue is, not assuming you know the issue. Irene is very good at pausing to listen to the children. Then usually she can figure out a much better solution because she knows what is going on. So having Kathy and April go to Irene's has been a good experience for us too.

There were also times early on where we asked certain things that she wasn't ready to give. We had to work out the limits of the relationship. The relationship has been very good the last couple of years because we all understand what the limits are. We know what is reasonable to request and what is not.

SUE: Irene does a Christmas party every year. Her birthday is in December so she gives a party in the late afternoon on the twentieth or twenty-first. Parents and children come, and the alumni come. Kathy looks forward to it every year because she can see some of her old friends from Irene's. Last summer she had a potluck picnic that was a success. The year before for her birthday the parents took Irene, Eddie, and Auntie out to the suburbs to dinner one night. We didn't repeat that this year. Even in that way, "life with Irene" is noninstitutional. Even things that are good we don't necessarily mark on our calendars for the next go round!

10

DAY CARE CENTER

We did not really worry about her mother and father; she was absolutely confident that they would always keep the window open for her to fly back by, and this gave her complete ease of mind.

J. M. Barrie, *Peter Pan*

The Coles have lived in New York City all their career lives. Rachel, four, their daughter, went to a private day care center from the age of three months. Phil, then a graduate student, delivered and fetched her, while Joanna continued to work as a book editor full time. Now Phil is a psychotherapist, and Joanna a free-lance writer of, among other things, juvenile science books. And Rachel, they say beaming, has "changed everything."

Like her parents, Rachel is using the best the city has to offer. Along with friends from her age group at the day care center, she has moved on to the Riverside Church Weekday Nursery School. She takes ballet and views the nearby American Museum of Natural History as her winter playground. She makes conversation with the doorman of their apartment house and eats spicy Chinese food at her favorite restaurant.

Rachel Cole was part of the first crop of Basic Trust Infant/Toddler Center, one of Manhattan's finest, when it moved out of the germ of the idea in an upper West Side apartment into a nearby brownstone basement. When I visited Basic Trust in 1979, the center had in its care twenty five children between the ages of six months and three years. Most of the children logged fifty hours a week there, and the minimum "load" was three full days per week.

These Basic Trust tots were among an elite of the approximately 122,000 American children two years old or younger enrolled in licensed day care centers, according to a national survey in 1976–1977.[1] In New York City, of the 65,000 children attending group day care, a mere 850 children were enrolled in full-day centers for children two months through three years of age. Seven out of ten of these children were in privately funded centers like Basic Trust. The statistics have grown but not dramatically since that time.

In every state, the licensing of child care centers serving children under three is very strict. A center must have a high ratio (in general one to three) of caregivers to children; separate space for eating, playing, and sleeping; refrigeration in the main activity room as well as in the kitchen; and a visit by a nurse once a week. To provide these important features, infant care becomes expensive per capita. Consequently, there are far fewer infant centers relative to demand than any other type of day care. Parents who hear that a center has a long waiting list may not have lucked into the Yale or Stanford of the genre; waiting lists are the norm. Jan Calderon Yocum, director of the Day Care Council of America, has said:

[1]Richard Ruopp, Jeffrey Travers, Frederic Glantz, and Craig Coelen, *Children at the Center: Final Report of the National Day Care Study—Summary Findings and Their Implications* (Cambridge, Mass.: Abt Associates, 1979), p. 198.

"Dissatisfied with a succession of sitters and wishing something of greater continuity, most parents are in a panic situation when seeking an infant day care center."

To see two dozen small children participating in a professionally constructed extended family is unsettling. It jolts our conventional idea of babyhood passed with a stay-at-home mommy. When I descended the flight of red stairs and pushed open the heavy red door at Basic Trust, I was feeling curious, and a little bristly. Everybody was just being put "down." The babies' sleeping room was closed and curtained off. In the darkened rear room ten cots had been set up and covered with sheets. On tiptoe I entered a drowsy scene for all the world like the underground home in *Peter Pan*. And felt as Mrs. Darling might have had she gone to see the Lost Boys.

Day care centers supported by private and public funds reflect a cross-mixture of economic and cultural groups. As a wholly private institution, Basic Trust draws more similar families. All have two professional-level career parents, with one or at the most two children. They can afford the $6,000-per-year cost, and they prefer the high-quality group care to care in their apartments for their infants and toddlers.

A day care center cannot be judged by an initial visit, which gives you images without the content. A thorough evaluation requires moving with a child through some of the day, seeing how the three vectors—child, caregiver, and parent—converge. How is it like a home, what's better or worse, and what's missing?

At Basic Trust each child is assigned an adult as primary caregiver. The toddlers all call the staff "my Debra," "my Peggy," "my Gail." The staff work in graduated shifts so there is no abrupt bisection of the day for the children. The older children's active speaking vocabularies, a teacher said, contain the first names of all the center's children and staff, plus the names of all the parents. The caregivers follow each child carefully through the day and are able to give parents a narrative report when they pick up their children.

From 8:00 to 9:00 A.M. is welcoming time at the center. Most of the children prefer eating a leisurely breakfast together instead of breakfast at home, including Rachel Cole. One of the parents I met was Philip Cole, who remarked that "Rachel is always happy to go to the center, but she wants to take her own sweet time about everything at this stage. Breakfast with the other children is much more her style right now." Cheese and rolls or bagels are the most popular breakfast. The older tots visit with the babies, and they split up at 9:30 when the toddlers have "Meeting."

"Meeting is a time to verbalize, to sing songs they have made up, in a small way to listen," Jan Miller, the founder and director of the center, explained. Often a parent joins the circle. That day at Meeting, Merrily Hansen, a curriculum specialist for the New York City Board of Education, and her son Christopher, age three, led the group in a new song, "Up, Up in the Sky," with hand motions. Christopher was proud to share the song—and his mommy—with his friends, but later he sat in her lap while she read a story to him and another boy, instead of going along to Woolworth's and the park.

In the back room, water play, blocks, and the play kitchen are constants. Every day there is something extra to do in an artistic way, such as fingerpainting, wood chip sculpture, collages, or molding with playdough. One child will stay with an activity a few minutes, another will shape playdough or construct with blocks for forty five minutes.

In the front room, I watched both infant caregivers (one young woman, one young man) talk with the children in a gentle, unhurried way. The babies do nothing fancy. No one is teaching them proto-math skills or their ABC's. It is just a cozy, caring environment with rhythms and routines similar to those in a home—changings, snacks, meals, being pushed in a carriage, exploring textures and shapes. The big difference, which may be good or bad, is that this is a much "busier box" of visual, aural, and tactile stimulation than many babies experience at home.

I saw a baby wave bye-bye cheerily to a delivering and departing parent, and I wondered about the pangs of separating. An infant teacher said, "Sophie accomplished it herself. At six months, she screamed every time her mother left; nothing satisfied her. Then she opened up to the environment. Now, at a year, Sophie's little legs kick with eagerness as she comes up the block."

Most day care centers aim for a balance between consistency and routine on the one hand and freedom on the other. To achieve this free flow in a city setting, Basic Trust concentrates mostly on outings and human relations. They capitalize on everyday real-life events and highlight everyday activities to enhance the community feeling. This means that morning and afternoon, small groups move out into the city for "trips." They go out and do all the errands a mother does—the week's grocery shopping, trips to the bank or the dry cleaner's. The branch library does special film showings for them. Twos and occasionally even one-year-olds enjoy an hour program of short films.

At Christmas time they ride on the bus to Rockefeller Center to see the skaters, to F.A.O. Schwartz to see the toys, and to the Metropolitan Museum of Art to see the tree. The American Museum of Natural History, a few blocks away from the center, is like their backyard. Two teachers, a couple of babies, and four tots spend an hour there regularly, especially in winter. Rarely on a visit to the center do you have an inkling of the total enrollment, the director explained, since most children are out and abroad twice daily. "I appreciate this," a father interviewing at the center said. "The biggest problem for kids in the city is being cooped up. I saw one loft nursery recently which was beautifully appointed, but it is more desirable for a program to use the resources of the city."

Older children are taken to visit where their parents work. One such visit for Rachel and her peers was to the children's book department at a New York publishing firm. There colleagues of editor Joanna Cole read them stories, after which each child chose a book to take home. At the United Nations, where a Brazilian mother works, they saw an African art exhibit and played in the garden by the river. Most memorably, they passed through revolving doors and rode an escalator to the cafeteria. On a trip to a school for the handicapped, where another mother works, they made friends with children in wheelchairs.

The children help make their lunches. All the food served, including snacks, is nutritious. Parents are encouraged to supply yogurt instead of ice cream at birthday parties, and a snack is often puffy white rice cakes spread with cream cheese. The toddlers love to cook. In groups of four they make a carrot cake in tuna cans or bake honey date loaves (three steps) in little pans. "They get hands, elbows, noses, and toes in too if they can fit them," said a young teacher wearing a peasant blouse, jeans, and apron, known to be a patient *maître-chef*. Often they make an extra batch, wrap the goodies in foil, and label them "From the kids in the back" to give to the infants and their families.

At naptime the children, looking more "baby" and sweetly vulnerable, stand or sit on their cots for a while. Then they settle in with a blanket, a toy, or a book. Going to sleep is a pleasant experience. The adults sing softly and rub the children's backs. Jan Miller related how one parent complained, "My baby used to take the bottle, now he says 'Rub my back.'"

Jan, a handsome, dark-haired woman with a deep, resonant voice, is an interesting combination of chic and unadorned, breezy and deep-thinking, intimate and impersonal. Divorced from her husband, a theatrical manager of Broadway shows, when her son, now fourteen, was in babyhood, Jan has succeeded in having close and friendly ties with both ex-husband and her son's stepmother. Therefore, she brings to her theoretical ideas about extended family special meaning. Besides being Basic Trust's founder-director, she is a parenting instructor at New York City's Elizabeth Bing Center for Parents.

Jan had to get special permission from the State of New York to name her center, because only banks are legally permitted to call themselves trusts. The center's name harks from the first of the eight stages of child development as outlined by Erik Erikson, trust versus mistrust. Erikson writes that mothers create a sense of trust in their children by a combination of "sensitive care of the baby's individual needs and a firm sense of personal trustworthiness within the trusted framework of their community's life style." On this basis a child develops a sense of identity that later will merge with a sense of being "all right" and of "becoming what other people trust one will become."[2] Jan Miller rested her eyes thoughtfully on an animated about-three-year-old who was quizzing me about my little boy and girl, and offered, "Essentially basic trust means how to have these kids trust the world and trust themselves."

When I visited Phil and Joanna Cole in their apartment on Manhattan's upper West Side, they had just packed Rachel off to her full-day nursery school. Nearly two years had passed since I first met Phil over Rachel's bright red galoshes at the start of a day care day. They had forgotten our appointment for the interview, so the scene I popped in on was as typical for them as atypical for most parents of young children: husband and wife both home, each greeting me from the direction of a lamp lit by an easy chair and pile of paper and books, with a tray of coffee things somewhere down center. No children's playthings were strewn around. Rachel has nevertheless "felt" in the poster-size paintings exploding with color and vividly teacher-annotated that line the room's stucco walls.

Phil is short, with a barrel chest and broad shoulders. If you were doing a Jim Henson-like mix of animal characters and people for *The Wind in the Willows*, it's Phil you would cast for a chess partner every bit as brilliant as Toad. Joanna has well-defined, slightly bird-like features and salt-and-pepper hair, close cropped in a neat cap around her face. Hers is the warm, listenable voice of a *tour docent*. Knowing she is a science writer, you picture yourself being led by Joanna to see wonders through a giant telescope or peer at lichen on a Canadian Atlantic island.

Befitting to their introspective, quiet natures and intellectual interests, the spacious apartment is furnished in comfortable dark-wood antiques and modern filing equipment and desks. Their home library is incredibly large and makes the apartment look distinctly (unless your mind flashes to Nero Wolf mysteries) un-Manhattanish. Some wool in a basket here, paints and palette there—respectively hers and his I learn—point to some nonbookish personal pursuits.

At the time of our interview, March, Rachel had just passed her fourth birthday. Because Phil and Joanna's strong coupleness points up the special qualities and problems of many first-time, one-time parents who

[2]Erik H. Erikson, *Identity: Youth and Crisis* (New York: Norton, 1968), p. 103.

As a city child Rachel Cole gets to fly down different slides on different walks.
Some are in Central Park and others in pocket playgrounds.

marry apace but *wait* to have children, we started our discussion there,
with their marriage.

The Coles' Commentary

PHIL: The history of our marriage—which is also Rachel's history—is long,
because I'm *old*. Presently I'm in school, working on a Ph.D. in psychology. I also am a clerk at an institute, a clinic, down in the Village where I see
patients as a therapist. This is called a clerkship because it's not paid, it's a

195

training program. I started back in school in September 1977, thanks to a modest family inheritance that allowed me to try something new. Before that I worked at New York Public Library for four years. Before that I was a couple of years getting an M.L.S. Before that I was a welfare worker for five years. Before that I was an employment interviewer for three years. And I was in the Army for three years. Joanna and I were married for eleven years before we had Rachel.

JOANNA: Phil's younger brother married my best friend's sister. Phil is nine years older than I am. When I was a teenager, Phil used to come out to my hometown to visit. He was 25 and was going to Columbia School of Business at the time, and I was in high school. I'd come over to my best friend's house, he'd be there, and we would talk. Then we met later when I was in college, on the street. We married about two weeks after! Actually for a long time we didn't want to have children. Then we simply changed our minds.

PHIL: Partly it happened because both my parents died within a short time frame; my father about two years after my mother. That had something to do with the change of heart in terms of a replacement of the family.

JOANNA: I remember being with some people who had children, and disagreeing with their child-rearing mode. The decision not to have children was built on my fear that I would not do it well.

PHIL: We practiced on Taffy! Although I didn't realize it at the time, Joanna had always wanted a dog. She had been nagging me to get a dog, because as a child she never had pets. I had, and knew what a nuisance animals are, how inconvenient they are if you want to travel. So Joanna finally talked me into buying a dog. She practiced on this dog for a year. Seeing she was able to raise this dog successfully, she thought she could handle a child. It turns out we weren't able to raise the dog successfully. It's a terrible dog. Totally unhousetrained and with no discipline at all. The only thing is she is very loving. We're hoping to do better with our child!

JOANNA: I think many people have the same feelings, fearing that they will reproduce their own faults in their child. We have both been in therapy for a long time, and I remember at one point being with people who had children who were talking about sitting down as a family and discussing the problems, and having things go better. I thought, "Maybe you don't have to reproduce your own problems. Maybe you can change things." So then I decided that having a child would be wonderful and interesting, and would

196

add a lot of love to our lives. I came home and said, "We have to have a baby!" It was right after Phil's father died. Phil said, "We do?"

PHIL: Looking back I can't understand why I didn't want to have children. It seems natural in a marriage. I guess I thought that they would change our life a lot. Rachel *has* changed our life a lot. It has little resemblance to before.

JOANNA: I was thirty-two. I had thought about having a baby ever since we first married, but then we always said no. Phil, and I too. I imagined it would be horrible because I never felt capable of parenting. At that time I had been an editor for quite a while. It is important for a woman having children to have an established career. I was able to be away from the office at times or delegate responsibility. That's so necessary when you become a mother. So many demands are placed on you if you work too. You have to have a degree of flexibility at the job.

Because Joanna's career was so important to her and she was so accustomed to her job life, staying home with her baby had no appeal. Continuing to work made career sense, and it made financial sense. They chose group care principally by what seems a contradiction. Because they were very private people, they could not conceive of a caregiver who would come to their house. Because they are independent thinkers and doers, they were unperturbed at flouting the common wisdom among professional couples that if you had to return to work, the second best for your child was a sitter who comes to you. They found one group care solution and liked it enough to try another.

JOANNA: The reason I wanted Rachel in group care was I really didn't want some lady coming to my house. I also felt it would be very hard to know in fact what was going on when we weren't there. Not that I was paranoid and thought that there was going to be a big deception happening, but think: She's a loving, maternal person when you're there, then you leave, and it's *all day long*. She says, "What an adorable baby?" What is she thinking? She may be depressed and stick the kid in the crib. How could any parent check on that? I thought in a group having several caregivers that I would know more what was going on.

PHIL: Also we felt, once we had looked at day care, that the people who were taking care of the kids in day care were probably people of a calibre you wouldn't get coming to your house. The Basic Trust staff is great.

JOANNA: They were people we felt of an equal social status to ourselves. We're socially friends with them. I didn't like the idea of a person who would in fact be a servant. That relationship made me uncomfortable.

PHIL: Furthermore, we thought that if you are not going to take care of the child yourself, it's better that they should be in a group with other kids to play with. A child shouldn't be all alone without other kids all day. How boring!

JOANNA: I went back to work when Rachel was three months old. Her first experience was quite different from Basic Trust. The day care was in somebody's apartment, and it was not tremendously professional. Two women in their thirties ran it. They were just taking care of kids. They had them of all ages and had tiny babies, starting from two months old. We liked the women a great deal.

PHIL: I wasn't happy about Rachel's being in day care at such an early age, but we had no choice. We both had jobs then. I tried to get off from the library, but they gave no paternity leaves then, although now they do. I had Thursday off and worked Saturday, so Rachel was with us three days a week.

JOANNA: Phil would take her up in the morning, and I would bring her home at night. The first two-and-a-half years of her life I left the office at four every day. I always felt it was very important to be with her. We both feel that. We don't go out a lot.

PHIL: We never did go out a lot. With some people, having a baby vastly disrupts their lives. If you go out three evenings a week, you have to worry about babysitters. We've never gone out much.

JOANNA: I've never felt that Rachel was deprived of our attention. I've always believe that Rachel was getting more of parents than a lot of kids do, because we are around. When she is home, she is with us. People would say to me when she was an infant, "Oh you must hardly ever see your baby" or—people are so obnoxious about day care!—"Oh she *has* to be in day care?" Then a look of pity spread across their faces. Well, when Rachel was an infant, she woke up at 5:30 or 6:00 in the morning, so I spent two or three hours with her before going to work. And I would spend the time *with her*. I would read her stories or whatever, because I'm not much on housework. Then I picked her up at 4:30. Babies nap in the daytime, so sometimes she would not go to sleep until ten at night. What a tired time that was! But her schedule had the advantage that we spent all that time with her. Sometimes I related to her nonstop six or seven hours. When I came home at night, I wouldn't do anything else except be with her until she went to sleep. I figure, how many parents spend seven hours talking to their child? I didn't see that she was being neglected. And she always seemed happy.

PHIL: We found the first day care group through an ad in the local paper. When babies are that age, you don't have a lot of choice. Basic Trust was in existence at that time, just around the corner in Jan Miller's apartment, but we didn't know about it. And Basic Trust doesn't take infants until six months.

JOANNA: The women were very warm, but they didn't have a good program for the older kids. With the older ones you sensed a lot of hanging around, which we didn't like. But Rachel was just hanging around in any case! The older kids seemed to go to the pet store an awful lot to see the fish, and they watched television a lot.

The babies *had* to have their bottles, be picked up when they cried, have their diapers changed. Rachel had a minor hip problem. Her diapers had to be put on in a certain way to keep her legs in a frog position. When I explained this I thought they might not take her, but they said, "Oh yes, Shawn had that, and we took care of it and he was fine." And the women did. We always felt concerned that the babies got a lot of attention at the expense of the older children. Altogether there were about ten, a small operation. It had a little backyard, which they called the garden, but it was a plot of matted-down dirt. One of the women loved Rachel. As soon as I came in, she would tell me everything that happened. I'll never forget her telling me about Rachel being in the swing, and every time the woman would come towards her Rachel would "laugh and laugh," she said, huge belly laughs. They let me know she was happy.

PHIL: The women had a St. Bernard dog that used to tromple all over the children. One of us would say it wasn't good to have the dog. The other would point out that the chances that the dog would go berserk were slight. It was very friendly, but in its enthusiasm to get to the garden it tended to walk over the children.

JOANNA: The kids loved it. This was a real home situation. We worried about it being a little too homey, not professional enough.

PHIL: We had assorted anxieties about it. But there didn't seem much we could do. Unless I gave up my job. We didn't have enough money then so I could do that.

JOANNA: We would worry, but everything seemed fine so we didn't change it. But then we heard about Basic Trust. When Jan Miller advertised her service in the paper, seeing it was right next door and the other place was on Eighty-ninth Street, which meant a bus trip, we thought, "Let's look." At first we didn't like it because it was so professional.

PHIL: No, I liked it. I felt happy about that.

JOANNA: My reaction was that the women up at the other place were regular people. They didn't have big theories about child development. They weren't going to interfere with my child according to their ideas. They would be saying, "Isn't she cute!" and hold her. And Jan of course has lots of theories. Everything seemed a little cold and clinical compared with the almost slovenly way of handling affairs that the other women had. And there was some separation anxiety on my part.

PHIL: I had worried about the degree of carelessness at the first facility. It was women taking care of children, in a very natural way, but it wasn't planned or thought out. They had no special equipment or particularly good physical activity space. It was merely an apartment, somebody lived there. Whereas Jan had a real school. Even in her apartment, when we made our initial visit, the very large room was all set up as a school. It looked inviting and was clean and had lots of equipment and rugs on the floor. We also knew that they were about to move to a new place. So I was only glad when we made the switch, even though we missed the other people.

JOANNA: Basic Trust was considerably more expensive than the other place; that was very cheap. But the price wasn't a concern. Basic Trust when we started Rachel there was $90 a week. The fee is over $130 four years later.

Continually, the Coles encountered problems in the separations from Rachel at the two seams in her home–day care center life. As self-analytic people they typically interpreted—and endeavored to diminish—these trouble spots as matters of psychological attitude.

PHIL: Rachel was about six months old when we took her to Basic Trust. I returned to school that year and had a lot of time on my hands. I guess I was also having big problems being back in school. So I spent a lot of time over at the center. I would go there at two o'clock and stay for two hours. Or go in the morning and stay for three hours. Jan thought I was staying too much, but I had a good time. I was practically a fixture that first year. I was there such an enormous amount of time I'm almost embarrassed. I enjoyed getting familiar with that age group. Up until then, to be in a room with kids who were six months to two-and-a-half years old, I would have thought it was like being with people from another world. After a while they just seemed like human beings!

JOANNA: The transition from one day care to the other we didn't think was hard for her. Although for several months she seemed quite subdued. Problems with adjusting came later. At the age of six months she was not experiencing stranger anxiety. She readily accepted another person as a caregiver. Jan very much wants the children to establish a bond with one person, and Rachel quickly did establish a bond with Debra, one that was close for both of them. Sometimes she called out for Debra in her sleep. Sometimes if Debra were holding her when I came to pick her up, and I reached out and said, "Rachel," she would tighten her hold around Debra. And I would moan, "Uhhh." One of the biggest advantages of group care for parents is that when this happened, there would be another parent there who would say to me, "Oh don't worry about that. Marissa did that with Peggy a couple of months back. She outgrew it." I always thought to myself, "If you were at home with one other lady caring for your baby, and you came in and the child wanted that person instead of you, it would be very hard to get perspective on it." At Basic Trust the parents are involved, they talk to each other. There was a basis for comparison. You knew if your child was biting, that the other children were biting too. You didn't feel, "My child is turning into a dog."

The Coles, concentrating in their work lives on solitary study and solitary writing, with no prior personal friends with children, and having the one child, rejoiced at the ready "extended family," both for themselves and for Rachel. They entered Basic Trust's life zestily and took a keen interest in the stages of the children's growth. The link with Basic Trust even, they said, helped sustain Phil's determination to perservere in the psychology doctoral program and influenced Joanna to trade her prestigious editor's job for the adventure of free-lance writing, which she found herself ready for.

PHIL: It's very helpful if you can be in a group of people who can talk with you about child rearing and give you feedback. In our case, we had no parents who raised us around to say, "This is the way it is, you were like that too at this age." The group meant a lot because we *didn't* have experience and *didn't* know anybody else who did. Without the group we would have been left to what we could read in Dr. Spock! The parents were very close. They still have parties where all the old parents will go back. We're still friends with all those people. In fact, we moved en mass from Basic Trust to the Riverside Nursery—about eight of the children. And we are possibly going to move to another school in something of a group. Also, Jan spends a lot of time educating parents. Jan does not view this as just taking care of children. She views group care as also an opportunity for parents to learn about their children and how to raise them well. . . . Thinking back on the babies, they really enjoyed being all together. I don't know whether you can say that they played *with* one another, but they would sit in their highchairs and bang on them in a circle together. They got so much out of having the older children there who came and played with the babies, too. The older children loved to visit the babies. When Rachel got older, *she* would go in the little room and play with the babies. She liked that a lot, and so did the babies.

JOANNA: When she went to the new school, Rachel said all the time, "I don't like Riverside, they don't have babies." When she was a mere three. I remember Rachel and Marissa, both three, sitting on either side of Sophie at the table. Sophie must have been one and a half—and they were teaching her how to talk. They would say, "What's this?" and she would say, "Ga." The older children would help. I remember seeing a two-year-old climb up to the book shelf, which was on top of the piano, and a baby down on the floor, and the two saying, "You want a book? Which book? The little book? The red book?" and then handing it down to the child. Rachel's first sentence was, "Joey cry." They were all in the front room, and the kids were waking up from their naps. When Joey woke up from his nap and cried, Rachel recognized his cry. So she said to the caregiver, "Joey cry." I always thought that was impressive. Rachel was a year or fourteen months.

Phil and Joanna found a coterie of people who shared their values about child care and combining careers with parenting, but what about judgments on them by society at large? Joanna's response was intense, that she had suffered, especially in quick takes that offered but little chance to describe the center and her happy child.

PHIL: Practically everybody we knew was there in Basic Trust. None of our old friends had children, at least certainly not friends in New York City, or they didn't have children as young as Rachel. We're so late! Everybody else's children seem to be entering college! I worried whether we chose the right thing. I was brought up at home, very traditionally. And I'm sure a lot of day care is bad. If you don't have continuity of caregiving, it *is* terrible. Basic Trust was very much like a great big family. But even so, without responding to any outside censure, we worried was it the right thing to do, instead of the more common route of having a woman come in daily and stay.

JOANNA: When I went back to work Rachel was three months old, I did not know personally another woman who had done that. There was so much talk about working mothers, but personally I didn't know anyone who hadn't taken time off. Most of the people I knew, the children were grown, or they wouldn't have children—this one was single, that one had an aversion to marrying, this couple was too bound up with career. So I felt like a pioneer. Like Phil, I worried about giving over so much care to a center, but then I kept looking at Rachel. She was so happy and so wonderful! I couldn't see that she was being damaged. . . . I think people disparaged day care more to me than to Phil. I would be going out to lunch with writers or agents, and the conversation would turn to my child. They would say, "Oh, do you have someone who comes in?" And I would say, "No, Rachel is in a day care center." This shadow passed over their faces. They imagined the baby farm of cribs with the wicked nurse coming through to give them a bowl of gruel. So I spent a lot of time informing people. I had a set pattern. When the shadow passed over their faces, I started my recording that said, "Oh but it's a wonderful place and it's designed for babies. It specializes in infant care." I would tell them all about it. But it was defensive. Sometimes I got tired of my Basic Trust spiel. But I couldn't let the shadow go without responding.

One point day care centers hold in common with other institutions like schools and offices is the pattern of coming and going to them that demarks the day. As noted earlier, these were often stressful times, for Phil especially because he was the person who returned to an empty apartment, a home without Rachel, for that nonparenting portion of his day. Contrastingly, it frazzled Joanna when she and Rachel locked horns about leaving Basic Trust at night. It repeatedly took a third party, the director, to smooth the seams in their day.

PHIL: I had a harder time than Joanna reconciling myself to using day care. Because I was at home. There was one period when Rachel did cry when I left her in the morning. She really didn't want me to leave. I would take her over and sit and stay for a half hour or forty-five minutes. Then I would leave, and she would cry and carry on. It was hard to leave, and when I came home, I felt, "Rachel could easily be here." Except of course if she had been here, she would have had nothing to do, no one to play with. And I couldn't have been studying. So I felt torn. Joanna had to go to work every morning so she didn't have any choice.

JOANNA: I feel more of that emotion now that I work at home. At Basic Trust I viewed the separation anxiety as an instinctual reflex. I didn't think Rachel was suffering in my absence. I knew that children have to cry when mothers leave, and that's fine. If she felt bad when I left, I wanted her to cry, that was normal and good. So I followed a ritual. I said goodbye, kissed her, gave her to Debra, her favorite, then went out and stopped by the window to wave goodbye and kissed her through the window again. By that time she was feeling a little better. So I never had any guilt about absenting myself. When you have a child and you work, you have to spend so much time away from your job to take your child to the doctor, or when she's sick, or to pick her up early, you almost feel you are never there in the office. But now that I work at home, I feel if Rachel says, "I don't want to go to school, I want to stay home and be with you," that it's *possible*. I've lost that tremendous pull to get to work and at least be there. I don't feel the same kind of warrant and confidence in our choice.

PHIL: But the fact is that if you did let her stay home, you couldn't work.

JOANNA: And she doesn't really like it. Around 12:30 she becomes very bored. Then the next day she finds out she missed something good at school. One time when she stayed home, the school had African day, and Mrs. Hoff said she was so sorry Rachel missed it because she would have loved it. Rachel wished she'd been there.

PHIL: Another factor, the nursery school is more like a school than Basic Trust was. At Basic Trust Rachel never wanted to stay at home all day. Sometimes I would say, "You don't have to go today." So we stayed home. At about 10:30 Rachel would say, "Let's go to Basic Trust." You could do that there. At Basic Trust I could call up and say we weren't coming, and then call up an hour later saying, "Now Rachel wants to come." Rachel would often do that. It wasn't that she didn't want to go to the center. She simply doesn't like to get moving in the morning. At Riverside you can't change your mind. You either go or don't. No bobbing in whenever you want. What Rachel resisted and often still resists is change itself. If she is home, she doesn't want to leave. All the time she was at Basic Trust, she never wanted to come home. It was much harder to try to get them to leave in the evening than to drop off. All the parents would have fights with their children!

There seems to be an age right after when children first learn to walk that going any place is impossible. Going from Basic Trust just around the block meant passing all those brownstones with their steps. Rachel would have to go up and down every brownstone. It took forty-five minutes to get her home. Sometimes we strapped her into the stroller so she couldn't get out. Crying all the way! She wanted to walk herself—and not walk home. Once we were in a taxi and passed a woman on Seventy-ninth Street walking up the hill with a toddler of two. The child had stopped to look at a fire hydrant, and the woman turned and rested her head against the building and went, "Oh, no!" We knew what she was feeling. She had been an hour probably walking this block, wondering in frustration would she ever reach home. Now Rachel is selective. Her favorite doorway is at our dog's veterinarian.

Parents had a lot of conflicts with their kids about the end of day.

JOANNA: And when the children reached, say, one and a half say, to three and it becomes hard to get snowsuits on, the parents would get them on and the children would take them off. Rachel would say, "Take your coat off, Mommy." That was her idea. She was so glad to see me, and "Let's all stay at Basic Trust for the evening" would be her idea of paradise. If her whole family could be at Basic Trust! So they would get a cracker when they were all dressed and ready to go out the door, and not before. I had some of the worst times getting her dressed. Awful! Sometimes I walked out without her. Jan had to have conferences with us about how to handle this. Because I would be at the end of my rope, that tired. Once she got out it was fine.

For the Coles group care anywhere from thirty-two to forty-five hours a week is how they have always raised their daughter. But from time to time they do speculate on how being in the group setting may have influenced her development.

PHIL: The few times we have been able to compare Rachel with the children about her age who have not been in day care we have noticed how much more socialized she is. She's had a great deal of that experience. She plays readily with other children, and knows how to take turns. But now it doesn't seem so obvious since Rachel seems to be going through a period of being pretty horrible sometimes with other children!

JOANNA: I don't notice Rachel is more sociable. She seems on a par with the other children with whom she plays in the building, even though they had sitters. She likes to read stories and tell them, to walk the dog and to dance. She doesn't care about toys much and never has. Is that because she is so accustomed to being with people? It would be easy to exaggerate the influence of group care on a child. What we see is Rachel growing to be a strong person out in the world, and having a home life and experiencing family values the way Phil and I might have as young children. Many of the values are not so different. Where they are, it is probably the result of group care's influence on us, her parents.

Jan Miller's Commentary

To amplify our initial discussion at Basic Trust in 1979, I visited Jan Miller at home. Our eight A.M. conversation began—Jan not being one to waste time—over the purr of the coffee mill while she ground me her delicious best. I admired the fifteen-inch-square, Marimekko-covered pillows Jan had just "run up," and she reminisced about the days when her apartment was the day care center.

Jan believes wholeheartedly in small-group day care. She stresses the fragility of the nuclear family and its isolation. In her opinion, small group day care is the best way for most children to form social relations, and meet the world, in their early years.

No mommy should be left all alone with a baby at home! The pioneer woman and her family felt she was deprived when she went off on a covered wagon and settled a stake with her husband, not only because of fewer comforts, but because she felt she was deprived of the support she would need, as a parent.

But adults can survive! It's the children who, if the unit is only the classic mother-father–child/children, are left with a more meager experience. In the past a child had a number of adults to go to and still do in a majority of contemporary cultures. This practice takes the burden off the biological parents and offers the opportunity to make deep relations with a number of people. If a child's personality is not a good match with the mother's—a passionate personality with an introspective, for example— the child can draw close to other adults with whom to form different kinds of links. The way we view the family on the nuclear model is *outmoded* and inadequate. The mother-child dyad puts too much burden on them both. You and your husband should not be *everything* to each other. Neither should her children be everything to a mother. She must fulfill herself in

Caregivers like Jan Miller who are alert to the needs of the moment know
how to improvise on the daily routine.

numerous ways. That tightly locked nuclear family leads to a lot of power
struggles and offers too few solutions.

At the parenting meetings, the Basic Trust parents say that they raise
their kids in groups because it gives them a broader expertise. I am there to
give the developmental and psychological information. The goal of my
center is not to interfere with the special intimacy of the family but to allow
children and parents to move beyond it. Care and nurturance of children is
a community responsibility. This is our covenant.

*Going from the general to the specific, Jan then talked about Rachel
Cole's experience at Basic Trust.*

Even though Rachel had *always* had mommy and daddy leave her and
go off to work or school and other concerns, at different times she nonethe-

less felt quite a bit of perfectly normal separation anxiety. You can play on the positive side of separation anxiety. It may come at six months or nine months. When mommy goes, the child cries, but the child goes to someone for comfort. Rachel went to Debra, and a close attachment formed between them.

Being a group junkie can be a problem in an urban upbringing—that is, being part of lots of different groups all the time. Children need a consistent group and maybe even one special person. Rachel had that special person in Debra. In Debra's heart Rachel will always be one of her first children. The one-to-one relationship lent a degree of intimacy and nurturance to the group setting, as the Coles recognized clearly. Not all children choose and get chosen! Usually it's mutual because love blossoms that way. When a caregiver finds it too heavy, the relations are "monitored" by the group setting. At times Debra would say to her colleagues, "Take her on a walk with you. I can't stand her whining." This gave Debra time off.

When Rachel was going through anxious times, Phil would stay at Basic Trust too long. I'd say, "Please go home." He *could* stay too long, and I could say, "Get your ass out." Phil stayed because *he* was going through separation anxiety with Rachel. He felt a need to answer the clinging. After fifteen or twenty minutes of abhorrent behavior, I'd ask, "Is it making it easier? Does she really want you to stay?" Phil would go saying, "I'll miss you, Rach, but here are your friends." Rachel would call out, "Don't, Daddy!" while reaching for me. Protest is part of her growth.

Rachel is also an extremely dramatic child who puts them through their paces! Some days she would experience real attachment and missing. She would say, "No, no, no, I want my Mommy!" I answered, "You're really feeling it today. Some days are like that." I reflected for her on what was happening, without putting too much emphasis on it.

One of Rachel's more novel responses to her mother's leaving was to go to the door and cry, "Out out out!" Joanna used to joke and say, "*I'm* a mother who's gone back to work to support my child's day care habit!"

When parents and kids go through rocky times, it helps to have others who love and live with them. A hard time for Rachel was at two-and-a-half to three. We had conferences. They even came to my place, and we had a drink together. This was an embattled time. Both the Coles had real conflicts about being an authority with her.

One day at home Rachel was fighting with her mother about putting on her "bunny suit," and she suddenly screamed, "I just can't stand it . . . when you're so WEAK!" I had told the Coles, "She wants you to be strong." So first Jan said it, then Rachel said it in her own way. "We'd better take heed." The Coles are very private people. It was wonderful to see that they could trust me, an outsider.

We have many group conferences on parenting, but there are times you need to open up over coffee and donuts or wine. They would get a sitter and come to my house. We talked and talked. You can't discuss anything about a child's behavior in one or two lines! What happens in the family can be threatening, and sometimes Phil and Joanna felt threatened. When they came over, I emphasized I had to trust them, and they me. Massaged by the leisurely mood, confidences and consultation came more easily. All of us had the chance to watch Rachel grow. She came and widened our world.

Rachel thrived in the group setting partly from a reason of character. Although she could lovingly manipulate her parents—she is a strong, separate person—at the center when one adult gave up, there was always another to take up the gauntlet. Her parents worked toward setting limits at home she knew had to be followed.

Rachel taught us a lot too. That whole first group taught me to trust children and to trust in the positive aspect of growth. The organism always grows to the positive, given the slightest chance.

Rachel loved to be told stories. Being read to was a high point for her many days. Our kids in general show a precocious interest in books. But I am a "late-reading person," and don't push letters and decoding. Rachel would spin tales, verbal fantasies, even on the potty. She explained to us and her parents how a baby is born—her version—when she was three. She was often the child who gave us the most verbally creative response. Her imagination soared. She used language as a tool for delight.

Rachel wasn't a child who could lose consciousness and go to sleep at naptime, once she passed babyhood. I put her down, and she rested and dozed a little. She would talk. She was a *rich* child to have, though not easy. Having conversations with her was always interesting. We stopped what we were doing when she had some intense comment to make.

Now that she's at the nursery school, Rachel expresses some of her Basic Trust past in her fantasies. She makes up Basic Trust stories about a little person who gets into trouble and needs help, and the other children and big people are *there* to help. It's all resolved when the small, powerless person succeeds. We call them Basic Trust Tales by Rachel. She told them not at school but back at home, and she has continued to tell them with a Basic Trust tag all year at her new nursery school.

The Coles' generation of children and parents show a remarkable cohesiveness. They feel, "These are *our* friends," and Basic Trust provides them with a like-minded group. There were lots of dinner parties, kids sleeping over at one another's. At Rachel's third birthday she invited the departed children and the infants, as well as her peers, to her party.

Eventually Merrily and Jeffrey Hansen led the way to the new nursery school. The families didn't want to break up the group. If they went together, the kids would have one another. All the parents are not completely satisfied, but the kids have done okay. Now the families are thinking of an alternative public school in East Harlem, Central Park East, which Mr. Hansen, a school administrator, helped to set up. It was a big compliment to me when they said, "The director reminds us of Jan." They are still looking for the same commitment to child development and inner growth that they believe our center provided.

CASTRO VALLEY BABYSITTING COOPERATIVE

Policy and Procedures

Amended December 1, 1977

Explanation

1. *Purpose*—The purpose of this Co-op is to enable mothers to go out without concern over their children's welfare and without financial restrictions. They should feel free from imposing on the sitter.
2. *Function*—Members receive competent babysitting in return for hours spent sitting for other members. The member who is leaving the home to go out is called the *gadder;* the one who cares for the children is the *sitter*.

The gadder does not necessarily sit for the member who sat for her.

This Co-op is basically established for the care of pre-school children during weekdays 9A.M. to 5P.M.

Some Co-op members are available for evening and weekend sitting.

Regular time shall be charged for evening and weekend sits.

The gadder is charged for the number of hours out. The sitter is credited for the same number of hours. Time is calculated from when the children arrive or from the time the gadder has requested that the sitter be ready (whichever is earlier). There is one *exception:*

Any member who sits for another member's three or more children shall be given time-and-a-half. The gadder shall be charged straight time. For four or more children the gadder is charged time-and-a-half and the sitter is credited with double time. Hours will be computed to the nearest half—one quarter will be rounded up to half and three-quarters will be round up to the next whole number.

Some Co-op members are available for overnight sits. The gadder is charged the *number of hours* from the time the child is left at the sitter's house until the child is quietly in bed for the night. *Three hours* is charged to the gadder for the night sit. *Additional time* is charged to the gadder for care giving services (feedings, etc.) in the middle of the night. The additional time charged to the gadder is an individual agreement between sitter and gadder. The gadder is charged the *number of hours* from the time the child awakens in the morning until the child is picked up by the parents. An additional half hour/child is charged to the gadder if the sitter provides breakfast.

3.   *Membership*—Membership shall be open to all interested mothers in the Castro Valley area.

Membership shall be limited to 30 active families. Less than 5 is not advisable.

Members shall pay annual dues of $2.00.

All active members are obligated to participate in the schedule. Every month each member shall sign up to be both a sitter and an alternate. It is advisable for new members to attend the meeting in the month they join.

Members are required to attend monthly meetings except in extremely difficult circumstances. Grace will be allowed for up to 5 absences, however, at the occurence of the sixth absence during a calendar year the member will be charged 6 hours, and 1 for each absence thereafter.

Members dropping out of the Co-op must give the Secretary or the President at least two weeks notice in order to repay debit hours by sitting. Those who leave with a minus balance will be expected to pay off their debt at 75¢ per hour. Should the member have bonus or plus hours they are dropped unless she goes inactive.

An inactive member is one who is leaving the Co-op but wants to use up her "plus" hours. Inactive members are allowed 6 months to use up their hours, after which time they are dropped. Inactive members are not required to meet the standard attendance requirement.

An Associate member is one who sits weekends and/or evenings ONLY.

Members may be dropped from the Co-op by a majority vote of the membership for repeated infractions of the rules. Grievances should be reported to the President.

Meetings

The purpose of meetings is to meet new members, become better acquainted with old members, fill out the calendar, discuss rule changes, and discuss problems or questions members wish to bring up (and sometimes to return lost items). Some brief "program" may be presented on a topic of interest to the group.

Meetings shall be held once a month except November/December which is combined and held early in December.

All rule changes shall be passed by majority vote of those present at the meeting.

All members are expected to attend and will be penalized 6 hours when the sixth meeting during one calendar year is missed and one hour thereafter for each missed meeting.

Duties of the President and Secretary

1. President—The President shall be elected by a majority vote and serve for a one year term (Jan.-Dec.).

She shall preside over the meeetings and greet new members. The president is to be called with information concerning new members.

She shall arrange programs for the meetings if the membership so desires.

She shall collect dues.

She shall keep a record of the attendance of all members for the purpose of penalties and possible dropping from the roster.

She is responsible for updating the member roster. This is a master list of each member's name, husband's name, address, home phone number, children's names and birthdates, emergency phone number (e.g., husband's work number), and pediatrician's name and phone number.

She shall give a copy of Policy and Procedures, emergency forms, calendar and membership roster to all new members.

She shall serve as Hours Secretary if the regular Secretary is indisposed.

She shall call special meetings if necessary and preside over them.

She shall receive a half hour each month from each member.

2. *Secretary*—the Secretary shall serve for one month.

This position shall be rotated among the members in the order that they joined the Co-op. The position may be passed up or postponed for a maximum of 3 months if the person so chooses.

She shall record the date of the sit, number of hours (plus for sitter and minus for gadder), and any extra hours.

She shall compile everyone's hours at the end of the month and present a tally sheet at the meeting.

She shall make up a calendar-like sitting schedule for the following month. This shall include a sitter and an alternate for each weekday date, except holidays. This schedule shall be compiled through and including the day after the next meeting. Members are responsible for informing the Secretary of what days they are available to sit.

She shall prepare copies of the hours and schedule and pass them out at the next meeting. She shall be responsible for getting copies to those members who were absent.

She shall pass the books on to the new Secretary for the following month, explain the procedures, and help her with compiling the next hours tally.

She shall earn one hour credit for each member for that month. This is credited to her at the end of her month. Each member will be debited one hour for the secretary.

Gadder's Responsibilities

The gadder shall arrange for her own sit. She does not necessarily have to call the member who is assigned for that day.

The gadder shall confirm date, time, and estimated number of hours with the sitter in advance (at least the night before).

A note of medical emergency permission must accompany each of the gadder's children. Any special emergency instructions should be attached.

The gadder must leave the address and phone number of her destination.

The gadder takes her children to the sitter's home. The children should not be transported elsewhere unless the gadder agrees to this before she leaves. When a child is transported, the sitter must take the child's emergency form along.

If feeding is involved, the gadder shall provide food and instructions or she shall award the sitter an extra half hour credit if the sitter provides the food.

It is a good idea for the gadder to bring along extra diapers and a change of clothes for infants.

Be prompt. Time is calculated from when the children arrive or from the time the gadder has requested that the sitter be ready (whichever is earlier). The sit ends when the gadder returns.

Be courteous. When returning to sitter's home gather children, belongings, etc., and leave, unless sitter invites you to stay.

The gadder shall inform the sitter of the time she will return (be realistic). If gadder expects to be a half hour or more later than she said, she is to call the sitter.

Time is figured in half hours. Fifteen or more minutes is counted as a full half hour. Less than fifteen minutes is not counted.

Gadder and sitter should discuss hours of sit so both agree.

A member who is more than 25 hours in debt is not permitted additional gadding privileges.

Sitter's Responsibilities

Any sitter who has to cancel is responsible for getting a replacement and advising the secretary and the alternate.

If the sitter does not receive a phone call by the night before the day she is scheduled to sit, she is not obligated to stay home that day.

The sitter shall not transport the gadder's children unless this has been agreed upon ahead of time.

If the gadder requests that the sitter provide transportation for her children (e.g., to or from school), an extra half hour credit is given to the sitter (an hour if transportation is provided both ways), and the gadder is debited the same amount.

The sitter must follow all the gadder's instructions.

If two members pool their children under one sitter, each member shall pay regular time and the sitter shall receive double time.

The sitter shall inform the gadder if she is taking care of more than one family when the gadder calls.

The sitter shall earn an extra half hour if she provides lunch for the gadder's children.

It is the sitter's responsibility to report her hours to the Secretary. This can be done by phone call or post card. She must inform the Secretary if she is eligible for any extra hours because of more than two children. This should be done as soon as possible. All hours must be reported *within 7 days* or forfeited.

Alternate's Responsibilities

After the monthly schedule has come out, if the alternate finds out that she is unable to sit on her assigned day, she is responsible for making arrangements for a substitute. She shall inform both the sitter and the secretary who her replacement is.

The alternate is obligated to sit when the assigned sitter has too many requests or when there is last minute illness in the sitter's family. She must stay home until 9:00A.M. on the day of the sit.

General Rules

Any illness, no matter how minor, should be discussed between the sitter and the gadder. Basic consideration should be shown in this respect. Members should not hesitate to refuse to take children with colds. Allergies should be noted. Mothers should mention allergies to certain foods.

It is suggested that members have comprehensive liability insurance for their own protection against any accidents to another child. The co-op does not hold itself responsible as a group.

Members should keep a personal record of the dates and times they use the Co-op.

Special privileges, such as sitting of extra nonmember children because of out-of-town guests, can be arranged. Double time is charged for such children unless the gadder is caring for the child on a permanent (day care) basis. In the case of the latter, the nonmember's children's names, birthdates, parent's names, address, phone number, emergency phone number, and pediatrician's name and phone number, etc. should appear on the roster under the name of the member who is caring for them. All children must have emergency medical permission slips made out.

Authorization to Consent to Treatment of Minor

We, the undersigned parents of the minor listed below do hereby authorize _____, an adult person into whose care the minor has been intrusted, as an agent for the undersigned to consent to any x-ray examinations, anesthetic, medical or surgical diagnosis or treatment and hospital care which is deemed advisable by, and is to be rendered under the general or special supervision of any physician and surgeon licensed under the provisions of the Medical Practice Act.

It is understood that this authorization is given in advance of any specific diagnosis, treatment or hospital care being required but is given to provide authority and power on the part of our aforesaid agent to give specific consent to any and all such diagnosis, treatment or hospital care which the aforementioned physician in the exercise of his best judgment may deem advisable. We assume all financial responsibility for such service.

Minor's name_____
Birthdate_____
Address_____Phone_____
Doctor's Name_____Address_____Phone_____
Medical Insurance_____Number_____
Allergies_____
Dated_____

                                          Mother_____
                                          Father_____

INDEX